For Gordon

'Just pull it to the front and lay it down the sides'

Gordon Stewart on the art of re-upholstery, the first and only instruction.

Jonathan Hankins

Acknowledgements

This research was part of a PhD carried out under the academic supervision of Prof Andrea Potestio at Bergamo University, with the Professional supervision of Dr Francesco Samorè at the Bassetti Foundation in Milan. It would not have been possible without the support of President Piero Bassetti and the other collaborators at the Bassetti Foundation and all of the academic and secretarial staff at the UNIBG Doctorate School, in particular Prof. Gian Paolo G. Scharf and Prof. Paolo Cesaretti for their editorial work on this book. My thanks goes to them all.

I have been supported throughout the process by a host of other individuals and academics, in particular Professors David Guston, Sally Randles, Ton Robben and the many members of the VIRI who offered advice and suggestions.

My thanks go to all of the members of the University of Utrecht SOSCO research group for their hospitality and input during my stay in Utrecht.

This research would not have been possible without the help of all of those who dedicated their time within the case studies presented in the thesis: Adam and Louise Black, Gordon Stewart, Piero Bassetti, René von Schomberg, Jos Malda, and Maurizio Montalti. I thank you all for sharing your experience, expertise and time.

My personal and heartfelt thanks go to Cristina, Angelo and Adelchi for making all of this possible.

Table of Contents

Introduction: A Narrative Approach to Responsible Innovation. 1

Chapter 1

Responsible Innovation, an Overview 7

1.1 Definitions of a Concept under Development 7

1.2 Overview of Definition Backgrounds 21

1.3 Responsible Innovation Today; an overview of the situation 36

1.4 Some Conclusions 39

Chapter 2

The Scholarly Narrative 42

2.1 The Groundwork 43

2.2 The Debate Around the Frontier Sciences 50

2.3 A Multidisciplinary Investigation 54

2.4 Further Fieldwork Within RI 58

2.5 International Handbook on Responsible Innovation 62

2.6 The Influence of Design 64

2.7 Some Conclusions 69

Chapter 3

The European Narrative 71

3.1 Projects Funded Under the FP7 Framework Programme (2007-2013) 84

3.2 Some Conclusions 91

3.3 René von Schomberg 93

3.4 René von Schomberg: An insider perspective...................97

3.5 Some Conclusions......................................104

Chapter 4

The Italian Narrative: The Bassetti Foundation in Milan...................106

4.1 An Overview of the Bassetti Foundation.......................109

4.2 President Bassetti in his own Words.....................113

4.3 Some Conclusions.......................................147

Chapter 5

Poiesis-Intensive Innovation.......................................149

5.1 Situated Learning.................................153

5.2 Skilled Visions...157

5.3 RI Definition and Poiesis Intensive Responsible Innovation (PIRI).......................................161

5.4 Some Conclusions.......................................169

Chapter 6

Apprenticeship: Learning to See, Learning to Do: The Upholsterer's narrative.......................................172

6.1 Methodology for the Recorded Conversations...........................191

6.2 An Analysis of the Recordings: Conversations with the Village Upholsterer........................................194

6.3 Concluding Remarks: The death of our mentor...........................226

Chapter 7

The Scientist's Narrative.......................................230

7.1 Jos Malda.................................231

7.2 The Laboratory.......................................236

7.3 Skilled vision: The Development of the Process on Display..........242

7.4 Similarities in Problem Solving Techniques *247*

7.5 Professor Jos Malda in his Own Words *254*

7.6 Some Conclusions..*265*

Chapter 8
Concluding Remarks..**270**

8.1 Chapter 1, Responsible Innovation: An Overview *274*

8.2 Chapter 2, The Scholarly Narrative *276*

8.3 Chapter 3, The European Narrative..*278*

*8.4 Chapter 4, The Italian Narrative: The Bassetti Foundation
in Milan* *279*

8.5 Chapter 5, Poiesis Intensive Innovation *282*

*8.6 Chapter 6, Apprenticeship, Learning to See, Learning to
Do: The Upholsterer's Narrative* *284*

8.7 Chapter 7, the Scientist's Narrative...*289*

BIBLIOGRAPHY **294**

List **of**
Figures..**265**

Introduction: A Narrative Approach to Responsible Innovation.

The aim of this research is to open a field of study within Responsible Innovation that sees narration, and in particular the narration of aesthetics, as playing a central analytical role within daily decision-making practices in small scale production situations.

The central tenant for this research is that a narrative develops in the workplace through everyday conversation, providing fundamental and non-reproducible measures in order to steer the production process. Within the narrative that I have chosen to analyze in most detail, a furniture restoration workshop in the UK, one of the most used and visible measures is beauty. I argue that the position of the production of beauty as a goal, and its appreciation in finished work, comes to represent the art of doing something correctly.

In the furniture restoration case study presented in Chapter 6, those responsible for producing beauty live through a formalized apprenticeship period that sees them not only learn the necessary production techniques, but that their living and working within the workplace narrative also leads to understanding the decision-making process and the rationale behind it in terms of what could and what should not be done (and how), and more importantly why that is so.

The concept of getting things right is typical of the high-quality artisan community. A finished piece of work is judged on its aesthetic value, not merely in terms of the skill required in its production process but also in terms of the choices made during that process. Each process is different, an individual development that grows out of the wishes of the customer, the economic restrictions or possibilities that frame each particular piece, and the shared in-situ understanding (born through apprenticeship) of whether the job has been done correctly in both technical and responsibility terms.

I will argue that the appreciation of beauty can be seen as the codification of the tacit knowledge shared by those working within the process, enabled by the learning of a skilled vision.

Although this argument is based upon an artisan approach to manufacturing, I believe that the artisan category can be expanded well beyond the traditional workshop that comes to mind with the use of such categories. Artisan working practices can be seen in science laboratories and in high technology engineering, with a host of similarities within working practices visible only to the skilled eye, and understood within that particular social group.

I would argue that the aesthetics of doing things right, and the ability for that understanding to be shared through apprenticeship style learning in different contexts, is one driving force within the decision-making process within any particular setting.

The furniture restorers who see the beauty of a traditionally stitched in horsehair seat, the multiple lines of stitching and roll edge, the use of a once common but now extremely expensive raw material and its equally painstaking and laborious techniques, the calico covering and cotton wadding (all of which is hidden to the customer), sees a job done correctly. Days of hidden work are on show to trained eyes; a moral judgement shared and enforced, framed in everyday conversation as responsibility to the process, the customer, the piece and the others working alongside.

Beauty, ethics and responsibility are related, responsibility and ethics embedded within the beauty of the finished article. They can all be appreciated by those who have the skills and the vision.

In this book I argue that these considerations should play a part in the development of the concept of Responsible Innovation (RI). The aim of getting things right is a fundamental idea, not only for a furniture restorer or piano repairer, but also for the biotechnology professor conducting research in a laboratory, or the engineer designing a prosthetic limb.

I believe that this concept (getting things right, doing things correctly) should be a fundamental argument at the core of the debate on responsible innovation. As this publication seeks to demonstrate, research into responsible innovation has not yet analyzed the fundamental problem of the relationship between the production of beauty and its relationship to responsibility, but as outlined in chapter 2, has largely focused on governance. I argue however that the idea of getting things right is a fundamental core principle for RI, even if it is not always framed in such language.

Interest in the relationship between aesthetics and responsibility has always run through the various fields of action undertaken by the Bassetti Foundation, the host institution for my PhD and current employer. I argue that this intuition expressed in its earliest moments should form a core concept for the study of RI, and believe that if RI is to be better understood, it should be analyzed through judgements made in skilled and shared situations, some of which are framed through aesthetics.

The chapters can be read individually as they are stand-alone pieces.

In order to develop this argument, the book is structured as follows:

Chapter 1 offers an introductory overview of how RI is perceived today. The most commonly used definitions are analyzed in terms of their provenance and the backgrounds to their development. Similarities and differences are described in terms of the aims of their authors, while the effect of their use and implementation is also discussed. A history of the development of the argument from its roots in technology assessment is also sketched, while the fundamental differences between various streams of articulation and implementation are discussed and contrasted.

Chapter 2 is a summary of an extensive literature review that traces the development of RI as the focus of academic study, describing several particular fields of research interest and following them longitudinally to the present.

Chapter 3 is an investigation into the use of the concept by the European Commission, particularly its positioning within the various FP 6,7 and 8 funding calls. The chapter offers a description of the development of the concept within the institution, before addressing the work of its architect in the field of policy-making on a European level René von Schomberg. The chapter includes transcription and analysis of conversation between von Schomberg and myself, offering an insider's perspective on the use and development of the concept within European policy making and research funding.

Chapter 4 describes the work of the Bassetti Foundation and its role in the development of the concept of RI. The analysis is based upon a series of recorded and transcribed interviews with President Piero Bassetti and documents from the Bassetti Foundation archives. The chapter concludes with an analysis of the minutes of the first and seminal meeting held on behalf of the Foundation in Alz.

This analysis of the Bassetti Foundation archives demonstrates that the motions acted upon in the founding moments of the Foundation were in fact those taken up by the wider RI community as it grew, demonstrating the position of the Foundation as visionary in its day.

Chapter 5 expands upon the concept introduced in chapter 4 of Poiesis-Intensive Innovation, addressing issues of situated learning and skilled visions. The rationale for the case studies is described and methodology discussed. My own interpretation of the Bassetti Foundation concept of Poiesis-Intensive Innovation is developed, leading to the concept of Poiesis Intensive Responsible Innovation (PIRI), a concept that is tested in the case studies that follow.

Chapter 6 is the first of two case studies. This case study involves a furniture restorer working in Manchester (UK). The case study revolves around ideas of beauty, organization and doing things the 'right' way. The analysis is based upon personal experience, fieldwork and recorded interviews, and is designed as a test bed for an analysis of the relationship between aesthetics and ethics within production processes.

Chapter 7 is the second large case study. This study is based upon interviews carried out in Utrecht (Netherlands) within a biology laboratory at the University of Utrecht. The laboratory specializes in the design and build of living implants for regenerative medical use. The 3D printing of human cells and development of bio-inks are the laboratory Director's specialty. This case study is compared and contrasted to the first, with arguments surrounding similarities and differences analyzed in terms of bricolage and organization.

Chapter 8 is the concluding chapter. It draws together the book's central arguments. The concept of Poiesis-Intensive Innovation is summarized, as is that of Poiesis Intensive Responsible Innovation, alongside investigation into its use as an analytical tool for the investigation of the relationship between responsibility and everyday working practices.

The chapter concludes with a description of the findings of the two case studies, demonstrating the similarities and differences between the working practices and their relationships to Responsible Innovation, including the influence of the concept of beauty as a measure of correct procedure within the workplace narrative.

Chapter 1

Responsible Innovation, an Overview

The terms Responsible Innovation (RI) and more recently Responsible Research and Innovation (RRI) are currently in use across several academic fields and within many policy documents. The terms are however relatively new, coming to prominence in these fields in the middle of the last decade (de Saille 2015). The aim of this chapter is to explain their provenance, how they have been defined, their uses, and to investigate the academic and in some cases political history behind the term.

The chapter begins with an overview of current definitions in use today in academic literature, before looking at the historical development of the concept through the actors involved. The concept is very much seen as having developed in Europe (Guston et.al, 2014), but as this chapter will demonstrate there have been several important developments led by US based institutions and academics. The focus of this chapter is predominantly the term's development in Europe as it has become institutionalised within both the European Commission and several different funding bodies, but it will also contain an analysis of on the various US actors' roles in its development and in particular the importance of their broad input for the spread of the concept through academic literature.

1.1 Definitions of a Concept under Development

As noted above, the concept of RI and the related RRI form is relatively new. As a young and developing concept, there is no single definition in use in academic literature, but a series of definitions that all aim to define the concept in its broadest terms from the positions of the authors of each definition.

René von Schomberg

The most widely quoted definition in use at the time of writing is that of René von Schomberg, who describes RI as:

> a transparent, interactive process by which societal actors and innovators become mutually responsive to each other with a view to the (ethical) acceptability, sustainability and societal desirability of the innovation process and its marketable products (in order to allow a proper embedding of scientific and technological advances in our society). (von Schomberg, 2011, p.9)

Von Schomberg has worked for many years within the European Commission, and his definition shows the reflective input of this role. His influence within the commission in terms of its adoption of the concept of RI is unparalleled, having first introduced the language and later having built conferences and meetings around the development of the concept, guiding its implementation within a series of calls for funding. This argument will be addressed in greater detail in chapter 3 in a section dedicated to von Schomberg and his work both within academia and the European Commission.

The influence of von Schomberg's working history in TA is also visible in this definition, with its openly stated aim of promoting the guidance of the process with an aim or goal in mind, for a presumed innovative result (Oudheusden, 2014). These goals are reflected in the aims that underpin von Schomberg's arguments, of the need for normative anchor points within the development of RI processes, a subject that will be addressed further in chapter 3 in a section dedicated to the development of the concept within the European Commission.

The definition reflects von Schomberg's interest in working towards positive societal impacts of science and innovation. This interest is grounded and influenced by various EU public policy statements that aim to promote responsible innovation in its aim to address the Grand Challenges facing the institution today (EC, 2011, EC, 2012, EC, 2013). He also often refers to the Lund Declaration's aims of promoting research that will bring positive benefits for society as a whole (Lund Declaration, 2009).

Von Schomberg develops a framework for RI around his definition, arguing for the need for normative anchor points for both the product and the process of innovation, arguing that they must be sustainable, ethically acceptable and socially desirable.

I would like to stress at this point however that he does not consider RI to be merely a project that could be addressed in participatory research programmes, something that might be assumed from the truncated description above, but believes that its creation requires the establishment of a new innovation paradigm enabled by institutional change. This will be further described in chapter 3 as part of a description of his proposed matrix for responsible innovation.

Stilgoe, Owen & MacNaghten

A second widely used definition is that of Stilgoe, Owen & MacNaghten:

> Responsible research and innovation means taking collective care for the future, through stewardship of innovation in the present (Stilgoe, Owen and MacNaghten, 2013, p.1570).

This is a broader definition than that offered by von Schomberg, that looks towards what Stilgoe described earlier as the 'democratic governance of intent' (Stilgoe, 2011) and the principal of 'science for society' as proposed by the authors themselves in an earlier publication. (Owen, Macnaghten and Stilgoe, 2012).

The definition above is presented in an article that goes on to outline 4 dimensions of RI, the authors arguing that to innovate responsibly entails a collective and continuous commitment to being: **anticipatory** (describing and analysing both intended and potentially unintended impacts); **reflective** (on underlying purposes, motivations and potential impacts); **deliberative** (inclusively opening up visions, purposes, questions and dilemmas); **responsive** (a collective reflexivity process sets innovation direction and influences its trajectory) (Stilgoe, Owen and MacNaghten, 2013).

This description of RI has been influential on an EU level, with the European Commission presenting a working definition based on a similar set of dimensions, often referred to as 'pillars'. The EU defined pillars will be further analysed in Chapter 3.

Regarding the Stilgoe et.al definition and using the language used in the article (Stilgoe et.al. 2013 pp1568–1580) their proposed dimensions are described as follows:

Anticipation

The call for anticipation within RI comes from both academic circles (Wynne, 1992, Wynne, 2002, Jasanoff, 2003) with interest mainly in the social and political stakes involved in scientific programs, and from environmental and other political concerns (Toffler, 1970, Carson, 1962). Stilgoe, Owen & MacNaghten argue that:

> anticipation involves systematic thinking aimed at increasing resilience, while revealing new opportunities

for innovation and the shaping of agendas for socially-robust research (Stilgoe et.al. 2013 p1569).

The authors propose methods of foresight, technology assessment, horizon scanning and scenario planning in order to promote anticipation within the process.

Reflexivity

Following Wynne, the authors argue for the need for institutional reflexivity in governance (Wynne 1993). They argue that:

> reflexivity means reflecting upon one's own activities, commitments and assumptions, while being aware of the limits of available knowledge and bearing in mind that a particular framing of an issue may not be universally held (Stilgoe et.al. 2013 p1570).

Inclusion

The inclusion of new voices in the innovation process is seen as a legitimating force. The authors call for the inclusion of consensus conferences, citizens' juries, deliberative mapping, deliberative polling and focus groups in order to bring the broadest public possible into the research process (see Chilvers, 2010 for further discussion of these techniques, and the description of the Bassetti Foundation work in partnership with the Regional Government of Lombardy on the creation of the Open Innovation Portal, and inclusion of consensus conferences within regional legislation described in chapter 4 for a practical examples). The authors also raise the issue of gender inclusion as a positive goal, but also point to power relations within public participation projects as a problematic to be addressed.

Responsiveness

The authors argue that Responsible innovation:

> requires a capacity to change shape or direction in response to stakeholder and public values and changing circumstances, arguing that an RI approach should work towards making systems as responsive as possible (Stilgoe et.al. 2013 p1571).

Responsiveness is seen as two-fold, involving both answering questions and reacting to responses and other stimuli. The authors conclude that responsiveness involves responding to new knowledge, views, norms and perspectives as they emerge.

Given the importance of this seminal publication and in order to better understand the development of this definition, I will now offer a more in-depth overview of the structure of the article here, as it provides background to the definition in terms of methodology and purpose.

The article is divided into three large sections and a short concluding section:

Part 1 is an introduction that raises several historical and philosophical questions related to issues surrounding RI, offering a description of the development of ideas surrounding the theme, very much as described in further detail in this book. This section also goes on to raise the question of a new scientific governance that takes into account the question of RI within its structure.

Part 2 is entitled 'Four Dimensions of Responsible Innovation', and the authors firstly offer the definition of Responsible innovation cited above before moving on to the dimensions.

The 4 dimensions cited above (anticipation, reflexivity, inclusion and responsiveness) are presented in a table, with the authors stating that these dimensions provide a framework for raising, discussing and responding to RI related questions.

The authors describe their dimensions in detail: Under anticipation they call for improved anticipation in governance, describe the limitations of risk-based models and push the actors involved to pose the question of 'what if?' They also point to the problem of responsibility in hype (a realistic presentation of the possible advantages of a development tract) and offer the examples of upstream public engagement and Constructive Technology Assessment (Rip et.al, 1995) as two techniques that involve anticipatory discussions of possible and desirable futures. They also point to Real-Time Technology Assessment as another model of anticipatory governance (Guston, 2013), and raise the idea of scenario planning as a possible approach (for further explanation see Cassia et.al, 2011).

Whilst addressing inclusion, the authors offer a critique of public engagement practitioners, raising questions of power relations within the organization of dialogue (for further discussion see Blok, 2014), but argue that public engagement although imperfect, politicized and uneven, must be seen as a good in itself. This is a topic that several RI authors have gone on to address as demonstrated in Chapter 2 (see Li et.al, 2015 for example).

The responsiveness section explains the institutional integration of the 4 dimensions. The authors argue that if responsible innovation is to be responsive, it must be situated in a political economy of science governance that considers both products and purposes, reflecting the movement from TA to RI as described in the following section of this chapter, and very much reflecting the views outlined above from von Schomberg.

The final section of Part 2 is entitled Integrating the Dimensions of Responsible Innovation.

The authors state that responsible innovation requires the embedding of their dimensions into governance, connecting as an integrated whole. An institutional commitment to a framework that integrates all four dimensions is vital, and as such a piecemeal process is insufficient.

Part 3 is a case study of a project the authors participated in, and provides the underpinning for their definition and the development of the framework. The case in question is the Stratospheric Particle Injection for Climate Engineering (SPICE) project[1], funded by the Engineering and Physical Sciences Research Council (EPSRC)[2]. The authors worked alongside the project, allowing them to develop, embed and develop their framework. The authors offer an overview of the project and the socio-political context for the case study before moving on a section entitled Embedding the Dimensions of Responsible Innovation within SPICE. This case study has become one of the most important within the field of RI, and a model for other research projects (Asantea, Owen and Williamson, 2014, Van de Burg and Swiersta, 2013).

The process of the authors' embedding involved the development of a stage gating system based upon the dimensions described above. The operation of the decision gate involved an independent panel evaluating the SPICE team's response to proposed criteria, leading to recommendations to the Research Councils on whether the testbed should proceed and, if so, under which conditions.

---

1 https://www.epsrc.ac.uk/newsevents/news/spiceupdateoct/ for description of the project. Last accessed 30/10/2019.

2 https://www.epsrc.ac.uk/ for further explanation of the organization and its work. Last accessed 30/10/2019.

The criteria are as follows:

1. Risks identified, managed and deemed acceptable

2. Compliant with relevant regulations

3. Clear communication of the nature and purpose of the project

4. Applications and impacts described and mechanisms put in place to review these

5. Mechanisms identified to understand public and stakeholder views

The authors argue that the EPSRC created the institutional conditions that allowed the testing of these new governance mechanism, and were willing, with leadership from senior staff, to interrogate their own institutional responsibilities, leading to institutional reflexivity.

As the project developed the authors argue that this level of debate seems to have affected proceedings, with the test-bed (testing of a small-scale distribution system using a balloon) being postponed upon advice from a stage gate panel. They argue that the symbolic and political implications of the test were at least partly realized as a result of external voices entering the debate and broadening discussions.

During preparation for a stage gate presentation a patent was discussed that had been filed by a co-investigator, leading to discussions of a conflict of interest. The debate itself and what followed led to the testbed being postponed and eventually cancelled, with both the conflict of interest and related regulatory issues cited as potential problems.

The authors clarify that it was the SPICE team that chose to cancel the test themselves, it was not an external order either from above or from the funding body.

The paper concludes with a reflections section in which the authors argue that the responsible innovation approach introduced reflection, anticipation, inclusive deliberation and responsiveness, influencing the direction of the research conducted.

The authors describe both the achievements and limitations of their approach, warning against the institutionalization of the phrase and process (a problem raised by von Schomberg later in this book). They state that they are also aware that their involvement in the project came about after it had already been funded and given the institutional go ahead, but that involvement in these earlier processes is necessary if a real move towards responsible innovation is to be enabled. This work was also influential as it led to the inclusion of the concept into future research funding requirements of the EPSRC itself in the UK[3].

Hankins

In a recent publication I offered a definition that attempts to expand upon the Stilgoe et.al definition cited above in consideration of the concept of local processes situated within a 'glocal' situation:

Responsible (research and) innovation means taking collective care for the future through a reflexive process within which all interested actors contribute to responsible choices within a 'glocal' and topical context (Hankins, 2019).

This definition demonstrates my interest in the local production of both artefacts and of knowledge, and offers the foundations

---

[3] The EPSRC publishes a Framework for Responsible Innovation document
https://www.epsrc.ac.uk/research/framework/ last accessed 30/10/2019.

for my analysis of the case studies found in chapters 6 and 7. The fieldwork that this definition is drawn from brings the personal knowledge and community of practice of those working within the innovation process to the fore (Lave and Wenger, 1991), using arguments of situated learning as apprenticeships into ethical and moral formation (Bijker, 2010, Pinch, 2010 and Ingold 2010). These arguments will be dealt with in further detail, alongside the rational for their application to the case studies in chapter 5.

The definition was developed during my dedicated research time for my PhD, spent with small businesses and organizations within which an artisan approach to innovation can be seen. My life experience of living and working in an artisan environment has led to the development of a practice-led understanding of responsible innovation - rather than the more theoretical or normative concepts offered in RRI studies and by policy-makers. The influence of the Bassetti Foundation concept of Poiesis-Intensive Innovation can be seen within this approach, with responsibility embedded in the beauty and functionality of the artefact produced. The background and early development of this concept is further described in chapter 4, and its methodological implications for the case studies in chapter 5. It is further expanded upon within the case studies leading to the proposal of a Poiesis Intensive Responsible Innovation (PIRI) model in Chapter 5 and in the concluding remarks of this book.

I argue that the type of holistic conception of RI represented within this definition makes sense to people working within small scale working environments, leading to an *aesthetics of responsibility* that is grounded in a particular type of society, in this case those implementing artisan style working practices within their work and research.

This aesthetics of responsibility is narrated in daily working life, through shared language in everyday work conversation. The appreciation of the aesthetics element can be seen as a tool that allows the narrative to come to a conclusion, in that it closes the section that relates to a single piece of work. It involves both the local perception of those working within the process intimately, and the global situation within which the piece is situated. It is a 'glocal' construction.

This leads to conceptualizing a responsible system within which responsibility is not an abstract normative principle but rather a shared practice regarding peer-actors, processes and objects of their design. To this embedded notion of responsibility, I argue the need to add the conditions surrounding production, such as norms, market dynamics etc., but argue that norms and market regulations should not be the source of RI itself. It should be seen as developing from within a system of practice.

Reflecting the argument of this book, the definition goes further than just acknowledging that craft embeds qualities into products that are then recognized by the market (see Callon et al 2002) but argues that the production of foundational knowledge about RI is facilitated through practice. This does not necessarily exclude the idea that it can be governed or that it can be an object of scrutiny by third-parties such as bureaucracies. It does however mean that scrutiny by peers in a review process would feed on sharing such foundational, practice-based knowledge. The concept of bricolage as developed by anthropologist Levi-Strauss describes how poetry (I draw a parallel here with my own use of poiesis) finds itself within the process when he states that:

the 'bricoleur' also, and indeed principally, derives his poetry from the fact that he does not confine himself to accomplishment and execution: he 'speaks' not only with things, but also through the medium of things: giving an account of his personality and life by the choices he makes between the limited possibilities (Levi-Strauss, 1962, p.14).

This argument is also closely linked to Sayer's concept of Lay Normativity (Sayer, 2011), as the production process of the artefact reflects and represents the norms of those producing it. I would argue that the process and artefact itself embody these norms, constituted through a decision-making process based upon a shared understanding of such norms within the workplace.

The development of this definition is further discussed in chapter 5 and developed in the case studies, in which I argue (following the rationale above) that RI process can be embodied in the process and the product, and that a skilled practitioner learns to see and appreciate this in the aesthetics of the final product, building upon Grasseni's definition of Skilled Visions' (Grasseni, 2007).

van den Hoven

Jeroen van den Hoven offers the following definition:

Responsible Innovation is an activity or a process which may give rise to previously unknown designs pertaining either to the physical world (e.g., designs of buildings or infrastructure), the conceptual world (e.g., conceptual frameworks, mathematics, logic, theory, software), the institutional world (social and legal institutions, procedures and organization) or combinations of these, which – when implemented – expand the set of relevant feasible options regarding solving a set of moral problems (van den Hoven, 2013, p.80).

The basis of van den Hoven's definition is his concept of moral overload (van den Hoven, 2013, p.77). Moral overload is a situation in which a designer or engineer has many objectives for the design in question. An example might be the needs for privacy, user friendly capability, sustainability and cost. The designer/innovator has the moral obligation to adhere to all of these wishes, but achieving them together may be difficult to obtain. Boosting one may inhibit another for example. The author argues that an innovation that may lead to achieving all (or a majority) of these aims in the future leads to a moral obligation to innovate in the present. A responsible innovation is therefore an innovation that improves on the present situation of moral dilemma in that it creates a situation of maximizing gain for the highest number of moral objectives.

This definition is not so broadly cited within the RI literature, although well used in Dutch literature. It does however form the basis of the Delft University online course, Responsible Innovation: Ethics, Safety and Technology: How to deal with risks and ethical questions raised by development of new technologies[4] and van den Hoven's concept of Value Sensitive design (van den Hoven, 2013). I describe these matters in greater detail in my description of this course in chapter 2.

Pavie and Carthy

Xavie Pavie and Daphne' Carthy offer a further but once more not so broadly cited definition:

---

4   EdEX offer the Delft University course online at https://www.edx.org/course/responsible-innovation-ethics-safety-delftx-ri101 last accesses 30/10/2019

Responsible-innovation is an iterative process throughout which the project's impacts on social, economic and environmental factors are, where possible, measured and otherwise taken into account at each step of development of the project, thereby guaranteeing control over, or at least awareness of, the innovation's impacts throughout the entire lifecycle. In the case of impacts which are not accurately measurable prior to the launch but are considered to potentially become critical risk factors once the project is on the market, a number of hypotheses should be formulated in order to be tested post-launch to determine whether the product should be re-integrated into a previous step of the process for amendment aiming to minimize negative impacts (Pavie and Carthy, 2013, p68).

This definition is based upon questioning how to implement RI across an organization. The authors take a technical approach in their analysis of the innovation system, in a publication that is aimed at the business community. The publication cited above attempts to offer a kind of manual approach for a working public. The authors work in marketing and innovation, the definition serving in teaching in a business school environment. It is rarely cited in broader RI academic literature.

1.2 Overview of Definition Backgrounds

These various definitions reflect broad fields found within RI research. The von Schomberg definition (alongside that of Stilgoe et.al. that I will come to later) can broadly be seen reflected within the approach taken by policy-makers. As touched upon above and expanded upon further in chapter 3, the European Commission has taken the concept of RI and applied it throughout its funding strategy as a cross-cutting issue. The von Schomberg definition reflects some of the particular EU approaches in its use of the concept of social desirability, relating to the 'Grand Social Challenges narrative' set forward as EU policy[5]. The definition also refers to products, a reflection of the position set out in the 1957 Treaty of Rome[6] that innovation must work for the betterment of the EU economy, the responsibility concept sitting within a broader economic imperative (a situation that is problematic for von Schomberg and that I will come to later). The inclusion of the innovation process as well as any marketable products lays the groundwork for the implementation of a funding system that applies RI as a criteria for project funding, much of which can be seen in the text of the 2009 Lund Declaration that called upon Member States and European Institutions to focus research on the grand challenges of our times by moving beyond rigid thematic approaches and aligning European and national strategies and instruments (Lund Declaration 2009)[7].

The Lund Declaration was the end product of a conference on research and innovation held in Lund, Sweden. The conference was hosted by the Swedish Presidency of the Council of the European Union, where approximately 350 researchers, policy makers and representatives from industry and research funding institutions participated. Those present agreed on a declaration published later in the year stating that European research policy

---

[5] The societal challnges are described on the EC Horizon 2020 website
https://ec.europa.eu/programmes/horizon2020/en/h2020-section/societal-challenges last accessed 30/10/2019.

[6] Treaty of Rome download
http://ec.europa.eu/archives/emu_history/documents/treaties/rometreaty2.pdf last accessed 30/10/2019.

[7] The Lund declaration can be downloaded here
https://www.vr.se/download/18.43a2830b15168a067b9dac74/1454326776513/The+Lund+Declaration+2015.pdf
last accessed 24/10/2019

should focus on global 'grand challenges' such as climate change, water shortage and pandemics. The views presented can be seen reflected within EU research funding policy today, a topic that I will expand on in the following section of this chapter[8].

The Stilgoe, Owen and MacNaghten definition (Stilgoe et.al. 2013 p1571) was produced from a background in the UK Research Councils and the scientific communities they support, and is based upon a set of questions that were drawn out of an analysis of public debate on Science and technology. This analysis was based upon the experience of involvement in 17 UK public dialogues, with the authors drawing particular attention to the results of categorizing questions as to whether they referred to innovation process or final product (see Macnaghten and Chilvers, 2013 for further details). This reflects the funding body standpoint regarding the implementation of responsibility awareness within the research process as a means rather, than addressing ethical issues within products.

The Hankins definition is very much drawn from my experiences working with the Bassetti Foundation (to which chapter 4 is dedicated) and fieldwork carried out in the UK, Italy and Netherlands during research for my PhD. It will be developed throughout this book so I will not go into further detail here.

The van den Hoven definition must be seen within the interests and funding framework of the Dutch NWO (Nederlandse Organisatie voor Wetenschappelijk Onderzoek)[9]. This is the Dutch Organization for Scientific Research, an independent

---

[8] For further information about the conference see the EC CORDIS website
http://cordis.europa.eu/news/rcn/31013_en.html last accessed 01/11/2019

[9] Further explanation of the work of the NWO can be found on its website: http://www.nwo.nl/over-nwo/wat+doet+nwo Last accessed 24/10/2019.

funding body. Jeroen van den Hoven was the founder and until 2016 Programme Chair of the Responsible Innovation Program, funded through the NWO[10]. This program grew out of the Ethics and public policy Program (*Ethiek en Belied* in Dutch) through which the foundations of the new program were laid in discussion between 2003 and 2007, and involves a broad partnership between Ministries, NGO's, universities and the private sector (van den Hoven 2014, p.4).

Definitions in Non-academic Use

There have also been non-academic definitions published in different environments. In 2013 an Expert Group to the EU's Directorate General for Research and Innovation produced a working definition in their report, although it is much less known in the academic literature:

> Responsible Research and Innovation (RRI) refers to the comprehensive approach of proceeding in research and innovation in ways that allow all stakeholders that are involved in the processes of research and innovation at an early stage (A) to obtain relevant knowledge on the consequences of the outcomes of their actions and on the range of options open to them and (B) to effectively evaluate both outcomes and options in terms of societal needs and moral values and (C) to use these considerations (under A and B) as functional requirements for design and development of new research, products and services. The RRI approach has to be a key part of the research and innovation process and should be established as a collective, inclusive and system-wide approach (Sutcliffe, 2011, pp.55–56).

---

[10] The Research Council on Responsible Innovation website has further details
http://www.nwo.nl/en/research-and-results/programmes/responsible+innovation Last accessed
24/10/2019.

This definition shows several similarities to the von Schomberg definition above, a fact that is unsurprising given the link between the report and von Schomberg himself, at that time working within the Directorate General for Research and Innovation and very much being the major promoter of the concept of RRI. Both definitions are aimed at the process of innovation, its inclusiveness and use. For greater detail see the section on this report in Chapter 3.

The European Foundation Centre (EFC), an EU-based philanthropic organization that works directly for EU policy-makers also produced a working definition of RRI in 2012 that summarizes the above in non-academic English:

> Building on the success of Science in Society projects in engaging the general public and civil society in debates around science, RR&I aims to go one step further and engage all societal actors – from researchers through policy makers, to citizens, businesses, etc. – to work together throughout the research and innovation process in order to ensure that the results meet the needs of the world we live in[11].

Academic and Societal Roots of the RI Concept

Several authors argue that the roots of RI can be found in anticipatory governance strategies (Barben et al., 2008, Karinen and Guston, 2010) and Technology Assessment (Grunwald, 2014, Stilgoe et.al. 2013).

These authors argue that the concepts and working practises surrounding RI and RRI can be seen as having developed from the idea of anticipatory governance and its later derivatives. The language of anticipation and governance can be found across the

---

[11] The EFC website can be accessed here: http://www.efc.be/ although the definition page is no longer available. It remains widely cited however. Last accessed 30/10/2019

entire swathe of RI and RRI literature.

As Hilary Sutcliffe points out in the report cited above commissioned for the EU Directorate general of Innovation:

> RRI is about trying to get better at anticipating problems, taking into account wider social, ethical and environmental issues and being able to create flexible and adaptive systems to deal with these unintended consequences. This is sometimes called Anticipatory Governance (Sutcliffe, 2011, p.3).

The concept of anticipatory governance has been greatly developed by David Guston, a leading name in RI as the Founding Editor in Chief of the Journal of Responsible Innovation[12] and Director of the Virtual Institute for Responsible Innovation[13].

 In the abstract for his article Understanding Anticipatory Governance, David Guston describes anticipatory governance as 'a broad-based capacity extended through society that can act on a variety of inputs to manage emerging knowledge-based technologies while such management is still possible' (Guston, 2008, p.1). The example used is taken from the early history of the National Nanotechnology Initiative in the United States, within which the particular form of anticipatory governance involved building capacity in foresight, engagement, and integration. As Guston explains, the concept is not without its critics (Fuller, 2009, Nordmann 2007), and can be traced back through two major strands, the first associated with public administration and management (e.g. Bächler, 2001), while the second associated with authors in environmental studies and

---

[12] The Journal of Responsible Innovation online http://www.tandfonline.com/toc/tjri20/3/2?nav=tocList last acessed 20/10/2019

[13] The VIRI is hosted by Arizona State University https://cns.asu.edu/viri last accessed 20/10/2019

policy (Gupta, 2001).

The use of the word anticipatory in the title is not however depicted as being similar to foresight or prediction. An analogy is drawn with weight lifting or training in a gym. The exercises practised by an individual are not aimed at preparing him or her for a single event in order to overcome a particular hurdle, but to prepare them to confront the unknown challenges that lie ahead. It is a form of preparation, thus anticipatory governance is 'more about practising, rehearsing, or exercising a capacity in a logically, spatially, or temporally prior way than it is about divining a future' (Guston, 2014, p.226).

Technology Assessment as an example of anticipatory governance

Technology Assessment (TA) strategies are based upon the argument that new forms of technology will bring about societal change that will be much broader than that which may be of interest to the developers themselves, and therefore should be assessed by expert bodies. The concept emerged in the 1970s through the development of advisory roles (Bimber, 1996), with the aim being to bring about the mitigation of risk in relation to new technologies through the intervention of expert bodies that would report to political bodies in authority. The R&D stage of these technological innovations was addressed later however with the development of Constructive Technology Assessment (CTA) which opened a new route into looking further up the developmental chain of the innovation process (Smits and Den Hertog, 2007, Rip et.al., 1995).

These developments are influenced by what has become known as the Collingridge Dilemma (Collingridge, 1980). The

Collingridge Dilemma is a double bind problem, bringing up two conflicting realities for a situation that both affect action and outcomes. The dilemmas are of information and power: in order to assess impact we need information about an innovation, but the further we move up the innovation chain the less information is available. Information becomes available with the development of the innovation. But as the innovation is developed it becomes more difficult to adjust due to the problem of power, the political and financial interests involved become ever more entrenched, all of which makes adjustment and change more difficult.

Grunwald argues that the roots of TA and later CTA lie in a growing critique of innovation that developed in the 1960's (Grunwald, 2014b). The questioning of technology was brought about by an expansion in the realization that technological progress brought unintended consequences, as seen through environmental problems and catastrophes, which also leads to a negative effect on economic growth. This awareness can be seen as leading to a move beyond the aim of warning of possible problems and into shaping technology at an earlier stage and the development of new models of anticipatory governance (Barben et al., 2008, Karinen and Guston, 2010) such as Constructive, Real-Time and other forms of technology assessment (Rip et al., 1995, Guston and Sarewitz, 2002, Grin and Grunwald, 2000), upstream engagement (Wynne, 2002, Wilsdon and Willis, 2004), value-sensitive design (Friedman, 1996, van den Hoven et al., 2012) and socio-technical integration (Fisher et al., 2006, Schuurbiers, 2011). All of these forms can be seen as underpinning the modern concepts of RI and RRI.

For an extended discussion see the Journal of Responsible Innovation Vol 4 Issue 2 Special Issue on the relationship between TA and RI[14].

The following series of explanations demonstrate how they develop into or expand the argument of anticipatory governance.

Constructive Technology Assessment or Real Time TA

Constructive or real-time technology assessment (CTA) is an attempt *"to broaden the design of new technologies"* through the *"[f]eedback of TA activities into the actual construction of technology"* (Schot and Rip, 1996, p.252). The aim is to move the assessment of the technology earlier up the development chain, in order to be able to address issues before the development process becomes too embedded and the aims and structure difficult to adjust. CTA involves socio-technical mapping and dialogue between producers and consumers, and is embedded in the knowledge creation process itself. Its methodology includes the use of reflexive measures such as public opinion polling, focus groups, and scenario development and planning to elicit values and explore alternative potential outcomes for technologies under development. It also favours the incremental development of technologies in order to more easily manage any possible negative effects upon society.

A well-developed case study is that of Socio Technical Integration Research (STIR) developed by Erik Fisher[15] which leads to Fisher's explication of midstream modulation (Fisher, 2007). The approach involves the placing of social scientists into natural science settings, engaging the natural scientists in critical reflection about their assumptions and processes. Discussions are mediated through a semi structured decision

---

[14] Journal of Responsible Innovation Special Issue https://www.tandfonline.com/toc/tjri20/4/2
Last issues 30/10/2019

[15] STIR is an International Laboratory Engagement Study based at ASU
https://cns.asu.edu/research/stir last accessed 20/10/2019

protocol, resulting in the drawing of three typologies of modulation: de-facto modulation, reflexive modulation and deliberative modulation. The methodology also involves the mapping of social and institutional relationships within the setting, with the feedback generated aiming to problematize these relationships and practices. This may lead to changes in strategy, material practices and the direction research may be pushed along (Fisher 2007). This case is further discussed below, representing an example of a long-term case study and development of the theories of Constructive Technology Assessment.

Socio-technical integration

As noted above the best documented case studies and approaches can be found within the long-time US based STIR Project cited above. The STIR Socio Technical Integration Project is based in Arizona State University and directed by Erik Fisher[16].

The STIR approach consists in bringing social scientists and the humanities into laboratories in order to collaborate within different technological development projects to increase the breadth of voices heard and conversations held within these particular settings. The aim of doing so is to draw out understandings and finally respond to societal wishes through adjustment in the research process. The aim is not only to understand and control unintended consequences, but to bring broader considerations into the process while it can still be modified. The concept of midstream modulation as described above is central to this approach.

The following aims and objectives are taken from the website

---

[16] See the STIR website https://cns.asu.edu/research/stir. Last accesses 31/11/2019

cited above:

Identify and compare external expectations and demands for laboratories to engage in responsible innovation;

Assess and compare the current responsiveness of laboratory practices to these pressures;

Investigate and compare how interdisciplinary collaborations may assist in elucidating, enhancing or stimulating responsiveness.

Doctoral students base their studies on a protocol developed by Fisher during an earlier laboratory engagement study. This study provided evidence that such activities enable laboratory work to become more sensitive to its potential societal implications, without compromising the research itself, education or strategic goals. The aim of the STIR project is to investigate whether these results are applicable across a diverse and globally distributed range of labs and if so, how?

The intellectual merit of the STIR project consists in its extension of the laboratory study as a basis for interdisciplinary collaborations; its timely and comparative investigation of emerging international pressures on research; its multi-sited investigation of the capacity for a diverse set of laboratories in 10 different countries to participate in responsible innovation; and the globally engaged and communal form of graduate education that it will pilot and for which it will establish a platform.

Upstream Engagement

The underlying theme visible throughout this type of research is the related argument of upstream engagement (Fisher et.al., 2006), or simply stated the need to bring the broader public into the research process at an early stage. Its proponents' aim to bring in societal aspects raised by the broader public, that then become additional design criteria within research and innovation processes (Willis and Wilsdon, 2004). Practitioners argue the need to expose the underlying assumptions that underpin the research and methodology to public scrutiny. Within this approach the argument is adopted that scientists have a moral obligation to be clear and communicative with the general public about their work, in the belief that this will lead to a broader based steering of the processes involved. This idea has also been the subject of criticism, both from within the scientific community who question the rational of bringing in a non-expert public (Tait, 2009) and within the RI community who raise issues of the politics and power relations within public participation methodologies and their real possibility of succeeding in bringing in a broader voice (Wynne, 2006).

Value Sensitive Design

As previously noted, the concept of Value Sensitive design (Van Hoven, 2013) is based upon the idea that a designer suffers from a situation of moral overload. He or she has competing goals and criteria, all of which must be addressed. A product must be sustainable in its build, strong and durable but also cost effective, it must be user friendly but also respect issues of security and privacy. Proponents argue that strategies to maximize the values in these competing categories within the design process can build these values into the product. The moral arguments that designers face have to be embedded into the design process, shaping the affordances and future uses of the end product, nudging the user along a preferred path of use for the product involved.

This approach is based upon the idea that technological systems are the product of a long series of design choices, some conscious and others not. Some are inserted however for what we might see as less legitimate reasons, to benefit the engineer or the company, due to financial pressures or a host of other possibilities. The argument states that social and moral values should be central to design, and advocates the modelling of moral imperatives in order to help designers in their task.

An Overview of Governmental Technology Assessment Organizations

Historically, Technology Assessment has typically been carried out in the name of states or evenmulti-state organizations. Various different governmental organizations whose scope is to carry out technology assessment have been founded in recent decades, predominantly in the post war years as a reaction to the development of nuclear technology. The following overview is not meant to be exhaustive, but to give an idea of how governments have sought to address the problems of societal interest and involvement in the development of technology.

The USA Office of Technology Assessment (OTA)

The Office of Technology Assessment (OTA) was an office of the United States Congress, in operation between 1972 and 1995. The purpose of the OTA was to provide Congressional members and committees with objective and authoritative analysis (in the form of technology assessment) of the complex scientific and technical issues of the day. At the time it was widely hailed as a leader in practising and encouraging the delivery of public services in innovative format, including early involvement in the distribution of government documents through electronic publishing. As we will see below, its model was extremely influential and copied around the world[17].

Although the OTA was authorized in 1972 it began its operations in 1974. The foundations were laid in 1969 through mandate from the US National Academy of Sciences. The mandate called for an emphasis to be given to foresight, but in practice this became secondary as the OTA found itself having to address current day concerns as they were presented to congress (Bimber, 1996).

The OTA ran through the National Science Foundation from 1975 and very much represents views aired during the debate on the creation of the NSF itself, as this quote from Scientist and educator Detlev Wulf Bronk demonstrates:

> Competent social scientists should work hand-in-hand with natural scientists, so that problems may be solved as they arise, and so that many of them may not arise in the first instance (Bronk, 1975, p.413)

The OTA closed in September 1995 amid political wrangling within the US Republican party, being de-funded, with the loss of 143 jobs. Many scientists have called for it to be re-established, arguing that the OTA offered independent views on technological development. Princetown University holds the complete library of OTA publications and make them freely available online[18]

European Parliamentary Technology Assessment (EPTA)

EPTA[19] was established in 1990 under the auspices of the Enriue Baron European Presidency. The creation of EPTA was supported by interest and input from a smaller TA office, that of

---

17 http://treasuryota.us/ for full details of the working of the OTA. Last accessed 01/11/2019.

[18] Princetown OTA dedicated website http://www.princeton.edu/~ota/ last accessed 2-11-2019

19 EPTA website http://www.eptanetwork.org/ last accesses 02-11-2019

the UK's parliamentary TA office POST[20] and shares similar goals. EPTA hosts a steering committee consisting of Members of Parliament and representatives of the various advisory boards that serve the committee. The Presidency of the EPTA network revolves every year through its permanent members, with each Presidency holding an annual conference and Directorship meeting.

The Partners have the task of advising parliaments on possible social, environmental and economic impacts related to the development of new science and technology. The stated goal is to provide the support needed for the democratic control of science and technological innovation.

Danish Board of Technology and Foundation (DBT)

The Danish Board of Technology Foundation continues the work of the Danish Board of Technology, an independent counselling institution connected to the Danish Ministry of Science, Innovation and Higher Education, devoted to and engaged in tasks and contributions concerning public matters that require knowledge of technology, values and widespread action in society[21].

The DBT was abolished by law in November 2011 and the DBT Foundation established as a non-profit foundation on June 20, 2012.

One of the best-known operations of the DBT is their consensus conference system, which has been regularly held since the start of the 1980's. Their aim is to create platforms for participants to pool their knowledge, finding sustainable and interdisciplinary

---

20 POST website http://www.parliament.uk/mps-lords-and-offices/offices/bicameral/post/ last accessed 3-11-2019

21 DBT Foundation website http://www.tekno.dk/about-dbt-foundation/?lang=en last accessed 02-11-2019

solutions to R&D and development problems. The DBT consensus conferences combine their knowledge about public and social conditions with their experience about processes. These conferences are probably the most widely quoted example of public participation in national policy decision making about science and technology today (Guston, 2014b).

The DBT Foundation is extremely active at the time of writing and its representatives are often seen at RI and related conferences, demonstrating the close relationship and mutual influence of TA and RI.

The DBT consensus conference system forms the basis of a similar approach currently spearheaded by the Bassetti Foundation in Milan within their political involvement and collaboration with the Regional Government of Lombardy. The Region's Open Innovation Platform[22] contains a responsible innovation section that is currently moderated through a Bassetti Foundation collaboration. See chapter 4 for further explanation.

These three US, Danish and European examples described above are the best known of all of the governmental technology assessment approaches, but this is by no means the full extent of this form of TA. Other institutions include the Centre for Technology Assessment (TA-SWISS), Bern, Switzerland; the Institute of Technology Assessment (ITA) of the Austrian Academy of Sciences, Vienna; the Institute for Technology Assessment and Systems Analysis, Karlsruhe Institute of Technology, Germany; the Norwegian Board of Technology, Oslo, Norway; the Netherlands Organization for Technology Assessment at the Rathenau Institute, The Hague, Netherlands;

[22] http://www.openinnovationlombardia.it/it/home-page?login=true&redirect=%2Fdirect%2Fcrud%2Flistview_dettaglio%2FNews%2Fnews%2F1888&redirect_mode=news
Last accessed 01/11/2019

the Science and Technology Options Assessment (STOA) panel of the European Parliament, Brussels; and the Science and Technology Policy Research (SPRU), Sussex, UK.

1.3 Responsible Innovation Today; an overview of the situation

Responsible Innovation (RI) and Responsible Research and Innovation (RRI) are terms that are often used interchangeably and without their differences being defined within this particular field of research activity. RI is often described as a European concept, and is less tied to the idea of scientific research than its counterpart RRI. RRI tends to be associated with scientific research, while RI is also used in the business field. The development of RRI as a discourse is closely tied to the attachment of the RI concept to funding organizations, and in particular the European Commission. I imagine that the addition of the word Research in the title may have been brought about due to its embedding into policy drawn by the Directorate General for Research and innovation, reflecting the work and title of the organization. I argue therefore that RRI can be seen as the adaption of the RI terminology to policy-making, be that research or political policy. The section on the development of RI within the EU context and interview with René von Schomberg in chapter 3 expands upon this argument.

As noted above the RI field is in rapid expansion, and currently boasts its own journal in the Taylor and Francis published Journal of Responsible Innovation[23], founded in 2014 by then Editor in Chief David Guston of Arizona State University (the position currently being held by Erik Fisher). Other recent

---

[23] Journal of Responsible Innovation
http://www.tandfonline.com/action/showAxaArticles?journalCode=tjri20 last accessed 02-11-2019

developments include Chair positions in RI in the UK (Richard Owen holds the Chair in RI at Exeter University, Jack Stilgoe in UCL), and the Netherlands (Phil Macnaghten in Wageningen, NL), and the adoption and development of the concept by the European Commission and its inclusion as a 'cross cutting issue' within the Science For Society and Horizon 2020 research call for funding series[24].

The RI debate has also evolved to incorporate those interested in entrepreneurship and small Business, banking, home-based science and scientific research (sometimes referred to as hacking or Bio-hacking) and a host of other fields. As noted above the European Commission has included the concept in many of its research calls (de Saille, 2015), as have various engineering and research funding bodies (Holbrook, 2014).

The Netherlands government also has a large funded RI project[25], and it seems that the concept is quickly becoming institutionalized although remaining broadly interpreted and with several competing definitions. The language is also used in China (von Schomberg, 2019)

s noted briefly above the growth of the RI community has led to the creation of the NSF-funded Virtual Institute of Responsible Innovation (VIRI)[26], headed by David Guston and based at the Center for Nanotechnology in Society at Arizona State University. VIRI brings an expanding network of both academic and non-academic partners together to work towards the diffusion of scholarly and action study around various RI related

---

[24] See https://ec.europa.eu/programmes/horizon2020/en/h2020-section/responsible-research-innovation for full details of the concept within the Horizon program. Last accessed 02-11-2019

[25] The NWO website offers an overview http://www.nwo.nl/en/research-andresults/programmes/responsible+innovation last accessed 02-11-2019

[26] See the VIRI website https://cns.asu.edu/viri last accessed 02-11-2019

topics. The network holds an annual conference, with longer term aims including the creation of teaching materials and courses in RI, with the website hosting a large downloadable library of related articles. I myself am a founding institutional member, representing the Bassetti Foundation.

The developments described above have produced a large body of literature in the academic, non-academic and institutional fields. Many EC funded FP7 projects are now publishing their final reports on projects whose aims were to develop the concept (see chapter 2 of this thesis for further development of this argument), several edited collections of articles have been published (van den Hoven et.al, 2015, Owen et.al, 2013) and think tanks and other NGO's publish materials and carry out projects within the field (Fondazione Bassetti, the subject of chapter 3 of this thesis and the London based think tank MATTER[27] being the most widely operating examples).

1.4 Some Conclusions

In this overview of the development of RI and RRI I have described the various definitions that are in regular use in both academic and non-academic communities working within the broad field of RI. As seen, these definitions are drawn through different interests and from different perspectives, and are aimed for the use of different sections of the community.

The von Schomberg definition has become adapted to the functional aims of policy makers while the Stilgoe et.al definition was actually born through national funding body experiences, reflecting these interests and population. The van den Hoven definition has grown from a philosophical perspective, but also reflects the concrete needs of the funding

---

[27] MATTER website http://www.matterforall.org/ last accessed 02-11-2019

body that promotes RI in the Netherlands, and its need to show practical results for the funding commitment.

My own definition reflects a particular perspective on RI practices as situated within particular social settings, presenting a more anthropological and sociological perspective than many of the others. The final two definitions are working definitions used in non-academic settings, although it should be borne in mind that the non-academic sector working within RI should be seen to have played a large part in its development.

A great deal of the academic development of the RI discipline, particularly from the point of view of science and technology development, has been driven by the mainly USA based Science and Technology Studies (STS) scholars such as David Guston, Erik Fisher and Sheila Jasanoff, while the policy side of the debate and development in governance from a policy perspective has been driven by the EC through its various funding regimes. For further discussion see the dedicated chapter 3 in this thesis on the European perspectives and the scholastic perspective described in the forthcoming chapter for extended discussion of these authors.

The relationships between developments in Technology Assessment and the growth of RI can be clearly seen through the overview above. The movement from assessment to management of the innovation process can be seen as a point along a continuum that involves moving the assessment point higher up the development process in the belief that the earlier the assessments are made the more chance researchers have to adjust their innovation process to address their findings.

RI differs from TA in several ways however. Some authors argue that the most important difference is that TA tends to look for risk, for possible problems and effects that a technology might bring to society (several authors do not agree with this simplification however, for an extended discussion see de Boer et.al., 2018 or Stemerding, 2019). The goal of RI goes further, in that it aims to shape the innovation process in order to make it more responsive to societal needs. The value of what might be good for society is introduced, working towards societally defined goals and within societally defined guidelines. The aim is a move to away from restraint and towards positive steering towards goals.

This approach is obviously not free from criticism. Many scholars raise the issue of cultural difference in defining the concept of 'good for society' (Macnaghten et.al, 2014), and it seems obvious that we cannot have societal agreement on which type of technical development is good for which type of society. This can be clearly seen in the loggerhead debate surrounding the adoption of GM foodstuffs in Europe. From one perspective genetic modification offers the possibility of cheap easy to produce nutritional food, but from the other it represents a pathway to the destruction of the natural balance on Earth (Hankins, 2015).

The definitions and working practices described above have tended to lead to a view of RI as represented in pillar or dimension form, resulting in a list of issues to address (transparency, responsiveness, societally beneficial, to name just a few among many in competing systems). This movement has led to the academic sector of the community moving towards a convergence of interest related to governance of innovation in many different forms, a movement that can be seen in the following chapter, a description of the development of the academic narrative on RI.

This chapter offered an overview of the current definitions of RI and RRI in use within academic and non-academic literature, offering an analysis of the historical development of these definitions and the institutional backgrounds that support and adopt their strategies. In the following chapter I offer an overview of the academic literature, demonstrating that the lines of inquiry followed within this literature in relation to the concepts of RI and RRI are largely related to the governance of innovation, science and technology; there have been few case studies within this body of work, with the exception of those carried out as part of EU funded projects described in greater detail in chapter 3. Very little scholarship has addressed the RI issue from a situated, glocal perspective, an avenue for research that this book aims to open.

Chapter 2

The Scholarly Narrative

The field or Responsible Innovation has grown extremely quickly, and as a result most of the academic publications related to the argument are recent. The earliest use of the term in scholarly publication in English dates to around 2012, with the rapid growth leading to the publication of several books and the creation of the Journal of Responsible Innovation in the following years.

Policy developments within the European Commission have also led to the funding of several large projects either directly addressing the RI theme or containing the concept as a theme within a broader project. This has led to the production of several end-of-project reports, which although sometimes not purely academic in nature nevertheless make up an important sector of RI scholarly literature.

This analysis of the scholarly narrative of RI takes the use of the terms Responsible Innovation (RI) and Responsible Research and Innovation (RRI) as its defining border, meaning that all of the reviewed publications below either have the phrase Responsible (Research and) Innovation in the title or were published in books or journals with that phrase in the title.

As the literature field is rapidly expanding but relatively new (as explained above), the narrative will run through a selection of publications in chronological order where possible. The aim of taking this approach is to view the literature content through its development and see the relationships between different authors and positions over time, in order to draw out the RI narrative as it unfolds. References will be made to later publications however when topics are addressed that have developed over time, in order to bring the reader forward and backwards in literature history within established relationships between arguments and topics, while returning to the same starting point in order to grasp not only the development of the argument but also to gain an overview from a particular historical perspective.

Its aim is to trace the development as it moves towards the case study research format that this research sits within and hopes to expand upon. It is a skeleton overview aimed at offering a pathway to place this research within the framework of existing literature.

2.1 The Groundwork

Responsible Innovation, Managing the Responsible Emergence of Science and Innovation in Society.

Edited by Richard Owen, John Bessant and Maggie Heintz, this publication was the first edited collection in English to use Responsible Innovation in the title. Published in 2013, it holds articles from many of the predominant scholars of the time.

The book introduces key themes from academic and business literature in order to redefine the relationship with innovation and technology, and its publication led to the concretization of a discipline that developed in the following years. Essentially multidisciplinary in nature, the themes that are addressed and went on to further development include:

1. Identifying and managing the risks of innovation in the present and future

2. Building reflexive capacity into science and innovation to identify and manage the unanticipated wider impacts of innovation

3. Opening up dialogue around innovation and emerging

technologies to understand wider acceptability and public concerns

4. Regulation, governance and adaptive management

5. Key questions regarding the concepts of responsibility, accountability and liability.

Throughout the book key aspects of Responsible Innovation are scrutinized, underpinned by what was current knowledge at the time, using case studies / examples for illustration. The collection concludes with a look forward that pulls together these various fields of understanding and knowledge to ask the question of how we can ensure the responsible emergence of innovation in democratic society.

Many fundamental issues are introduced including the position of innovation in the twenty first century and the concept of value sensitive design. The book addresses the fundamental issues of governance, proposing a model of adaptive governance, problems of communicating science, debate and dialogue, anticipation and hype. As the first collection this book gathered together several authors and articles that had been published in different forms across other platforms, becoming one of the foundation stones of the developing narrative.

The collection very much points the way for the further direction that academic study in RI would take. A large number of the contributions focus on governance (Simakova and Coenen, 2013, Muniesa and Lenglet, 2013, Lee and Petts, 2013, Fisher and Rip, 2013 and Guston, 2013), a debate that forms the basis of many of the developments to come in the following years.

The overview below analyzes two of the articles that refer most explicitly to the interests of this book.

The book contains *Value Sensitive Design and responsible Innovation* (van den Hoven, 2013*)*, in which Jeroen van den Hoven introduces his mainstay of the concept of moral overload (outlined in chapter 1) within the process of innovation in relation to its move towards responsibility. Van den Hoven argues that with any product and during any innovation process a designer will be faced with a series of requirements that may in some cases not all be attainable. For example, a product should be sustainable, recyclable and cheap, or user friendly but secure. The author describes how an innovation process sits within a spider web of these needs and expectations, offering a form of matrix to help the design fulfil as many of the objectives to the greatest possibility. He offers several examples of failure to implement such techniques from recent Dutch history, including that of the failed introduction of the smart electric meter, abandoned after public concerns over privacy. He argues that such issues and values can be introduced and addressed in the product design stage.

The issue of ethics is taken up in *What is "Responsible" about Responsible Innovation? Understanding the Ethical Issues* (Grinbaum and Groves, 2013), in which Alexi Grinbaum and Christopher Groves describe the changing meaning of the word responsibility as it moves from corporation to the individual.

The authors argue for non-consequentialist individual responsibility and collective political responsibility, leading future thinking in RI in an argument that has been further developed since this early publication (Volume 6, Issue 2 of the Journal of Responsibility carries several articles that build upon these foundations).

Movers and Shakers

Bernd Carsten Stahl authored and co-authored two early articles on RI related topics in 2013, and following an open publication philosophy they are both freely available through open access platforms. These articles can be seen as foundation-stones within the emerging RI debate as a series of authors followed this investigative line.

Responsible research and innovation: The role of privacy in an emerging framework is published through the *Science and Public Policy journal* (Stahl 2013).

In this article Stahl describes Responsible Research and Innovation (RRI) as a 'higher-level responsibility or meta-responsibility' (Stahl, 2013). This article laid the path for a series of authors to write on what putting RI and RRI into practice could actually mean.

Stahl argues that as a meta or higher-level responsibility, RRI aims to shape, align, develop and coordinate research processes in order to ensure acceptable outcomes. He defines meta-responsibility in terms of its maintenance, development and coordination of existing responsibilities tying both individuals and society (including political and individual actors) into the responsibility argument.

More recently Stahl has co-authored two chapters in the international Handbook on Responsible Innovation (Stahl et. al., 2019, Rainey et.al, 2019) in which these arguments are further developed within the fields of ICT and the Human Brain Project.

Many other authors have followed up on Stahl's line of reasoning and questioning how a broader frame of actors can be brought into the responsibility debate.

One example of how the debate has been furthered can be found *in Knowledge kills action – why principles should play a limited role in policy-making* by J. Britt Holbrooka and Adam Briggle (Holbrooka and Briggle, 2014). The authors offer an analysis of two principles, one that aims to prevent or restrain an activity until cause–effect relations are better understood (precaution), and the other whose aim is to generally promote the activity while learning more about cause–effect relations along the way (proaction).

Holbrooka and Briggle argue that there is a middle ground shared by these two perspectives, but that their descriptions in extreme terms mask this. They conclude that the significant middle ground shared by the two principles means that they could be used to arrive at very similar policy prescriptions. The issues raised in this article have become fundamental within the RI debate, as the precautionary principle as expressed in Europe[28] and often criticized in the USA mainstream and innovation media has been brought in question. Precaution is often described as stifling in the media, and several RI proposals have tended to lean towards ideas of proaction and fit within the reflexivity debate outlined above (also see the Stilgoe, Owen and Macnaghten definition, 2013, and von Schomberg, 2013, both of which propose a precautionary approach although von Schomberg holds a pro-active view on the role of ethics). The need to describe innovation in economic terms (for example in EU policy decision language) has also had an effect on this passage.

The debate is moved further by Wickson and Carewe (Wickson and Carewe, 2014).

---

28 http://eur-lex.europa.eu/legal-content/EN/TXT/?uri=celex:52000DC0001
    See the 2000 Communication from the European Commission on the precautionary principle, last accessed 30/10/2019

In *Quality criteria and indicators for responsible research and innovation: learning from transdisciplinarity*, Fern Wickson and Anna L. Carewe describe the process of creating an evaluative rubric of performance indicators to address the challenge of articulating quality criteria and approaches to evaluate RRI. Through their experience of hosting a two-day workshop designed with this aim in purpose, the authors first present the criteria developed after looking at common characteristics of RRI, before creating a rubric.

The process described is extremely interesting because the rubric itself seems to make headway into the problem of how to measure RI in a comparative way. Possible results are described in a spider diagram, with issues of institutional and practical obstacles to carrying out an RI process also addressed. The article concludes with a call to critique and develop the rubric further.

Current movement towards the development of standards within RI practices (Forsberg, 2019) and the related development of the British Standards Institution Guidance on the Responsible Governance of Innovative Technologies[29] demonstrate the continuation of these earlier developments.

In a second Stahl co-authored article *The empathic care robot: A prototype of responsible research and innovation*, published in the *Technological Forecasting and Social Change* journal (Stahl et.al 2013), the author with Neil McBride, Kutoma Wakunuma and Catherine Flick raise the issue of depiction and expectation within innovation through their analysis of the 'science fiction prototyping' approach to visualizing or representing novel

---

[29] At the time of writing the BSI has published a call for comments on the development (in draft form) of the standard: https://standardsdevelopment.bsigroup.com/projects/2019-01085
Last accessed 31/10/2019

technologies and other techno-scientific innovations.

This is a methodological article about how different forms of presentation, in this case a fake radio play, can be used to raise complex ethical issues[30].

This article also led to several authors addressing the problems surrounding depictions of the future in various forms, such as the following examples.

In *The hermeneutic side of responsible research and innovation,* (Grunwald, 2014), Armin Grunwald argues the need for a deeper analysis of the social construction of imagined futures and so-called 'technofutures' (see Simakova and Coanen 2013 for an earlier publication). Grunwald argues that the social construction of their creation and diffusion may have effects upon public policy and societal opinion towards specific technologies, and therefore that a better understanding of their make-up would help in working towards the development of RI approaches.

Grunwald believes that such an approach could demystify techno-futures, and in particular help with understanding complexity issues, which is necessary for democratic debate to function in the present regarding technological development and its processes.

This argument is further developed by Groves et.al (Groves et.al, 2016). In *The grit in the oyster: using energy biographies to question socio-technical imaginaries of 'smartness',*

---

[30] In 2009 I published an article on the Bassetti Foundation website about US Professor Richard G Epstein's work on alternative ways to teach ethics. Epstein uses similar methodologies to raise issues about nanotechnology, robotics and intelligent computing. Epstein was one of the earliest exponents of such ideas.
http://www.fondazionebassetti.org/it/focus/2009/08/a_little_ethical_light_reading.html
Last accessed 1/11/2019

Christopher Groves, Karen Henwood, Fiona Shirani, Catherine Butler, Karen Parkhill and Nick Pidgeon show how a novel combination of narrative interviews and multimodal methods can help explore future imaginaries of smartness through the lens of biographical experiences of socio-technical changes in domestic energy use.

The paper conducts an analysis of different individual perspectives drawn from interviews in which people with divergent social experiences and lifestyles discuss their relationships to energy use.

The authors begin from the idea that social technology assessment requires a critical space in which to explore the 'worlds' of future imaginaries, arguing the need for thick ethnographic data in order to describe the forms of life that different types of technology make possible, an approach that I fully support. They argue that such data is necessary to inform deliberation about possible futures, questioning the argument that the social assessment of technologies and their imaginaries can only take place through explicitly constituted public arenas such as citizens' juries and consensus conferences.

2.2 The Debate Around the Frontier Sciences

The S.NET Conference Publications

A further font of publication has been the S.NET group. S.NET is the Society for the Study of Nanoscience and Emerging Technologies, and their series of publications lead the way in an entire section of publications related to the governance of science and scientific research.

S.NET is an international community of both practitioners and (mainly) social science scholars interested in nanotechnology and other emergent technoscience fields. Each annual meeting gathers contributions from diverse academic and non-academic fields, resulting in the publication of a collection of papers. Many arguments run through several of these volumes.

At the time of writing there have been eight dedicated edited volumes of papers based upon presentations given at S.NET meetings or of their members' research. The governance of science and technology issue is addressed across the series of publications, and within it that of regulation, a key theme that runs throughout RI literature.

The RI themes have run throughout the series of annual conference publications, coming to the fore in the fourth 2012 edition (Konrad et.al. 2012). Amongst a host of related chapters, the fourth issue of the S.NET book series contains a Regulatory Governance section that includes an article by Aline Reichow and Barbel Dorbeck-Jung in which they present a soft regulation classification scheme as a tool for supporting RI. In *How Can We Characterize Nano Specific Soft regulation? Lessons From Occupational Health and Safety Governance*, (Reichow and Dorbeck-Jung, 2012, pp. 83-102) Reichow and Dorbeck-Jung set out categories of soft regulation established to support risk management and risk assessment. They define soft regulation as 'standards, guidelines, communications, benchmarks and codes of conduct' (p. 83), in an argument very much related to that on standards cited above. They define six categories including policy goals, compliance and the authority of those regulating, arguing that such a scheme could make a potential contribution to regulatory policy.

Issues surrounding both soft and hard forms and approaches to regulation are addressed in Chris Bosso's *Nano Risk Governance, soft Law and the US Regulatory Regime* in the fifth issue (Bosso, 2014, pp. 7-18).

Arguments surrounding politics and decision-making run through several of the other papers in the book series, drawing environmental issues into the argument. In *From Lab Bench to Fuel Pump: Researchers' Choices in the Development of Lignocellulosic Biofuels*, Maria Fernanda Campa, Amy Wolfe, David Bjornstad and Barry Shumpert describe research conducted at the US Department of Energy's BioEnergy Science Center, a facility that was founded to help develop the nation's bio-energy future. (Campa et.al. 2014). The authors explore 'decision junctures', in order to see which considerations are given the most weight in the decision-making process. Their findings are interesting in that they relate to personal and institutional driving factors, adding a further layer of complexity to the question of how to define RI in a real world situation, and very much reflecting the interests of the Bassetti Foundation that I will expand upon in chapter 4 and my own interests in the shared and situated construction of responsibilities.

Problems surrounding politics and governance have been addressed by other authors across the RI community in various other formats, including those sitting firmly within what I argue can be seen as the science sector of RI publication.

In *Mapping 'social responsibility' in science*, Cecilie Glerup & Maja Horst employ the Foucauldian notion of 'political rationality' to map discussions and ideals about the responsibility of science toward society, mirroring their interest in the importance of media and communication within the RI debate. The authors ask the following three questions of papers taken from a sample of academic journals:

How is the specific problem (or problems) about lack of

responsibility in science articulated? What are the central aspects of science (or its relation to society) that need to be changed according to each articulation? And what kinds of solutions to the problems are imagined in these articulations and how are these solutions supposed to be put into place?

In a ground-breaking article that highlights several implications and issues within the field of RI governance, four different political rationalities of the social responsibility of science are identified as reflexivity, contribution, demarcation and integration. These can be seen in relation to the pillars and characteristics of the RI approach as described in chapter 1, with the most obvious similarity being reflexivity. Contribution is also markedly linked however, as it implies that science contributes to the well-being of society, and is therefore related to the grand challenge arguments, (von Schomberg 2013,). The demarcation rationality also relates in terms of access to information, pressure on academics to publish and make careers, while the integration rationality relates to science being firmly rooted within society. I will argue that the concept of integration can also form an analysis for other forms of working relationships, such as those described in my first case study in chapter 6. Integration within society brings responsibility for the artisan, as well as for the scientist. This issue will be further investigated in the case studies later in this publication.

The governance argument is further developed in *Responsible Innovation: An Approach for Extracting Public Values Concerning Advanced Biofuels* by Gabriela Capurro, Holly Longstaff, Patricia Hanney and David M. Secko (in Capurro et.al, 2015).

This article draws a science journalism perspective into the academic literature[31]. The authors explore how a deliberative 'mini-public' views the need for advanced lignocellulosic biofuels and their recommendations for supporting or opposing its development and production. Participants of the study engaged in four days of deliberation on their value-based considerations concerning the social acceptability of this technology, before developing a series of recommendations.

Five key factors were first identified that support the need for public deliberation, the event was recorded and transcribed, a list of stakeholders, benefits and concerns was drawn up from the data. A further task was to set the agenda for further deliberations, with nine distinct issues identified. The authors follow up with a discussion of their findings and reflection over the process. The article concludes by emphasizing that the public values reported here are not only important to global discussion over the future of advanced biofuels, but are also one approach to meet the challenge of their politically legitimate extraction as part of socially responsive RI frameworks.

2.3 A Multidisciplinary Investigation

As a pillar of RI, public deliberation discussions are further developed in several subsequent more recent articles, once more written from multiple disciplinary perspectives: communication, cognitive sciences, policy-making just to mention a few, leading to the introduction of case study and ethnographic analysis within RI research.

In *Policy Decision-making, Public Involvement and Nuclear Energy: What do Expert Stakeholders Think and Why?*, Nan Li, Dominique Brossard, Leona Yi-Fan Su, Xuan Liang, Michael

---

31 Authorship is accredited to The Concordia Science Journalism Project (CSJP)
   http://www.csjp.ca/about-us/
Last accessed 30/10/2019.

Xenos and Dietram Scheufele explore how a series of social, cognitive, and communication factors relate to expert stakeholders' attitudes toward public involvement in energy policy-making (Li et.al. 2015).

This study intends to identify all relevant stakeholders involved in making high-level decisions on managing the nuclear fuel cycle in the USA, examining how stakeholders with specialized knowledge and professional experiences develop their attitudes toward public participation as a function of institutional identity, perception of public opinion, and media use. Data were collected with a mail survey of US expert stakeholders involved in making high-level decisions on nuclear energy and other uses of nuclear power, and tables of results were published that the authors follow with a discussion.

In the conclusion the authors state that:

> non-profit stakeholders and scientists working for various institutions value public involvement regardless of their perceived split in opinion, whereas governmental stakeholders are more likely to embrace the input of a divided public than a united one. Governmental stakeholders usually serve as the conduits between lay citizens and other expert stakeholders and are primarily responsible for initiating any form of public form. They go on to argue that their study offers a baseline understanding of the effects of online media attention on expert audiences and that expert stakeholders' attitudes toward public involvement in decision-making related to nuclear energy is shaped by a range of social, cognitive, and communication factors. The issue of involving members of the lay public in science policy-making merits further

exploration. Given the close relationship between public opinion perception and online media use, it is worth exploring the causal links between online discourse of energy issues and elites' perceptions of public opinion or other dimensions of public sphere. Also, how these factors would ultimately influence the quality and outcome of policy decisions is a more intriguing question to answer (Li et.al, 2015, p.277).

Continuing the debate surrounding governance, communication and perception of RI, in an article entitled *Governance of new product development and perceptions of responsible innovation in the financial sector: insights from an ethnographic case study*, Keren Asantea, Richard Owen and Glenn Williamson describe an ethnographic study within a global asset management company whose aim is to understand the process and governance of new product development and perceptions of responsible innovation (Asantea et.al, 2015).

The piece offers a finely-honed description of the innovation process using stage gates (see Stilgoe et.al 2013 for further discussion of the stage gating process described in chapter 1), and suggests that inserting RI into a more holistic version of these processes might be a good approach. This study into de-facto governance (Randles and Laasch, 2015) very much reflects my interests as expressed in this book about the need for ethnographic research in fields much broader than those of the traditional science and innovation studies field. This has however remained an underdeveloped field within RI (with the exception of the Responsible Innovation Series published by Springer, van den Hoven et.al. (eds) 2019), an issue that my case studies section in this book aims to address.

The Politics of Publics

A further question addressed by several authors surrounds the constitution of publics and the politics involved in public participation in decision-making processes.

In Look who's talking: responsible innovation, the paradox of dialogue and the voice of the other in communication and negotiation processes, Management Science Professor Vincent Blok develops a concept of stakeholder dialogue in responsible innovation (RI) processes. The author raises two main questions during the article, pertaining to the role of stakeholder dialogue in the assessment of the grand challenges and the risks and uncertainties involved in RI processes to address these challenges, asking which concept of dialogue is able to respect both the necessity of openness towards other stakeholders and the fundamental differences among the actors involved.

Blok refers to the self-responsive nature of those involved in the dialogue, involving both self-destruction and self-constitution as the relationship of dialogue between the parties develops. The author argues that he has encountered four characteristics of stakeholder dialogue in RI processes, which are displayed in a table (found on p.186), concluding that

> the input of the communication process is found in the grand challenges of our time. The grand challenges block our routine responses, show the inadequacy of our current innovation strategies and call for our dialogical responsiveness to the other. The grand challenges are the input of stakeholder dialogue, since grand challenges destroy myself and demand that I become responsive to these challenges together with multiple stakeholders. The throughput of the communication process is characterized

> by the continuous and unceasing interplay between self-constitution amidst others (self-referentiality as a prerequisite to finding a common ground among stakeholders during the dialogue) and self-destruction amidst others (responsiveness to the appeal of the other during the dialogue) (Blok, 2014, pp186).

Blok further develops this argument in his 2019 article *From Participation to Interuption: Towards an Ethics of Stakeholder Engagement, Participation and Partnership in Corporate Social Responsibility and Responsible Innovation* (Blok 2019).

Blok's arguments are complemented in *New avenues within community engagement: addressing the ingenuity gap in our approach to health research and future provision of health care* by health research specialists Don Chalmers, Rebekah E. McWhirter, Dianne Nicol , Tess Whitton, Margaret Otlowski, Michael M. Burgess, Simon Foote, Christine Critchley and Joanne Dickinson (Chalmers et.al, 2014).

In this article the authors describe their experience of working within a Public consultation project involving deliberative democracy. They recount a public consultation experience in Tasmania regarding problems with public perception of the ethical issues involved in the creation of a biobank, predominantly related to consent and security. The authors argue that the use of deliberative democracy is bringing an essential new dimension to public engagement in the genomic medicine era, using their experience in the field to develop and describe community engagement techniques.

As is apparent, several of these articles are based upon field work or experience, a methodology that forms the basis for my own interpretation of RI and led to a joint publication with anthropologist Cristina Grasseni on collective food purchasing networks in Italy.

2.4 Further Fieldwork Within RI

Collective Food Purchasing Networks in Italy as a Case Study of Responsible Innovation (Hankins and Grasseni, 2014) is based upon fieldwork in Italy and the USA. The authors present work-in-progress insights into solidarity economies, and in particular alternative food networks, as a form of active citizenship that could re-orient the current debate on responsible innovation.

In this article we argue that the responsible innovation debate could be enhanced by using a bottom up or grassroots approach to analyze how structures that appear to show similarities to a responsible innovation model are organized and function. Many of the lessons learned during this fieldwork have been applied to this more recent research project as aspects of this argument continue to run throughout this book.

Several further articles have also drawn conclusions based on fieldwork.

In *Communicating through vulnerability: knowledge politics, inclusion and responsiveness in responsible research and innovation*, Gabriela Di Giulio, Christopher Groves, Marko Monteiro and Renzo Taddei (Di Giulio et.al, 2016) consider why and how inclusion and responsiveness need to be sensitive to more 'local' understandings of vulnerability and need, drawing on research that explores such understandings in different cultural contexts (conducted in north east Brazil, the north coast of São Paulo and England and Wales), using a variety of qualitative methods including narrative, biographical interviews, action research and intervention research.

Several of the case studies described above and below have influenced aspects of my own methodological choices and approaches, not only in terms of action or intervention research that in the case of this research has led to a form of co-production of data.

The case studies mentioned involve discussions surrounding individual and group reactions to problems of environmental concern, such as risk of flooding or landslides, seen from institutional and personal perspectives, reflections upon changes brought about in people's lives as they are moved due to dam construction, and the construction of narratives of energy use respectively. The themes of identity and the creation of social order run through the case studies, and are addressed through the lenses of inclusion and responsiveness as proposed by various RI authors within definitions and descriptions of RI.

The authors argue that such virtues (responsiveness and inclusion) must be characterized by a sensitivity to and understanding of the dimensions of knowledge politics as explored by environmental and development justice advocates, if vulnerabilities are not to be ignored and the complexity of entanglements between identities, risks, vulnerabilities, practices and technologies missed.

The case studies present personal interpretations of situations as a tool for understanding how actions taken both by individuals and third parties are interpreted, accepted or not and justified, opening a particular viewpoint from an RI analysis of what responsiveness and inclusion might actually mean.

This is an important new line of investigation within RI as it relates to how people feel about both their own actions and those of others, raising issues of 'lay normativity' as described by Sayer, an argument that I will return to later (Sayer, 2011).

A further case study has recently been published (de Hoop et.al., 2016) that demonstrates how qualitative research techniques can lead to an understanding of possible barriers to the implementation of RI.

In *Limits to responsible innovation*, Evelien de Hoop, Auke Pols and Henny Romijn present a case study on biofuel innovation in Hassan, South India. This case study demonstrates that there are important barriers that may make it difficult to introduce innovation according to RI values (Hoop et.al. 2016)

The authors come to the conclusion that he case study clearly displays a number of factors that may limit or threaten RI. Factors include material barriers to innovation, the price of 'exnovation' of competing practices and innovations (namely the effect upon previous existing practices), various factors related to the difficulty of stakeholder involvement, and the absence of theories on how to turn the decision to discontinue a particular innovation process into as much a valid outcome of an RI process as the decision to innovate.

The authors represent these problems of the main tenants of RI as follows:

Responsiveness; researchers and farmers in Hassan were aware of material barriers. Farmers limited their participation in the project. The project's researchers were unable to find a solution to the barriers identified, such as water shortages and the price of exnovating an existing practice.

Anticipation: RI literature does not explicitly discuss the importance of taking the exnovation of existing practices into account in an RI process. The case study demonstrates that the researchers at Hassan Bio-Fuel Park and policy-makers showed very little concern with exnovation, while the farmers clearly did take this into account, leading to their partial participation in the project.

Inclusiveness: both farmers and researchers argued they had no other option but to operate within existing power structures. They were all aware of the difficulties that these power structures created but sometimes were able to use them to their own advantage.

Reflexivity: The responsiveness barrier particularly applies to the effect of the project's researchers trying to generate political support for their project goals.

The authors argue that all of these factors above need and deserve to be included and adequately theorized in the RI literature in order to move towards a framework that helps make innovation (if it should take place at all) more responsible.

Once again, the case studies show several similarities to the case studies that I present. The issue of understanding why people chose a particular path is fundamental, whether down to technical issues of personal beliefs, availability of materials and relational capacities.

The case studies in chapter 6 and 7 aim to further develop the literature surrounding how RI is interpreted on a personal level.

2.5 International Handbook on Responsible Innovation

The International Handbook on Responsible Innovation. A Global Resource is the largest collection available to date. Released in 2019 and edited by René von Schomberg and myself, the handbook gathers together 65 authors and 36 chapters bringing together the main developments within the field since its inception.

In the co-authored introduction, von Schomberg and myself outline the development of the concept of RI and its promotion and uptake by several large funding bodies (not least the European Union) before describing how the body of work presented in the Handbook addresses the conceptual issues underlying responsible innovation (Part I), the link with societal desirable outcomes in terms of grand societal challenges (Part II), emerging technologies (Part III) and cultural and regional dimensions (Part IV) (von Schomberg and Hankins, 2019).

Given the scope of the handbook and in such a broad field, any collection reflecting the various standpoints and positions will also have to be broad, and this collection is certainly so. In the introduction the co-editors argue that all of the authors share something in common however, commonalities that are reflected in von Schomberg's definition of Responsible Research and Innovation cited and described in Chapter 1.

As editors we explain however that the definition was proposed as a starting point for a field rather than an end result. It is meant to be the representation of a framework for action through which (via the work presented in the collection) the issues addressed in the definition can be addressed and investigated.

The collection opens von Schomberg's overview chapter in which he identifies several deficits of the research and innovation system: existing market failure to deliver on societally desirable innovation outcomes; lack of open research and scholarship; lack of normative design of technologies and foresight. Together these deficits form the basis for a plea for responsible innovation to be embedded in public policy.

The deficits described are derived from the exclusive focus on risk and safety issues as state responsibility, the lack of any public governance of outcomes of research and innovation and the non-alignment of public values under public research and innovation policies that overemphasize the macro-economic benefits of innovation.

This chapter very much reflects the data taken from my earlier meetings with von Schomberg and presented later in this book while the other chapters offer an enormous variety of arguments and approaches from across the field and the world.

The release of the handbook was accompanied by an (at the time of writing) ongoing tour of events under the title of Challenges for Responsible Innovation. The aim is to build upon the issue raised in the handbook and discuss challenges as well as possible approaches to follow building into the future. The Bassetti Foundation website holds a dedicated section that includes abstracts for each chapter written by the authors themselves as well as an overview of the handbook, details of the events and reports on each event including overviews of the issues raised[32].

My own chapter in the Handbook introduces the Poiesis Intensive Responsible Innovation approach that forms the basis for the research described in this book using a different set of case studies, all of which complement those chosen for

---

[32] The Bassetti Foundation website holds a dedicated section on the handbook and the events
https://www.fondazionebassetti.org/tags/The%20International%20Handbook%20on%20Responsible%20Innovation
Last accesed 30/10/2019

expansion here as they formed part of the fieldwork for this research and very much informed the approach adopted.

2.6 The Influence of Design

Delft University Responsible Innovation: Ethics Safety and technology MOOC

As part of the research for my PhD I completed *the Responsible Innovation: Ethics Safety and technology* MOOC offered by Delft University of Technology (NL). At the time this course was the only freely available MOOC that covered the topic of RI, addressing the concept from the perspective of design for engineers. My interest was drawn to the course as it relates to the case studies in chapters 6 and 7 in that the course approaches the design process as representative of a decision-making process[33].

Rather reflecting von Schomberg's standpoint, in his introductory lecture Jeroen van den Hoven argues that technology is always value laden, that responsible innovations have to have the aim of solving the so-called grand challenges, and that they themselves also have to be expressions of our shared moral values. He argues that this should not be seen as a problem and that the situation may help to push innovation. In chapter 5 I make a similar argument, that the creation of the artisan process involves the construction of a narrative of shared values, which offers certain possible approaches to the exclusion of others.

Van den Hoven argues that RI involves both a substantive and process aspect. The substantive is described as addressing problems in order to improve on current situations, with the

---

[33] The course ran over a period of 7 weeks, with a different area covered each week. Each topic was addressed through a series of video lectures, with readings to download, a quiz to complete and various extras for the diligent student.

process aspect including the criteria for being held responsible.

In his lecture he summarizes this concept in his definition of RI mentioned in chapter 1 as

> an activity or process which may give rise to previously unknown design and functionality either pertaining to the physical world (e.g. designs of buildings and infrastructure), the conceptual world (e.g. conceptual frameworks, mathematics, logic, theory, software), the institutional world (social and legal institutions, procedures and organization) or combinations of these, which - when implemented - expand the set of relevant feasible options regarding solving a set of moral problems. I thus suggest a core conception of responsible innovation which refers to, among other things, a transition to a new situation, and which has as its defining characteristic the amplification of possibilities to meet more obligations and honor more duties to fellow human beings, the environment, the planet and future generation than before.

This is an interesting definition because it appears to suggest that technical improvement can be defined as responsible innovation if it addresses some of the moral and practical problems that exist within current technology. This broadly drawn definition in fact lies at the base of the MOOC content, as it develops into a practical framework for attempting such developments. I see this as a topic for analysis myself, as the framework within which these developments occur is locally defined and developed (see chapter 5 for further discussion).

As the title suggests, the course is aimed at engineers, and the well-known trolley problem[34] is used to make the argument that

---

34 The trolley problem presents a situation within which an individual can affect the outcome of an

engineers can build systems that will avoid dramatic decision-making quandaries (as in deciding between competing disastrous consequences) through design. The ground is laid with a discussion about individual and collective responsibility and the related many hands problem[35].

The course goes on to introduce the dilemma of moral overload, with an explanation of the difficulties of fulfilling a series of differing and competing moral obligations. Emotions, values and decision-making scenarios are brought into the discussion, and it is at this point that the course opens what is a particular line within RI, in aiming to show where (on a series of graphs) an acceptable solution (in RI terms) might sit in terms of its moral obligations. According to the argument offered, there are optimum places to situate the proposed solution that are deemed acceptable, because they come closest to fulfilling as many of the moral obligations as possible. This seems to form a basis for the Value Sensitive Design model that is developed in the rest of the course.

My understanding of this model is that any proposed solution or development cannot please everybody, and cannot fulfil all criteria of moral expectation, but that it can be engineered to fulfil as many as possible. The closer the project comes to fulfilling them all, the more responsible it is, within certain margins deemed acceptable.

A further issue that is raised is the importance of the institutional context within which a technology is being developed and implemented. The course describes how the way

---

accident. The trolley is out of control, but an individual has access to a lever that will change the trolley's direction. The moral decision over whether to change the direction to kill less people is theme of the discussion.

35 The problem of many hands relates to the taking of individual responsibility within a complex multi-actor process.

the public is involved and treated during the planning and development process affects the outcomes of possibly contentious engineering projects going ahead. There is little concern here shown to any discussion of the ethical issues involved in public participation however, and the course seems to hint at the idea that the general public are more likely to accept a new innovation if they feel that they have some involvement in the development trajectory followed, without however offering any critique of this issue (Glerup and Horst, 2014).

The debate then moves on to risk, Technology Assesment (TA), and constructive TA, arguing that the well-known RI framework developed by Owen et al. described earlier owes a lot to the historical development of these fields, a line that I developed in chapter 1. The precautionary principle is also discussed and some suggestions of how to deal with uncertainties in the future (such as the use of pilot schemes) are also made.

At this point the course veers off into what is for me a new dimension within RI, that of balancing risk, safety and cost, and moves into quantitative methodologies and mathematical modelling, later moving into innovation management, and the economic determinants of innovation. Management structure to promote innovation was discussed, but I found the relationship between management structure and responsible innovation seemed under developed. A discussion about frugal innovations followed, but it was very much framed in terms of market properties. A frugal innovation is described as offering a product to a particular type of user, at low cost but high reliability that should in some way improve their life. Arguments around stakeholder engagement in the design process were underdeveloped however, as were problems of exploitation in market terms as developments were framed as offering business opportunities for already developed industries in developing countries.

The course closed with a series of lectures related to designing for values, very much representing the culmination of the debate. It was very much based around case studies in artificial intelligence and autonomous weaponry, with the value sensitive design argument running throughout, with a theoretical model also presented for designing for trust and presence, raising the issue of designing for participation on the one hand or surveillance on the other.

The course aims are to develop a workable and applicable model of RI that can be put into practice today by engineers, and the organizers should be lauded for embarking upon such a difficult task. I feel however that if RI aims to go beyond risk assessment and mitigation, it needs to highlight the 'post TA' aspects of RI (namely the more social elements involved in the innovation process and the aims of such processes). These aspects seem underdeveloped in this course however. It should of course be borne in mind however that Delft is a technical university, and the stripping down of the concept of RI to a workable model and engineering design technique could well have exhausted their goal.

2.7 Some Conclusions

In recent years the rapid development of the concept of RI has created a vast field full of different interpretations and approaches. As this review has shown, there has been a move towards using case studies, although predominantly based within the hard sciences in laboratory settings, with my research offering an extension of this trend. I believe that my approach represents a completely fresh line however within this movement as it analyzes artisan working practices and applies the conclusions drawn related to ideas of doing the job 'right' to a science laboratory.

The interest for this approach lies in demonstrating how a procedure comes to be defined as having been correctly followed within a particular social setting and from the perspectives of the actors involved in the process themselves, though the construction of a narrative. These correct process are constructed within the work space and are fluid and subject to change. Each process is viewed on its own merit within a narrated framework of possibilities, and importantly is seen to have been done correctly.

This approach however represents the first critique within RI that is related to the concept of doing things right as appreciated via an aesthetic conceptualization alongside an ethical one, investigating the social construction of how this works in practice.

Mainstream RI literature has generally put its focus on governance, be that from a funding or action perspective. I believe that my own research is novel in that it aims to investigate how actions are narrated and negotiated in real time within small social groups, and how moral choices are displayed and appreciated in the beauty of the artefacts or processes in action, a topic that has not to date been represented in the literature.

In the following chapter I analyze the adoption of the concept of RI by the European Commission, its insertion and development within funding possibilities and some approaches taken by EU funded projects. A documentary review is supported with the analysis of recorded data from René Von Schomberg, widely seen as the architect of these developments.

Chapter 3

The European Narrative

As noted earlier, RI and RRI have been adopted as concepts within the European Union funding mechanism. RRI has become a cross-cutting issue in the Horizon 2020 call, after growing in importance in the FP6 and FP7 calls.

In this chapter I will first describe the development of RI interest and implementation within the European Commission, before presenting an interview with an individual who is widely seen as the architect of this involvement, René von Schomberg. The interview was conducted in 2016, recorded and transcribed, and represents the culmination of a research collaboration with von Schomberg that was built up over the duration of my PhD period. The working relationship has continued and recently led to the co-edited publication of the International Handbook on Responsible Innovation described in the previous chapter (von Schomberg and Hankins, 2019) and a series of presentations under the title Challenges for Responsible Innovation. This interview offers a first-hand description of how the concept came into use, offering a much broader understanding of the development process within the European Commission than that offered merely by an analysis of their publications.

RI/RRI Terminology in Use

The terminology of RI, adopted in the RRI form by the European Commission, first appeared through a workshop for invited experts hosted by the European Commission's Directorate-General for Research and Innovation in May 2011 (de Saille, 2015).

The European Commission uses the term RRI (Responsible

Research and Innovation) rather than RI, reflecting the importance of innovation and research for its funding system. The terminology is predominantly found in relation to funding calls for research projects, hence the inclusion of the term Research in the title, within the geographic field of the European Research Area (ERA). I also believe that its relationship with the Directorate General for Research and Innovation highlights this connection between research funding and innovation within the European Commission. Its inclusion and diffusion reflects a paradigm shift in the way the Commission sees its role in scientific research, from top-down government to more reciprocal forms of governance, basing action upon a *'new social contract'* creating a *'shared responsibility between science, policy and society'*, to ensure that science promotes *'socially beneficial action as well as freedom of thought'* (EC, 2009, de Saille, 2015).

The basis for this shift can be found in the 2007 Lisbon Treaty (EC, 2007). The treaty states that policy-makers and legislators must *'maintain an open, transparent, and regular dialogue with representative associations and civil society'* (art. 8b.2), and *'carry out broad consultations with parties concerned'* (art. 8b.3). In 2012 the Directorate General for Research and Innovation (DG Innovation) published a document outlining the European Commission's approach, and describing the 6 keys of a framework for Responsible Innovation (EC, 2012): Engagement (choose together, with the joint participation of researchers, industry, policymakers and civil society in the research and innovation process); gender equality; science education (preparing the new generation by giving them the tools necessary to fulfil their responsibilities); open access (making publicly funded research freely available); ethics (a respect of rights and following the highest ethical standards); and governance (policy makers must also take responsibility in terms of developing research trajectories (EC. 2012).

It should be noted at this point that all of these aims as put forward within this document should also be seen from a political and economic perspective. These developments were born out of a perceived loss of competitiveness between Europe and those countries that spent a larger proportion of their Gross Domestic Product (GDP) on Research and Design (R&D). A closing of the investment gap and its resulting drain of young researchers to countries where funding opportunities were higher were seen as goals alongside an aim to *'stimulate the competitiveness and growth of European industry and promote employment and the quality of life of Europe's* citizens' (EC 1997, 4).

Innovation is thus seen as the primary vehicle for resolving (or working towards addressing) both social and economic problems within the EU, a fact that is very much reflected in the Horizon 2020 funding call. This movement and aim can be seen from as long ago as 2002, with the steady path of increment of the themes that are now defined as RRI issues drawn to the fore with the launch of the FP6 funding regime, moving through what was initially the *Science and Society* theme within the FP6 funding call to the *Science in Society* theme of FP7 and the current *Science with and for Society*, a further development of the 'For Society, By Society and With Society' concept outlined in an earlier newsletter (EC, 2011, Owen, Macnaghten and Stilgoe, 2012).

The term 'Responsible Research and Innovation' first appeared in a constructive technology assessment workshop dealing with nanotechnology, in the Netherlands in 2007 (Robinson 2009). This appearance was not casual however, as nanotechnology had become the main vehicle for the advancement of the arguments outlined above, due to its growing economic importance alongside a parallel growth in understanding of its potential to cause societal conflict. Its development was seen as necessary and advantageous, but the problems associated with public perception of the technology had to be avoided (at that time genetic modification of plant life was taken as an example of how non-involvement of the public had led to it viewing the technology with suspicion and resulting in conflict (von Schomberg 2007).

The term was first used within policy-making in May 2011 within a conference organized by DG Innovation (partly by von Schomberg personally), whose aim was to bring experts from funding bodies, consultancy and academia to address the problem of tensions previously experienced, with innovation seen as a tool for wealth and job creation on the one hand and as a provider of solutions for Europe's social problems on the other (the background and developments of this meeting are further discussed in the interview with von Schomberg later in this chapter).

Almost a year after this meeting a larger and much more comprehensive conference was held. The *Science in Dialogue – Towards a European Model for Responsible Research and Innovation Conference* was held in April 2012 in Odense, Denmark. The conference led to the publication of an information leaflet, *Responsible Research and Innovation: Europe's Ability to Respond to Societal Challenges* cited above (EC 2012) that promised *'a smarter, greener economy, where our prosperity will come from research and innovation ...*

[which] must respond to the needs and ambitions of society, reflect its values and be responsible'. The leaflet lays out the six 'keys' of RRI: (1) inclusive engagement, (2) a commitment to gender equality, (3) more science education, (4) ethics, defined as shared values reflecting fundamental rights, (5) open access to data and (6) developing new models of governance (de Saille, 2015).

These recommendations eventually became the bedrock of the H2020 call as follows:

> With the aim of deepening the relationship between science and society and reinforcing public confidence in science, Horizon 2020 should favour an informed engagement of citizens and civil society on research and innovation matters by promoting science education, by making scientific knowledge more accessible, by developing responsible research and innovation agendas that meet citizens' and civil society's concerns and expectations and by facilitating their participation in Horizon 2020 activities. (COM, 2011, 809 final, para 20).

The commission went on to define the RRI process for the follow up Science in Society work program as:

> societal actors (researchers, citizens, policy makers, businesses, civil society, … work(ing) together during the whole research and innovation process in order to better align the process and the results with the expectations of society (EC, 2011, 5023, 5)

The Horizon 2020 website defines the RI approach within the call as follows:

> Responsible research and innovation is an approach that anticipates and assesses potential implications and societal

expectations with regard to research and innovation, with the aim to foster the design of inclusive and sustainable research and innovation[36].

The description continues by explaining that Responsible Research and Innovation (RRI) implies that societal actors work together during the whole research and innovation process in order to better align both the process and its outcomes with the values, needs and expectations of society.

The website goes on to specify the following:

> In practice, RRI is implemented as a package that includes multi-actor and public engagement in research and innovation, enabling easier access to scientific results, the take up of gender and ethics in the research and innovation content and process, and formal and informal science education.

> Responsible research and innovation is a key action of the 'Science with and for Society' objective. RRI actions will be promoted via 'Science with and for Society' objective through action carried out on thematic elements of RRI (public engagement, open access, gender, ethics, science education), and via integrated actions that for example promote institutional change, to foster the uptake of the RRI approach by stakeholders and institutions.

> RRI is furthermore a 'cross-cutting issue' in Horizon 2020 and promoted throughout Horizon 2020 objectives. In many cases, inter- and transdisciplinary solutions will be developed which cut across the multiple specific objectives of Horizon 2020. Within the specific objectives

---

[36] Horizon 2020 website https://ec.europa.eu/programmes/horizon2020/en/h2020-section/responsible-research-innovation last accessed 01-11-2019

of the programme, actions can focus on thematic elements of RRI, as well as on more integrated approaches to promote RRI uptake.

In a factsheet published in 2013 entitled *Science With and For Society in Horizon 2020*[37] the commission further explained its position regarding RRI within the Horizon 2020 funding regime:

'Science with and for Society' (SWAFS) will be instrumental in addressing the European societal challenges tackled by Horizon 2020, building capacities and developing innovative ways of connecting science to society. It will make science more attractive, raise the appetite of society for innovation, and open up research and innovation activities; allowing all societal actors to work together during the whole research and innovation process in order to better align both the process and its outcomes with the values, needs and expectations of European society. This approach is called Responsible Research and Innovation (RRI) and is mainstreamed throughout Horizon 2020.

The document commits the Commission to the allocation of 462 million Euros to the implementation of the project described above, concluding that:

Science with and for Society will have its own Work Programme comprising of calls, grants to identified beneficiaries, expert groups and public procurements grouped together under 'other actions' to further develop, disseminate and support good RRI practices all across Europe. In addition, because Responsible Research and Innovation

---

[37] Download from the EC website
https://ec.europa.eu/programmes/horizon2020/sites/horizon2020/files/FactSheet_Science_with_and_for_Society.pdf last accessed 01-11-2019

(RRI) is a cross-cutting action that will be implemented throughout Horizon 2020, 0.5% of the budgets for the 'Societal Challenges' and 'Industrial Leadership' pillars of Horizon 2020 will be earmarked for RRI/Science with and for Society actions. This means in practice that other Work Programmes in Horizon 2020 will include actions relating to public engagement, gender equality, science education, ethics and Open Access (EC. 2013).

The largest dedicated publication directly related to the EC approach to RI and RRI was the Report of the Expert Group on the State of Art in Europe on Responsible Research and Innovation entitled *Options for Strengthening Responsible Research and Innovation* (EC 2013). The Chair of this report was Jeroen van den Hoven whose RI definition and approaches have been documented in chapter 1 and 2, with the aims of the report to identify policy options for strengthening Responsible Research and Innovation.

The need for action is first demonstrated through examples in which the outcomes of research have been contested in society, because societal impacts and ethical aspects have not adequately been taken into consideration in the development of innovation. Policy objectives are then defined within the remit of the Horizon 2020 aims as described above. There follows the presentation of four main policy scenarios:

Option 1, 'business as usual' implies that the existing approaches to address RRI in EU funding programmes would continue to be the main tools for its promotion at EU level.

Option 2 is an 'improved business as usual', with specific funding for RRI.

Option 3 entails 'Improved coordination with the EU Member

States without a legally binding initiative'

Option 4 is 'Improved coordination with the Member States with a legally binding initiative'.

The report presents an analysis of the impacts of the various policy options, before offering a comparative perspective on the options deemed available, and briefly laying out the options for policy monitoring and evaluation, and can thus be seen as a direct development of the 2012 information leaflet cited above (EC, 2012).

Following on from these documents on RRI, recent history has brought two more important documents for its development and direction, the 2014 *Rome Declaration on Responsible Research and Innovation in Europe* and the 2015 *Lund Declaration*.

The 2014 Rome Declaration[38] was issued under the Italian Presidency of the European union, in agreement with the participants and organisers of the *Science, Innovation and Society: achieving Responsible Research and Innovation* conference[39] held in Rome on 19-21 November 2014.

The declaration was approved on the basis that:

the benefits of Responsible Research and Innovation go beyond alignment with society: it ensures that research and innovation deliver on the promise of smart, inclusive and sustainable solutions to our societal challenges; it engages new perspectives, new innovators and new talent from across our diverse European society, allowing to identify solutions which would otherwise go unnoticed; it builds trust between

---

[38] Rome Declaration on RRI is available for download at
https://ec.europa.eu/research/swafs/pdf/rome_declaration_RRI_final_21_November.pdf last accessed 01-11-2019
[39] Details of the conference are available through the Engage 2020 website
http://engage2020.eu/activities/activity/sis-rri-conference-in-rome/ last accessed 01-11-2019

citizens, and public and private institutions in supporting research and innovation; and it reassures society about embracing innovative products and services; it assesses the risks and the way these risks should be managed[40].

The declaration calls on European Institutions, Member States, Regional Authorities and Research and Innovation Funding Organisations to:

Build capacity for RRI by: Promoting and securing resources for RRI activities at the national, regional and local level; Integrating RRI in the design and implementation of research and innovation programmes; Networking existing initiatives that support RRI knowhow, expertise and competence, within and between EU Member States and between sectors; Supporting global RRI initiatives in view of the global nature of our grand challenges.

Review and adapt metrics and narratives for research and innovation by: Monitoring the performance of Research and Innovation Funding and Performing Organisations with respect to RRI as well as the socio-economic impacts of RRI; Providing guidelines for the implementation and assessment of RRI; Setting and communicating a forward looking vision of RRI. We call on public and private Research and Innovation Performing Organisations to:

Implement institutional changes that foster RRI by: Reviewing their own procedures and practices in order to identify possible RRI barriers and opportunities at organisation level; Creating experimental spaces to engage civil society actors in the research process as sources of

---

[40] Quote taken from European Commission Digital Single Market Website https://ec.europa.eu/digital-single-market/en/news/rome-declaration-responsible-research-and-innovation-europe last accessed 01-11-2019

knowledge and partners in innovation; Developing and implementing strategies and guidelines for the acknowledgment and promotion of RRI; Adapting curricula and developing trainings to foster awareness, know-how, expertise and competence of RRI; Including RRI criteria in the evaluation and assessment of research staff (all quotes taken from the Rome Declaration on RRI, 2014).

The *Lund Declaration 2015* is a reflection upon the Lund Declaration made in 2009[41]. The 2015 version reflects failings seen in relation to the original document and opens with a subtitle in capital letters:

EUROPE MUST SPEED UP SOLUTIONS TO TACKLE GRAND CHALLENGES THROUGH ALIGNMENT, RESEARCH, GLOBAL COOPERATION AND ACHIEVING IMPACT[42].

The 2009 document stated the following:

> European research must focus on the Grand Challenges of our time moving beyond current rigid thematic approaches. This calls for a new deal among European institutions and Member States, in which European and national instruments are well aligned and cooperation builds on transparency and trust.
>
> Identifying and responding to Grand Challenges should involve stakeholders from both public and private sectors in transparent processes taking into account the global dimension.

---

[41] The Lund declaration 2009 http://www.vr.se/download/18.7dac901212646d84fd38000336/ last accessed 01-11-2019

[42] The Lund Declaration 2015 https://www.vr.se/download/18.43a2830b15168a067b9dac74/1454326776513/The+Lund+Declaration+2015.pdf last accessed 01-11-2019

The Lund conference has started a new phase in a process on how to respond to the Grand Challenges. It calls upon the Council and the European Parliament to take this process forward in partnership with the Commission (Lund Declaration, 2009).

The 2015 document readdresses these issues, arguing that:

The Lund Declaration 2009 called upon Member States and European Institutions to focus research on the grand challenges of our times by moving beyond rigid thematic approaches and aligning European and national strategies and instruments. During the last six years European institutions, member states and associated countries have taken important steps to align and coordinate resources and shift the focus towards society's major challenges. Today Europe still faces a wide range of major challenges and business as usual is not an option. The Lund Declaration 2015 therefore emphasises the urgency of increased efforts in alignment at national and European level and that investments in research and innovation better and more rapidly be exploited to the benefit of society. It identifies four priority areas, each with defined priority actions, and calls on all stakeholders to take these priorities into account in their field of responsibility (Lund Declaration, 2015).

The document calls for the ERA to take the following priority actions:

Alignment: Provide high-level political support ensuring active participation of all Member States and associated countries in addressing grand societal challenges; step-up efforts to align national strategies, instruments, resources and actors to ensure an efficient and effective European approach including smart specialisation strategies; improve framework conditions within the European research and innovation system and speed up necessary structural changes in Member States to increase interoperability and openness of programmes, notably in the context of national era roadmaps; agree on a common approach and design a process for 'smart alignment' that allows Member States to jointly identify and address new challenges.

Frontier Research and European Knowledge Base: Investing in and strengthen excellence in frontier research and research infrastructures and ensure that these are effectively organised to enable interdisciplinary projects; foster a new generation of researchers with the right set of skills that include creativity, entrepreneurship, mobility and innovation; strengthen open science including open access to both publications and data as well as the fostering of knowledge exchange.

Global Cooperation: Connect with partners in advanced, emerging and developing countries to address societal challenges at global level; ensure that European initiatives better exploit their potential to attract the world's best researchers and innovators and private sector investment.

Impact on Challenges: Incentivise Europe's public research organisations to strengthen the interface and collaboration with stakeholders and actors outside the academic community; strengthen pro-active involvement of end-users, public sector and industry in addressing societal challenges including demand-side actions (all information taken from the download available on the website).

I would argue that these requests and recommendations, in particular aimed at addressing the perceived 'Grand Challenges', very much guide the trajectory of RRI and RI as seen from the EU perspective. The grand challenges narrative runs throughout calls for funding and projects, and currently drives research, as it has become a necessary objective in research projects. It appears in much of the academic literature attributed to Von Schomberg (Von Schomberg, 2013), and is an issue that is addressed in the interview material that is included in this chapter.

3.1 Projects Funded Under the FP7 Framework Programme (2007-2013).

Under the auspices of the FP7 Framework Program, several large projects specifically aimed at developing tools for and arguments surrounding RRI were funded. The major projects were: RRI Tools, GREAT, Res-AGorA, PROGRESS, RESPONSIBILITY and Responsible Industry. There were other smaller projects funded, but these generally are seen within RRI as the biggest and most influential. The following is a brief description of each of these projects, the aim of which is to offer an overview of how these concepts have been operationalized in multinational EU funded projects.

Much of the following information has been taken from the projects' dedicated websites.

RRI Tools[43]

RRI Tools was created in order to *empower all actors to contribute their share to the Responsible Research and Innovation initiative, the final outcome of RRI Tools being the*

---

[43] RRI tools website can be found here http://www.rri-tools.eu/project-description. Last visited 01-11-2019

development of a set of digital resources to advocate, train, disseminate and implement RRI.

The project was carried out by a multidisciplinary consortium consisting of 26 institutions, led by la Caixa Foundation (Spain). The project used a system of hubs, each hub being responsible for different geographical areas. Hub members were drawn from different types of organizations, including various foundations, NGOs and University structures.

The main output from the project was the RRI Toolkit[44]. The greater aim of the project was to help in building a Europe-wide community of practice in RRI that can use, maintain and add to the toolkit launched by the consortium.

The toolkit itself is accessed through its own search engine, with tools available that address issues including co-construction methodology, science engagement techniques, ethics and responsibility awareness tools, and criteria for gender inclusion.

The project ran training days for anyone who wished to learn more and use or maintain the toolkit.

The project has also published various reports, including The State of the Art in RRI, a working definition of RRI and a report on the quality criteria of good practice standards in RRI. These can all be accessed through the RRI Tools website linked above.

GREAT[45]

The GREAT acronym refers to Governance for Responsible Innovation. The aim of the project was to *develop an empirically based and theoretically sound model of the role of*

---

[44] Link to the online tool kit http://www.rri-tools.eu/search-engine Last visited 01-10-2019

[45] The website offers an overview of the project http://www.great-project.eu/. Last accessed Last visited 01-10-2019

responsible research and innovation governance, in order to bridge what the project leaders describe as *the gap that would allow evidence-based planning, implementation and evaluation of responsible research and innovation.*

In order to do this, the project investigated current RRI practices in order to develop a procedure that would be adaptable to modern scenarios. The research involved a series of case studies, beginning with a survey approach before moving into more qualitative research approaches.

The project resulted in several academic publications as well as a long series of reports to the EU funding body (Hartswood et.al., 2014, Grimpe et.al., 2014, Grimpe et.al, 2014b, Hartswood et.al, 2013). This project closed in February 2016.

ResAGorA[46]

Res-AGorA project takes the acronym from *Responsible Research and Innovation in a Distributed Anticipatory Governance Frame. A Constructive Socio-normative Approach.* Its goals were to develop a normative and comprehensive governance framework for (RRI). The project was carried out by a consortium of eight universities from across Europe, and contained three core empirical elements: *A series of case studies examining in depth existing RRI governance across technological domains; a systematic country monitoring disseminated through a web portal; and a number of 'co-constructive' workshops bringing together key stakeholders.*

This project produced a sizable amount of literature all of which is freely available through the website[47]. All of the case studies were presented through reports in three different stages. The

---

case studies included synthetic biology, occupational health and a critical examination of self-regulation models. Many of these reports were presented as papers in various conferences, and I myself saw several. I was also involved as an expert in one of the working groups and attended a two-day conference in Vienna whose focus was on GM food[48].

I feel that some of the methodology used within this project shares a lot of similarities to my own research. The case study approach adopted led to the publication of a report for each individual case which then all fed into a final large publication, before being compared and analysed in order to draw conclusions.

The final document, *Navigating Towards Shared Responsibility in Research and Innovation. Approach, Process and Results of the Res-AGorA Project*[49] was very broad in terms of where the input came from, describing the passage from the case studies to the final deliverable, *The Responsibility Navigator* and the development of the co-construction method (Lindler et.al., 2016). The two publications together work to introduce differing working practices into different fields with the aim of helping those actors become more reflexive in their decision-making processes. The aim of the co-construction methodology in particular is to introduce upstream self-reflection through workshops, and is presented in a manual format.

The Responsibility Navigator has similar aims but the methodology differs, involving a set of questions that an individual or group would have to answer in order to move towards a more responsible model. The principles are gathered

---

[48] The Vienna conference took place on 23 -24 March 2015

[49] The book is available to download through the website http://res-agora.eu/publications/res-agora-book-now-available/ last accessed 29-10-2019

into three groups, ensuring Quality of Interaction, positioning and Orchestration and developing supportive environments, all of which are supported with evidence from the case studies outlined above.

Progress[50]

The Progress team take their name from the full project title Promoting Global Responsible Research and Social and Scientific innovation. From their mission statement (taken from the website cited above) their aim is *to establish a global network on responsible research and innovation (RRI) involving academia, SME's, international organizations, policy advisors, research funders, NGO's and industry.*

Through interactive discussions with relevant societal actors as well as innovators, the project's goal was to move RRI debates from the national or regional to the global level and achieve the following objectives:

> Link existing international networks of RRI with relevant societal actors on a global scale to focus innovation on societal desirability; complete a major fact-finding mission comparing science funding strategies and innovation policies in Europe, the US, China, Japan, India, Australia, and South Africa; advocate a European normative model for RRI globally, using constitutional values as a driver to inform societal desirability; develop a strategy for fostering the convergence of regional innovation systems at the global level.

---

[50] Progress Project website http://www.progressproject.eu/ last accessed 22-08-2019

The project involved running a series of workshops, minutes from which are available on the website cited above. One topic addressed of particular interest for my research is that of social desirability. The issue was raised as a problem within the project, in other words how could we measure agreement in terms of social desirability? Another topic addressed was that of inclusive innovation, and a further problem addressed that of how to define broad impact criterion.

The project closed with the publication of findings and an agreed RRI convergence strategy. This was a truly global strategy with input from across the continents that brought about the case studies, with a global, multidisciplinary, participatory and inclusive form of RRI. As with all of these projects the deliverables are all freely downloadable through the website.

Responsibility[51]

The Responsibility website describes its project as *A Global Model and Observatory For International Responsible Research and Innovation Coordination*. The project was structured into three main components; the forum, the observatory and training.

The project's aim was to build a network of stakeholders and develop a shared understanding of RRI through the network. The project included the building of a virtual observatory for RRI in order to support these goals, work towards the diffusion of knowledge and promote tools to this end. The project Coordination and Support Action developed the observatory, enabling users and readers who have relevant interests to find, bookmark, comment on and share resources on social media. The main fields of interest were current and emerging

---

[51] The Responsibility Project website: http://responsibility-rri.eu/. Last accessed 22-08-2019

technologies and the issues they are likely to raise for RRI, governance arrangements suitable for addressing RRI and a series of case studies, examples of good practice and training materials in RRI.

Again, the project was run by a Europe-wide consortium of universities from whom various representatives attended a host of conferences to promote the platform. The project led to the publication of a series of reports detailing how it had developed, and offered training and developed training material for use across Europe and beyond to interested groups.

Responsible Industry[52]

The aim of this project was to explore how private corporations can conduct their research and innovation activities responsibly. This project is quite different from the others that have been funded as the community it aims to target is the business community. Their main field of interest is in ICT, and within that field elderly care is predominant.

According to the website cited above, the goals of the project are to:

> Synthesize current discourses on RRI in the industrial context, based on an extensive literature review, 30 in-depth interviews with industry thought leaders, 5 bottom-up case studies and 2 Horizon Scanning reports.

> Investigate, through practical cases and in depth dialogue with stakeholders (industry, CSOs, policy makers and emerging global stakeholders), of processes, challenges and opportunities leading to responsible innovation along specific value chains of products and applications.

---

[52] The Responsible Industry website: http://www.responsible-industry.eu/. Last accessed 21-10-2019

> Conduct an International Delphi Study of RRI in industry involving 130-150 stakeholders and an international Multi-Stakeholder workshop.

> The development of a detailed implementation plan to be tested in at least 4 pilot projects.

> Reflection on the viability of the implementation plan, supported by least 15 industry-driven focus groups.

> The development of models of RRI in industry as a basis of specific recommendations to be disseminated to the various stakeholders through an Exemplar Implementation Plan of RRI in Industry.

At the time of writing the project has recently closed, having produced a host of reports and proposals throughout 2017 that are still available through the website.

As noted above many other projects have been funded since 2014 under what is known as the SWAFS (Science With and For Society) work programme section of Horizon 2020, many of which have recently seen completion. An overview is available on von Schomberg's personal blog[53]. The overview hosts a table that contains links to the projects with a brief summary of their aims and objectives written by von Schomberg, so I will not duplicate the table or its contents here but guide readers towards the website.

3.2 Some Conclusions

The gradual and constant integration of RI principles into the EU funding structure has certainly brought the concept to the

---

[53] Downloadable PDF of von Schomberg's overview is available here
https://renevonschomberg.files.wordpress.com/2018/10/overview-of-projects-on-open-science-and-responsiblle-research-and-innovation11.pdf
Last accessed 01/11/2019

attention of the broader academic and industrial public. In the cases described above many of the goals have involved case study work that investigates how RRI practices have been developed and defined in different situations, how they have been perceived and approached, and to raise questions about how the concept can better be implemented through the funding structure. The projects have involved the bringing together of large numbers of experts and operators in a broad range of fields, raising awareness of the debate within the partner countries and providing large amounts of data for the EU in return. The various tools and all of the literature produced has been made open access and accessible in terms of the language used and their operability.

From a critical perspective however, I feel that this systematic funding has led to an analysis of RI from a particular perspective, that of policy and funding. The definitions of RI that are used throughout this series of projects is that of the European Commission, leading to those who wish to develop definitions or concepts that may be more critical in nature having to frame their arguments within this structure or face exclusion from the funding regime. While it may be good for citizens, I feel that it might have led to a less critical approach within the study of the concept of RI itself.

This regime has had an immediate effect upon those working within the field of RI, as it has presented large amounts of funding enabling the development of collaborations and the production of tools to integrate into innovation systems. Almost all of the organizations that I have dealt with during this research period have participated in EU funded projects, which has galvanized and focused the development of the concept, bringing together interests from within academia, civil society and industry, creating new opportunities but also changing the way social research in the field is conducted; interdisciplinary has become the norm, non-profit organizations have become involved, and reports and publication use different language and are structured differently. All of which reflects the goals and aims of RI as described in the various definitions in chapter 1.

As noted in chapter 1 and 2, the driving force behind the inclusion of the concept of RI and its insertion as RRI within the European funding system is widely seen to have been due the influence of René von Schomberg. In the section that follows I analyse the development of the concept from his personal position through conversational and interview data, before offering a selection of comments drawn from recorded interviews organized as part of my research project.

3.3 René von Schomberg

René von Schomberg is widely viewed as having been the architect of introducing and promoting arguments surrounding responsibility in innovation and research within the European Commission.

He is widely accredited with one of the widest quoted definitions of RI and RRI (Von Schomberg, 2011) and is the central figure within the field as related to policy making.

An overview of his position: The Responsible Innovation Matrix, 2011/2012

As noted, René von Schomberg has worked within the European Commission since 1998, as (amongst other things) Team-leader in Science Policy within the Directorate General for Research and innovation. He has a great interest in responsible research and innovation, is a well-respected member of the RI community, and has very much taken the lead in developing the idea within EU research policy. He has consistently held the position that a series of specific developments are necessary if the transformation of research and innovation is to proceed towards a more responsible position. These necessary changes include a change in incentive and rewards systems within research, public authorities becoming proactive in compensating for market failure (through public, private, or public/private partnerships) and innovation management through market standards and codes of conduct. These changes underpin the need for a move towards the governance of outcomes rather than the current form of a governance of constraints (von Schomberg, 2019).

Von Schomberg first published an article and a 'Responsible Research and Innovation matrix' on his blog[54], which he has further developed in Owen's edited collection described in chapter 2 (Owen et.al, 2013), his chapter in the International Handbook on Responsible Innovation (von Schomberg, 2019) and beyond.

The matrix should be read and interpreted via a parallel reading of the article published in 2013 as *A Vision of Responsible Innovation'* (von Schomberg 2013).

The matrix article as it appears on the website opens with a historical overview of how the definition of responsibility has developed and changed over the years in terms of its relation to discovery and innovation. The author argues that ancient inventions were *controlled by a central agent to avoid abuse* but that today *Economic exploitation of innovations implies a loss of a sole control agent.*

The article opens up a debate into how to define and promote a form of innovation that would have a desirable social outcome in terms of benefits and risks, (a stated aim of EU policy), before describing current EU legislation. The author states that there are many difficulties in formally measuring the possible benefits and risks for society, arguing that the process is in some way flawed and artificial. He argues that it may be difficult to reach a consensus on what is beneficial for society, as it may be difficult to see relational and networking uses and possibilities. He uses the example of video gaming technology used in surgical techniques to express the difficulties involved as unforeseen uses emerge for new technology.

The author continues by discussing the problem of defining the right impacts and outcomes of research and the subjective nature of the so called 'good life', before outlining how EU public policy statements aim to promote responsible innovation, offering what he describes as *normative anchoring points*. Von Schomberg regularly returns to this debate (von Schomberg, 2014) as demonstrated by his 2016 lecture at the conference of the same title[55].

The author then addresses the Grand Challenges and the direction of innovation development, explaining how the Lund Declaration offers an alternative description of the role of innovation in Europe, criticizing the prevailing view that innovation is good per-se and a viable mechanism through which jobs and well-being will be created. The following quote summarizes von Schomberg's general theme; *The idea is clear; to steer the innovation process towards societally-beneficial objectives* (taken from the Wordpress blog cited above). He

---

[55] The Conference on Responsible Research and Innovation (RRI): The Problematic Quest for right Impacts was held at Donostia International Physice Centre on 10 – 11 March 2016.

concludes that the aim as outlined in the declaration is to fund research that will bring particular positive outcomes for society as a whole.

The second section in the article is entitled *Responsible Research and Innovation: Organizing collective responsibility*. In this section the author describes how possible unforeseen and undesirable effects are not merely the responsibility of an individual, but are in fact side effects of collective action. He goes on to give some examples of what we might be able to describe as 'irresponsible innovation', categorizing four types: a) technology push, b) neglect of fundamental ethical principles,) policy pull, and d) lack of precautionary measures and technology foresight.

The example offered of technology push is Monsanto's attempt to break into the European market with genetically modified soya in the 1990's. The Dutch government's electronic patient record system (EPRS) project is his example of the neglect of fundamental ethical principles. The introduction of security technologies, such as the use of biometrics for passports, asylum applications and whole body image technology (body scanners) at airports is given as an example of policy pull and he cites the report *Late Lessons from Early Warning*s (EEA, 2001) for a string of examples of lack of precautionary measures and technology foresight.

Under the title *A framework for Responsible Research and Innovation*, von Schomberg offers his well-known definition of responsible innovation cited in chapter 1, before continuing by describing possible normative anchor points for both the product and process dimensions of innovation, stating that they should be ethically acceptable, sustainable and socially desirable, before introducing and explaining his matrix of examples of lead questions to be answered by stakeholders, either from a product or process perspective in order to fully implement an RRI scheme.

He uses five different headings: Use of Technology Assessment and Technology Foresight; Application of Precautionary Principle; Innovation Governance; Ethics as a 'Design' factor of Technology; and Increasing Social-ethical Reflexivity in Research Practices and Deliberative Mechanisms for Allowing Feedback with Policymakers: devising models for responsible governance and public engagement/public debate.

The article concludes with a section entitled Outlook. Within this section the author summarizes the current situation within the RI debate and its effect upon policy-making before outlining his ideas about how an agenda for responsible innovation could be nurtured and developed. The final line is particularly worthy of note as it states that *RRI should become a research and innovation "design" strategy which drives innovation and gives some "steer" towards achieving societal desirable goals.*

I would argue that this was very much how the concept became perceived by the European Commission in its passage through the different research agendas described above, showing von Schomberg's clear influence on the field in question. It is apparent to all of those working in the community that these developments can be directly attributed to the work, interest and influence of Von Schomberg within the commission, making him by far the most influential character in the policy-making field and the most cited author across the field.

3.4 René von Schomberg: An insider perspective

Through my work within the Bassetti Foundation I was able to initiate online conversation and eventually develop a research collaboration with Von Schomberg, leading to several meetings, both at conferences related to RI and also through visiting his place of work in Brussels, and leading eventually to our collaboration on the International Handbook on Responsible Innovation (2019) and Challenges to Responsible Innovation (2019) book tour.

Developing this relationship allowed me to build a working relationship that has led to my attending many conferences that he has spoken at, and given me the chance to produce large amounts of recorded data in order to better contextualize his remarks within a broader RI experience. The arguments that follow are based upon this experience, and in particular a recorded interview held in Brussels in 2016.

In this section I argue four main point related to von Schomberg's position on RI, and his view of the development and implementation of the concept. The points are as follows:

1. The various pillars used to describe RI should not be taken as a definition of RI or RI practices;

2. RI could be spelt out as the need to cultivate responsibility as a social need and objective;

3. The development of the concept was brought about by the need to move beyond the idea that innovation is a good in itself;

4. Arguments surrounding RI and the fallibility of innovation are difficult to make within a form of governance whose consensus depends on growth and jobs.

I would like to support these arguments above using short quotes from my recoded interview.

1. The various pillars used to describe RI should not be taken as a definition of RI or RI practices:

While talking about the key action structure and the development of the pillars of RI, von Schomberg describes how their creation was more of an organization change than the search for a definition of a new way of working:

> My recollection is that the pillars were never meant to be pillars of RRI. They were just pillars of a unit that was assembled together from pre-existing units from the Science and Society Directorate, it was just an organizational change. We had people from science education and ethics and governance of science and they had all come together in one department. And the idea was of course to integrate this into one unit, and the pillars were actually a reflection of elements partly from previous departments. It had an internal sense to have these 6 pillars to sort of represent what it is that brings them together and what they do.

Von Schomberg argues that the pillars came to be seen as a process through which RRI could be understood and practiced, but they were not intended for this use, they represent a pathway to transformation but in many ways are not really representative of his view of RI.

> But the step that it takes, that well this is now RRI, is a mistake. And this was also never my idea. My point was more that each of these pillars is important but they need to be transformed each for each. So ethics has to transform from an ethics of constraint to an ethics of innovative design, science communication has to change from communication from some kind of central agent who tries to enlighten the public to distribute the science communication where it is

actually in the hands of each actor that does the innovation, so each of these pillars need a radical change if they are to be part of RRI, otherwise in my view they have nothing to do with RRI. It can still be sensible to do but it has nothing to do with RI.

2. RI could be spelt out as the need to cultivate responsibility as a social need and objective.

I was based a long time in the then science of society directorate of DG research so this was about in the mid 2000's and I was at that point developing a concept that had its beginning while I was at university about responsibility, and that was the basis that I used later for the concept of responsible innovation. The idea of doing RI in DG research came about on a reflection on the Science of Society program as it was then.

Von Schomberg explains the deficit that he felt was visible in the concepts and practices of the time.

We had all these activities like consensus conferences and ethics research, a lot about the risks of technology and so on. So in my view these things were all good but there was a deficit, and they were that first of all there was always a focus on the risks on different technologies such as synbio and nano and whatever, and its technological potential and the criticism thereof, but not so much about what actually is this innovation all about? And it was not about innovation processes as such. It was very much about technologies themselves and the risks of these technologies, so the negative aspects of technology.

As the Science and Society program was transformed into the Science in Society program the need to cultivate responsibility as a social need was brought to the fore.

So this brings us to the following big issue which was also not in the science and society program then of how do you steer innovation processes towards the grand challenges, because this was actually a new thing in the European agenda. And well you could say that there you have the opportunity connected to citizen values and so on. So against this whole background, a sort of deficit of the science and society program on the one hand with an exclusive focus on risk, and ethics in a very constrained way, and so RI would be an answer to this deficit, plus it would go much deeper into the wider innovation process and not just look into particular key enabling technologies.

So that was by the end of 2009 I believe if I remember this well, we had then the first ideas and workshops to bring this forward and we were able to have RRI anchored in the H2020 program which in the meantime had acquired an enormous budget increase for this area compared to that of the science and society.

Von Schomberg also addressed the use of his current definition and the others that steer the policies followed by the EU, which also relates to the social need objective.

Well the pillar depiction is hopeless, if it doesn't mean the transformation that I was talking about, and regarding my own definition, looking back to it, maybe I should sharpen it a bit. Actors should become mutually responsive to each other. Probably we have to strengthen this a bit. This responsiveness should be translated into some kind of commitment towards a social objective.

He offers a further example of this thinking related to the pillar argument taken up above in point 1 and describes how he seen the paradigm shift required for a move towards RI, that introduces the argument of point 3.

> We have ethics and so on then you get these pillar stories, you know we should do education and everything else, we should do this this and this and then you have RI. But this of course is a very problematic approach because each of these are precisely the shortcomings that I was reflecting upon before. It is not about an ethics of constraint where you say well you should not do that in your research and innovation, for RRI you have to have a normative design of tec. And we should use ethics as a driving force for innovation, it is more about normative design. Maybe the normative design of innovation systems rather than technologies as such.

3 The development of the concept was brought about by the need to move beyond the idea that innovation is a good in itself.

Von Schomberg maintains that the development of the concept of RI must be seen from the perspective of requiring a critical view of innovation.

> There is a paradigm shift not just looking at the conditions and the risk and the classic task of the state but a move to making the actors responsible for the outcomes, so beyond the market. Because now you say that the benefit equals market output and so the idea is that the state should also become responsible for what you get out of it and not only for having good safety measure or something which is of course also important.

He continues this theme.

> I think that if you look to the genesis of the concept further, I

think that this element is not really articulated. I think that one still needs to articulate it further, we are not just talking about having better stakeholder participation or something else but it is about stakeholder commitment or societal objectives and not technological potential.

The following quote leads directly to addressing point 4, regarding the position of the EU regarding economic growth and job creation.

Innovation was not the focus but it was rather different technologies and the second question was the output. What do you want to get out of it? And the third goes with the first in that it is a general criticism of how science and technology are always justified in the commission, if you look at the justifications, the paradox is that science and technology funding was always very consensual. If you look to the history of the EU then research was one of the first things to do and was never really controversial, and progressively over decades got more and more money with big steps in budgets and this is all against the background that science and technology is inherently good, and embedded in a theory of macroeconomic justification that it will produce jobs and growth.

4. Arguments surrounding RI and the fallibility of innovation are difficult to make within a form of governance whose consensus depends on growth and jobs.

This clarification further explains his position.

And this was again for Horizon 2020 when it was still under development, it was again a big challenge. It was all about innovating jobs and growth and this connection. So my reflection started there by saying we have this paradox, a consensus, but at the same time non embedded like the other policies of the commission, which go back to the treaty of Rome where we link it to fundamental values of what citizens actually want the EU to do.

So my idea was to bring science and technology into the same context as the other policies, which means not merely a justification in economic terms, apart from the fact that the economic rationale in itself is wrong. So you can see that the idea of RI was a criticism of a particular economic paradigm which falsely believed that this will bring enormous jobs and growth and secondly whether you can do it in this way by just providing framework conditions, namely money.

3.5 Some Conclusions

Through my working relationship with Renè von Schomberg I have been able to gain invaluable insight into the development of RI practice and discourse within the European Union. The excerpts from the recorded interview cited above add context to the literature and practice reviewed, while offering suggestions for improvement of the RI project and the speaker's position within it. What appears clear is that von Schomberg is calling for a transformation in the system, and not merely the adjustment of an existing mechanism. This position can be seen in his 2019 article in the Handbook on Responsible Innovation via his description of deficits in the global research and innovation systems (von Schomberg, 2019).

The interview above demonstrates how von Schomberg has been central to developments within the European Commission, how the framing of science and innovation as well as economic imperative has played a large part in this development, and how issues surrounding the implementation of a radical change in thinking at the level of trans-national governance should be approached.

In the following chapter I turn to the Bassetti Foundation's contribution to the RI debate, counting milestone conceptualizations of responsibility, innovation and more specifically Poiesis-Intensive innovation. My research consists in linking these conceptualizations to the wider RI scholarship and in contributing relevant case studies to this latter notion of Poiesis-Intensive Innovation with respect to RI, in a way that I would summarize as derived from a narrative that leads to an aesthetics of responsibility.

I will first introduce the Bassetti Foundation and its vision and mission, then dwell on its unique context and concept of Poiesis-Intensive Innovation. Finally, I will trace the steps through which the Bassetti Foundation historically laid the groundwork for conceptualizing responsible innovation.

Chapter 4

The Italian Narrative: The Bassetti Foundation in Milan

The Bassetti Foundation has held a prominent position within debate surrounding Responsible Innovation since its very inception. The organization was one of the very first to use the term, using variations on the theme (responsibility in innovation being the main example) in use on the website from as early as 1999. The Foundation has the promotion of the concept as its mission, and was the first foundation created to further debate and action in this specific (and at the time almost self-named) field. Many of those at the forefront of the RI debate today have visited the Foundation over its long history, delivering lectures, participating in round-table debates and other projects. Bryan Wynne, Sheila Jasanoff, David Guston, and René von Schomberg have all presented their research and work, as the Foundation has very much been an engine for the development of the idea of RI and its possible implementation.

The Foundation is also particular in being one of the very few non-academic operators in the field. Having non-academic roots, the objectives of the Foundation are currently and have always been to effect change through action, and not merely the furthering of academic debate. One of the results brought to the broader community was the tangible effect the Foundation had upon the politics and Statute of the Region of Lombardy.

Quoting the Foundation, Giuseppe Adamoli, President of the Special Statute Commission, made reference to responsible innovation during the 3 July 2007 meeting of the Regional Council of Lombardy. The concept was later included in the new Statute, approved in the spring of 2008.

In his remarks, Giuseppe Adamoli referred to a speech delivered by Foundation President Piero Bassetti:

> There is also a great challenge which our Region must face. It is a challenge referred to by Piero Bassetti, the first President of the Region of Lombardy[56], at a conference on Technical and scientific innovation, democratic innovation. Bassetti spoke about responsibility in innovation and expressed his hope that Lombardy would face this responsibility directly and commit itself to governing this issue in its own Statute, leading the way for other Italian regions. It is a complex issue that calls for the participation of society's leading innovative forces in the administrative and legislative procedures I mentioned previously[57].

The Foundation has recently participated in the drafting of further regional legislation, known as the Legge regionale 24 settembre 2015 - n. 26 Manifattura diffusa creativa e tecnologica 4.0, and even more recently the Legge regionale 23 Novembre 2016 – n.29. The aims of these pieces of legislation is to support and allow financial assistance for promoting innovative manufacturing processes, and the small businesses that put their development into practice[58]

The influence of the Foundation on regional politics is clear in this case and is a subject that I will return to later in this chapter, with other examples of where the influence of President

---

[56] The Region of Lombardy contains just over 10 million inhabitants, and produces about 20% of GDP for the entire nation.

[57] Quote taken from
http://www.fondazionebassetti.org/en/focus/2007/07/political_responsibility_in_in.html
Last accessed 01/11/2019

[58] Documentation and the full text of the law is available on the Capire.org website.
http://www.capire.org/attivita/clausole_valutative/lr20150924lombardia.pdf last accessed 28-03-2019.

Bassetti's personal experiences in politics can be clearly seen.

Foundation President Piero Bassetti was in fact Board member and Councillor within Milan City Council from 1956 to 1967, going on to become the first President of the Region of Lombardy from 1970 to 1974. A Member of Parliament from 1976 to 1982, he was also President of the Chamber of Commerce and Agriculture in Milan (1982-1997) as well as President of the Union of Italian Chambers of Commerce (1983-1992). From 1993 to 1999 he was also President of the Association of Chambers of Commerce Abroad (CCIE).

Today he is President of the Bassetti Foundation and also President of Globus et Locus, an association of institutions whose objective is to analyse global and local relations.

Under President Bassetti's leadership, the Foundation participates in large EU sponsored projects and has an international presence and global network of collaborators. I myself have collaborated extensively with the institution, representing the Foundation since 2006 in a role that developed into that of Foreign Scientific Correspondent, and saw myself based in Boston USA for 3 of those years. The Boston posting reflected a time of great expansion in the Foundation position within the RI debate, provoked mainly by the rapid take-up of the idea by academia across the world and within the various funding and governance organizations as described in chapter 1. The Foundation is recognized as having played a pivotal role in this development, specifically in laying the earliest foundations of the present debate.

The Foundation has developed a particular perspective on RI over these years of activity, with several notable differences to operators from the academic sector. Innovation is not seen as necessarily science nor investment heavy (as is prevalent in most of the scholarly perspectives described in chapter 2), focusing an entire strand of political and philosophical thought on responsibility within entrepreneurship and local, national and international governance (see the Lombardy governance example above).

In the following section I describe the development of the Foundation since its inception using documents available in the Foundation archives, before looking at some of the most important turning points in Foundation history.

I then analyse a selection of my recently recorded interviews with President and Founder Piero Bassetti in order to describe these developments in much deeper terms, as much as possible in his own words, using short extracts from much more extensive recorded interviews in order to offer a much denser and personal description of the Foundation's particular approach.

Much of the data is taken from recorded meetings, discussions and interviews that took place in Milan, at the Foundation offices and conference suite. Some of the data used is taken from an interview that took place between President Bassetti and Professor Sally Randles from the Manchester Metropolitan University as part of her *Voices* Project and later became a chapter in the International Handbook on Innovation (Randles, 2019), and much of this section owes a great deal to her inspiration and collaboration. Where discussion was provoked by questions offered by Professor Randles I mark so in the text, and I also mark where my observations involve interactions that were not recorded but experienced first-hand in my position as collaborator or invitee.

4.1 An Overview of the Bassetti Foundation

The Bassetti Foundation (Foundazione Giannino Bassetti in Italian) is a not for profit social research organization, founded in its current format in 1993 to honour the name of Giannino Bassetti, former head of the family business, with the aim to promote debate surrounding the idea of responsible innovation.

The Bassetti family owned a large textile company throughout much of the last century, for many of those years under the guidance of Giannino Bassetti and his brothers. From early roots in the hand weaving business, the company became extremely well known in Italy and across Europe for its high-quality household textiles.

Under the leadership of the Bassetti brothers, and later under the direction of Giannino (as the brothers became more specialized they took on different roles) the Bassetti Textiles company became mechanized (moved from hand loom use to mechanized techniques) between 1906 and 1908, and underwent a rapid expansion over the following years that was only curtailed due to the outbreak of the Second World War, at which point the company employed 1500 workers, rising in the years immediately after the war to almost 4000[59].

The business was of note for its political line towards its employees and those living in the areas around the factories, a characteristic that I feel is very much the base and reflected within the modern Bassetti Foundation. Influenced by ideas of solidarity predicated through the Catholic Church, the business promoted a relationship of mutual collaboration with its stakeholders, including the formation of a committee that

---

[59] For a detailed history see the Treccanni website (in Italian)
   http://www.treccani.it/enciclopedia/giovanni-bassetti_(Dizionario-Biografico)/ last visited 21-11-2019

included members from each sector described above and supported by a large Italian Workers union (CISL) in a form of co-management. The aim was stated as being the examination of all of the company's productive and organizational needs preventatively and together, with the scope of obtaining understanding, participation and fair solutions to problems for all parties concerned.

Giannino Bassetti's death in 1980 lead to the creation of the modern Foundation, to honour his social and business achievements. The social approach outlined above can be seen as the roots of the political and socio-philosophical line that the Foundation has followed over the years.

Since its inception it has worked towards the creation of a network of interested parties, in order to further research and promote action aimed at the proliferation of the ideas surrounding RI, with the aim of promoting real change. At the time of writing, the Foundation website[60] holds almost 20 years of reflections, articles and interventions surrounding ideas related to RI, published through a Creative Commons license in keeping with a policy of giving open access to all publications to interested parties and individuals[61].

The Foundation participates in an array of different RI related projects, being part of an International network of relationships, thus allowing its collaborators a privileged viewpoint on the global development of the concept of RI. The foundation is action oriented, and as a result works with many different institutions within the fields of academia, politics and civil

---

[60] The Bassetti Foundation website: http://www.fondazionebassetti.org/
Last accessed 02/11/2019

[61] Further details are available through the Bassetti Foundation website cited above

interest. Research and interventions are always geared towards real-world results, as research informs policy proposals and political action.

To be precise, the aim of the foundation is stated in its mission as

> the promotion of the development of responsible behaviour in innovation, in both the national and international context, through assisting institutional, private and associative subjects to orient themselves and their goals towards the improvement of society as a whole.

This aim holds not only for the technoscientific fields, but also within the creative economy, entrepreneurism and also governance.

The aims of the Foundation can be further expressed in the following points:

To make all of those actors who participate in innovative decision-making more aware of the consequences and responsibilities that their roles entail;

To help in building a relationship between civil society and institutions, contributing to scientific research while developing instruments for the diffusion of responsibility in the technosciences, lifesciences, biomedical and oncological laboratories, in bioethics, governance, finance and business;

To participate in projects and international consortia to work towards understanding, developing and spreading understanding of the work the European Union has conducted in developing the concept of RI, while contributing to strengthen and enrich this work;

> To collaborate with local government and other organizations in order to develop governance programs that gain from the Foundation's specific competences, collaborating with such structures and proposing projects with such entities[62].

Lines of research and investigation have involved many different partners from different fields in public and business life. One line has been the role of finance within responsibility, investigated through a partnership with Allianz Insurance Company that culminated in a lecture given by Michael Bruch at Bocconi University in 2013[63] . The role of financing has also been a topic of debate related to funding bodies and the roles that they hold, with several large projects carried out with Banking Foundations and financed through regional banks, the largest recent example being the WAVE event hosted in Milan in 2015[64].

To summarize the above, the Statute finalized in 1994 states the objective to be to create a new and updated understanding and a new and widespread sense of social, civil and political responsibility within those who innovate.

4.2 President Bassetti in his own Words

A great deal of discussion has taken place over these years regarding how to define the concept of RI, and within it both the concepts of responsibility and of innovation. Innovation has been defined by Piero Bassetti as *the achievement of the improbable* which is taken as meaning much more than the discovery of something new and therefore applicable within a

---

[62] Aims taken from the Foundation Statute, available through the Bassetti Foundation website cited above.

[63] Video of the lecture is available through the Foundation website http://www.fondazionebassetti.org/en/focus/2013/01/risk_and_responsibility_in_inn_1.html last accessed 29/10/2019

[64] Posta about the WAVE event http://www.fondazionebassetti.org/tags/Wave last accessed 29/10/2019

broad range of fields. The following quote is taken from a recorded conversation with President Bassetti. Bassetti is talking about how the discussion of responsibility was approached at one of the most important meetings in the development of the thinking of the Foundation which took place in Alz, and will be described in further detail later in this chapter. It is an extended explanation of the Bassetti Foundation definition of innovation and how it leads to raise the issue of responsibility:

We started defining innovation as the realization of the improbable, this was our first definition. I think you would say achievement in English because in Italian 'realizazzione' means something that is between implementation and realization. The idea is that when you are innovating you are dealing with the implementation of something that is improbable, and we think this is important because it is an action which regards the appearance of something that is not impossible, is not forecast-able but is improbable. Therefore, is in a sense economically and sometimes physically risky.

We think that innovation is performed through the availability of a surplus of power and knowledge; You must know something more, but you must have the power to implement it, therefore the base requirements for innovation are something unknown and something non existing.

At the end of the process you have something that we could in a sense see as new. Therefore an innovation is an absolute novelty. We (at the Foundation) think that this introduction of something absolutely new and unknown is a risk and as such has to be handled responsibly. This leads us to addressing the strange fact that many things have been implemented by entrepreneurs without them taking full charge of the consequences of what they were about to implement[65](taken from Randles, 2019).

The problem of how to define responsibility however is not such an easy one to conquer. Issues of social meaning, values and geographic differences have all come to the fore both within the Foundation itself and in the broader literature on RI as described in chapter 2. The following quote comes from Bassetti as he describes a fundamental moment in the Foundation's history, the meeting in Alz. In this short second section Bassetti outlines some of the problems involved in trying to define the concept of responsibility, referring to the 10 commandments as the point of departure in Europe, and discussing the problem in terms of the development of the atomic bomb raising issues of power and implementation.

> What didn't come out at that time was that when we were talking about responsibility, all of those present thought that the concept was clear, in terms that an irresponsible person is bad, and a responsible person is good. So what did we mean by being responsible? Behave in a correct manner. But what do we mean by correctly? We mean ethically correct. But what does ethical mean? Well in substance we mean the 10 commandments.

> And seeing that this was obvious it became a contribution that was very positive to the debate. And this leads to some of the most important achievements for the Foundation. Firstly, the definition of innovation as the achievement of the

---

65 This quote and the series that follow was taken from an interview conducted with Sally Randles as part of her Voices project, and transcribed and used with her permission. The interview later became a chapter in the International Handbook on Responsible Innovation

improbable, and secondly the concept of the impact of innovation, which is that innovation does not always have positive impacts. Which seems obvious, but at that time it wasn't. So innovation can have negative impacts.

Let's take the atomic bomb for an example, at that time the problem of the bomb was really evident. So with the bomb we are talking about innovation. The decision to develop the bomb was not taken by Einstein or Oppenheimer but by Truman. So from this we get the concept of innovation that I developed, that innovation is a plus of knowledge and a plus of power. When these two plusses meet, innovation can emerge. At this point for the problem of verifying if something is or isn't responsible then the definition of what we mean by responsibility becomes fundamental.

And here we needed some time, several years, because the idea of responsibility was not something that was clear. This was a difficult problem to overcome, because responsibility is the ethics of behaviour, and so for example the ethical boards in the hospitals were one case. We followed the ethical issues within health, for example therapies that are responsible if ethical.

At this point we came to the conclusion that the criteria of ethics were extremely fragile, and at this time the idea of the fragility of ethics was not well known. We had not had all of these battles over the sciences of life in which all of these ethical problems have emerged so much that nobody now knows where they stand any more.

In those days there was a lay ethics, that said that we will not accept the ethics of the church, but what is lay ethics? We needed 2 or 3 years to come to the conclusion that the concept of responsibility was an extremely vague one.

Much of the early work of the foundation was initially dedicated to reflecting upon what innovation is, but as this moved on to looking at what responsibility actually is or might be perceived as, many difficulties came to the surface. Bassetti argues that this is because we can understand innovation, but responsibility is connected to ethics, and if you forget about a purely religious approach, responsibility is something that is difficult to locate, organize and to approach.

The loss of absolute values is a topic that is often brought into play during conversations within the Foundation, in some ways the question could boil down to one of how to determine right and wrong in an age without God. One solution proposed is that of deliberative democracy. Bassetti argues that democratically taken decisions will be better decisions in terms of the good of society. For him this sits under the umbrella role of politics, as the following quote summarizes:

> Within the term responsibility, etymologically, you respond (from Latin, 'respondere'). But you respond to whom and for what? So it sounds like a clear affair but it is not. When you move into the significance and meaning we find a lot of approaches. There was a Latin idea of responsibility, with many different approaches. But if you assume a political look then responsibility is the impact on history. How do you change history through innovation and what is the space for responsibility in making history? This is the role of politics, and in a democratic country it has to be decided by majority or minority assumption of responsibility. We went through this in our work in the foundation and spent a lot of time thinking about what we assumed (and assume) to mean by

responsibility. I think that should be much more clarified, particularly by those in political authority. We must spend more time over this. I have issues with some institutions because we don't believe in the significance of corporate social responsibility. This is theorized in a simplified and misleading way, and we believe that the problem of theorizing responsibility in innovation is still unsolved.

This brought us to the point of saying that responsibility was the anticipation of the effects. So if you tell me what effect the innovation will have then everyone can decide knowingly, but that does not mean responsibly, even if today there is still a tendency to say that knowingly means responsibly. If you think about it, if I do something knowingly then I obviously do it bearing in mind my morality, and here we have the legal responsibility problem.

The following line summarizes the standpoint:

we are not interested if an innovation is responsible, we are interested in whether it is democratic or not. And if those democratic are responsible.

The argument seems clear: if we improve the method of decision-making we should arrive at a better decision from the broadest point of view, those including responsibility, efficiency, productivity, and risk. Instead of analysing a system it should be put into the hands of the population, but which population? Some populations will make better decisions than other populations. People who do not know anything about a topic cannot be asked to make a decision upon that subject as there are no grounds for their decision-making. Bassetti argues that the population should make the decisions over who can make decisions, representing a reflection upon one of the central pillars of RI, that of inclusion. He continues the clarification:

> So I think that what is happening in the foundation is the entrance of political logic in the ethical or purely rational logic, about probability and knowledge.

> I agree but I think that this fault of problematizing is extremely serious for humanity. We are handling the relevant innovations in an irresponsible way. We take OGM (Genetically Modified Organisms) or nano or bio technology and the neuro-sciences and we play with innovation in an irresponsible way. In that sense the road we have run is very short compared to the risks that humanity is dealing with historically. That is the production of the relationship with science and knowledge. This brings us back to the problem with Adam and Eve and the apple. Regarding science, it appears we do not yet have control of it. This has been a problem for the foundation, because when we started to pose the question the reaction was 'oh you want to put a limit on the innovative capacity of humanity so you are a reactionary!'. Well that does make sense in a way, but it is also part of the problem. We must problematize our love for innovation. As I say you have innovation when you really change something, not when you discover something. This is the difference, innovation is the implementation of discovery, and you change things so it is connected to power and in economics is connected to money. You need a surplus of power to implement innovation.

> Not many people think like we do, but in a way, humanity is forced to face this problem because I think that we are jeopardizing humanity by playing with technology and the supplement of power that it gives us without sufficient

understanding of the consequences. That is an enormous political problem that is not properly dealt with. In that sense I think that capitalism is fully contradictory with responsibility, for example in dealing with the limits of the planet. If we do not change our economic approach and move for example towards the sharing economies or the commons approach..... well I am glad to be old and not be there when the problem comes up.

As argued above, the origin of the thinking that underpins the Foundation lies within the family's connection to textile production, and in particular innovation within that field. One instance that is often mentioned within debate and discussion is emblematic of how daily decision-making and choices can affect the world and had led to defining the Foundation's position.

Several years ago, the family business introduced a new product to the Italian market. The product was a new sheet, a bottom sheet that meant that beds could be made in a much simpler way. The sheets had corners, it was what we now know as the first fitted sheet. In doing this the business had affected the way men and women deal with something in practical terms, in this case the daily chore of making the bed. The following words are from Bassetti himself:

When I noticed the changes this provoked, in such a relevant area as sleeping, I began to realize how full of implication, and very important this process had been. The fact that we could change the way people interact with the bed without responding to any other authority apart from that of profit which was of course the matter of interest to the business, led to the question I first asked my uncle (the then Director of the family business); 'but to whom did you ask the authority of changing the bed for the Italian family?' Well he replied 'I don't know, but we do make a profit!'

Bassetti does not however find this an adequate response. He was a student of Schumpeter and this is very much reflected in his thinking on this matter. The question for Bassetti is where do we find the authority or responsibility of implementing innovation?

> Schumpeter argues that wherever you have something of increasing value you have profit. Therefore, the judgment on the validity and value of innovation in his theory is referred to as the existence of profit. Profit is the compensation for a valuable innovation.

Bassetti however does not accept this argument and often refers to the development of the atomic bomb as example of why innovation has to be responsible. The fact of dealing with the bomb, and the responsibility that that entails, demonstrates that innovation must be responsible.

Today the Foundation focuses on different fields for innovation but the Foundation's question remains the same: Where is the responsibility within innovation, with whom does it lie and to whom are the innovators responsible? Out of this perspective the view grows that risks associated with biotech or synthetic biology are enormous, as risks have moved into areas of unknown consequences, and can no longer be measured in terms of percentages. Bassetti often uses the example of shipping to explain risk and its shortcomings today. He argues that if we take the risk associated with sea transport we can expect a certain number of failures, one ship in every 10 for example will be lost, but if we are looking at synthetic biology or the development of nano technology we can no longer measure the risks in the same way. And we cannot see the possible effects of these risks, they are in some ways absolute risk.

A further example that is often used in the Foundation is that of the events in the USA on 9/11. Following from the argument above about absolute risk, we would have to ask the question that if you don't know the consequences of your action, in this case an innovation process, how can you carry out a risk assessment? What are the risks? They are unknown risks, so how can their frequency be determined?

The example of 9/11 can be described in this way: September 11 was an innovation, an irresponsible innovation but never the less an innovation. The insurance company Allianz lost eight billion dollars on that day[66] and legal battles continued for many years as insurance companies found themselves insured for losses that were provoked by an event that from their point of view was totally impossible to predict. We can use this example to make the statement that the criteria of probabilistic risk does not exclude somebody (or a company) from the problem of the extent or type of responsibility they take when you construct something (in this case towers), or indeed of those who insure them.

Once the event has occurred once however the risk can be seen, if not measured, and attempts to prevent it occurring again can be made. But in the case of the towers in hand, it becomes obvious that defending a structure of that size is very difficult. Where will the next attacks come from? They might come from

---

66 See *Ten Years After 9/11: Property Insurance Lessons learned* by Scott G. Johnson for further explanation of the complexities of insurance losses after the attack at the Twin Towers http://www.robinskaplan.com/~/media/pdfs/ten%20years%20after%209%2011%20property%20ins urance%20lessons%20learned.pdf?la=en, last accessed 24/11/2015

under the ground, or from another as yes unforeseen route, and how could the towers be protected from such unknown risk?

The Foundation line is that the way to address the problem of unforeseen risk is through responsibility. Responsibility is not here seen as legal responsibility however in terms of blame, or after the event responsibility, but a forward-looking responsibility. But the question that is often raised is that of how someone can take responsibility for something that they cannot foresee.

The tower problem can be easily seen in other fields. If we take synthetic biology or genome editing, we find similar issues. Today genome editing is not only the realm of scientists in labs, but also of bio hackers and biology students. It has become easy to modify a genome, but the modification is not necessarily a modification that merely lives in the present. Modifications can be passed on through the generations as organisms reproduce the modification in their offspring, in effect changing the historical course of the entire future of the organism, bringing the question of unknown risk over an unknown timescale.

If we look to President Bassetti's work experience we see where these arguments were born.

The business experiences of the family textile company have had a steering effect upon the development of the Foundation's approach. A look back to these operating practices allows the reconstruction of the early building blocks.

When Preseident Bassetti started his participation in the family business it was a monopolistic producer of domestic goods such as sheets and other textiles, but mainly bedding. The firm was particularly innovative in marketing. It was the first textile firm in Europe to spend a lot of money on advertising. It was a prestigious very well-known and accepted name, mainly producing products for the rapidly growing middle classes. This meant that when the company suggested changes in behaviour and the acceptance of new ways of seeing and furnishing the house it held a lot of influence. The company also had ties with Pirelli, and worked with them regarding ways of producing mattresses.

The way people dealt with the bed and its surroundings were extremely diverse at the point in which the company started modernizing the market.

Bassetti Textiles were the first in Europe to use the broad support of psychological analysis, with experts within the company analysing the relationship between people and the bed. The bed was seen as a strong, important part of life and the home, where you are born, you reproduce and sleep. The company gained an insight into the importance of changes in the relationship between people and the bed, leading to it being able to perceive the relevance of changes in social, cultural and political terms of this relationship between people and beds, to see the relevance in changes in consumers and supply of beds and its organization.

This was particular to the firm, which was very advanced in dealing with cultural approaches to marketing in this field. Going as far back as the 1950's the company was already acquainted with the relevance of change, not only in terms of standardization and industrialized organization, but also in the changes in the relationship between the psychology, attitudes and habits of their consumers. This led to the company stressing the importance of change.

Bassetti sums up the experience with a familiar analogy:

It was a family firm and so dealt with a complex sensibility. Our family was peculiar, catholic with a strong sense of values and social responsibility.

Bassetti did not however remain within the family business for long, moving into politics, another experience that can be seen as playing an important role in the future direction of the Foundation.

Now I was born into that family and I was the natural candidate to become a manager within the business, and so I started working in the field before following my vocation into politics. I have in fact led a life of politics. I was in the city government, I was a founder of the Italian Regions, first President of the Region of Lombardy, I sat in parliament etc. My career is marked by politics, so this is a reflection on a decision that was routine, as it is in every firm. When you have an idea and it is successful you don't spend too much time reflecting upon the responsibility you have taken outside the fact of whether you have made some profit or not.

Bassetti summarizes his education and work experiences in the following quote, taken from his interview with Sally Randles. In just these few words we find many of the cornerstones of the foundation's approach, the necessity of power, the importance of civil society, the importance of beauty and practicality, and the influence of economics.

In a sense I understand that my personal experience somehow changed, because as you have probably noticed I was born into a situation. I followed a normal course of classics studies, in the humanities as most Italians do, then I went through the normal experience of a ruling class member, military experience and university. I won a fellowship and spent 2 terms in the USA at Cornell, then another in London to study the privatization of steel. I spent six months studying the re-privatisation of the UK iron and steel industry. Then I went through the initiation into my management career, as I said I soon discovered my vocation towards a civil service experience. I was elected into the local city council. But my educational experience was a strange mixture. I have an education in economic sciences, mainly theoretical economics, so I have a mixture of science experience, and management, so power experience, but also in a way a sensibility connected to the humanities experience.

So I agree (in a sense) that the approach to a normal managerial decision taken not only through the rationale of economics but together with values and political consequences, is what facilitated the perception of a connection with that strange affair that is responsibility (Randles, 2019).

As hinted at above, the Foundation's position is that the tool required to achieve more responsibility in innovation is the democratization of decision-making. This standpoint is steeped in President Bassetti's political experiences in terms of politics as service to society.

As often stated by President Bassetti, the aim of the Foundation is to promote change and not merely academic debate. In order to better move towards this goal, the Foundation has created a large network of collaborators and partners over its lifetime, and has recently undergone a change in its statute. The Foundation has become a Foundation of Participation, allowing partner organizations to hold a seat on the Board of Directors and offering mutual advantage to those involved.

One thing is a foundation that proposes the discussion of a problem, but a foundation that proposes to address a problem is another thing. And it is clear that in the second case you need a set of instruments that is more developed and finer and probably more powerful. The foundation did not have and could not have within the limits of its capital the answer to this problem, and so there was a need to find alliances. And this having been a dominant question, where do you find alliances?

As I have argued above, President Bassetti has spent most of his working life in the field of politics, notably within the Lombardy Regional Government as President of the region, and the answer to the question above lies within these experiences.

Well in the first case you find it in a public structure that is nearby and as you know I was president of the Region of Lombardy so in a certain way I still have a judgment that is brought about through familiarity with the political structure as a whole but more so with the region, so the first thought was the region.

In order to address the scientific side of the debate the Foundation is looking to appoint a scientific institution to the Board. At the time of writing negotiations are ongoing, and as I result, I cannot name those involved. Bassetti describes the logic of these choices:

Looking at the institutional and legal possibilities and seeing the possibility of the participatory foundation, newly appeared in our system, we decided 2 things:

First to abandon our previous way of working because it was destined to become inadequate. Because of course if we had the possibility of investing millions then we would have kept everything within the existing set up, but in reality, we don't have these possibilities. But if we go and involve institutions that are willing and capable of political responsibility, because in politics you cannot get away from your responsibilities, scientific responsibility, and to the responsibility of the life sciences, which are part of the same problem in a sense, innovation that is capital and science intensive, we needed a different statute, and this is what we have done.

In effect this set up maintains the driving force for the foundation and the family to steer the history of the story of innovation, because it gives all of the power to the family, but it also opens the possibility of participation from a structure such as a Polytechnic University or another institute that works within the life sciences, but could also be spread more widely.

Finance and Banking have also been fields of interest for the Foundation, not only as possible partners but also as topics of critique and reflection. As noted, President Bassetti studied economics and much of the thinking underlying the Foundation's approach owes its basic principles to his experience as a student of Schumpeter.

Risk is an issue that has run through RI debate since its inception, and the Foundation promotes debate on the subject matter through various relationships. The Lecture involving Allianz cited above being one example.

Bassetti feels that certain aspects within this debate have not been problematized, and he sees the case from his own experiences as having had to take on responsibility through the family business at an early age:

There are problems tied to innovation which are connected to the limits of humankind, and which are based in the concept of risk, which is another topic that is also not problematized. The experience of humankind has always been tied to power and the risk of exerting it. If you grow up in a position of power, you grow up in the risk of your condition. If you are limited in your possibility you probably have less contact with risk.

The quote above returns to the problem of power, the power to both innovate and change the world but also the power to risk relationship. Issues of politics come in to the discourse around power, as does the related problem of moral responsibility:

You cannot propose a limitation in the increase of power, in the sense of the will of power as Nietzsche used, the term as used in German and Italian meaning "potenza", so not power in political terms but in absolute terms. I agree that we have a strong wish for power, and the sense and value of life lies in exerting this will. The Prometheus myth is false, you can contain but not restrain the main push that he represents. If you do not have clear absolutes as humanity did when it believed in God, all seeing, all knowing, when you had these terms then God was responsible, but we have disposed of him. Having killed him, we must assume the responsibility of driving the destiny of humanity.

For Bassetti this leads to the acceptance of the problem of risk within politics:

That is a real problem, if you transfer it in political terms you see that the only way to gain an understanding of the problem is advocating risk. Because when you mention risk everybody understands that power may be a risky affair in absolute terms, not only historical. The risk of losing a war doesn't change the history of the planet. But increasing the population to 7 billion people might, can they be sustained? This is a demographic risk, the only limit that you can assume as an objective is risk. Risk has been at the source of capitalism, you can insure a boat using a model of probability, so 1 boat in 10 will sink, and you cannot have capitalism without insurance, but the concept of risk was based on probability, now we are dealing with absolute risk.

Another aspect that has become an important topic of discussion and practice, is that certain types of innovation create a dramatic problem with the governance of innovation. Because the current model of governance designed for industrial society is built upon industrial innovation, it does not easily apply to today where there are different types of innovation. He raises the question of how such new soft forms of innovation can be governed (oft-cited examples include Air B&B or Uber).

Bassetti argues that legislators face the issue of having to understand that they can no longer obtain the criteria of responsibility from norms and ethics. This is problematic because all of the bureaucracies in the world lean upon norms. And norms always lean on ethics. He argues that this therefore requires a new approach.

Poiesis-Intensive Innovation

Poiesis Intensive Innovation is one of the central concepts for this thesis, and grows out of developments at the Bassetti Foundation. My own interpretation and definition of the term will be expanded upon in chapter 5, with what follows describing the early development of the concept and Bassetti's influence.

A search on the website reveals the earliest published use of the term Poiesis-Intensive Innovation in February 2006[67], with the concept further developed in the following years and culminating in a lecture held on April 2014 at ISTUD Foundation Business School[68]. In this lecture entitled *Poiesis-Intensive Innovation: responsibility and culture for the third industrial revolution*, Foundation President Piero Bassetti argues that innovation is the implementation of new knowledge through the addition of power and praxis. He adds that innovation processes can be divided within two broad categories; science-intensive and *poiesis*-intensive. Through this articulation, the speaker claims that *Poiesis*-Intensive Innovation does not come from science, but rather from knowing how to do things. As a result, it does not need to be capital-intensive and is characterized by working practices that are different and more varied than those developed in science and technology.

Bassetti argues that within the industrial and entrepreneurial context, science-intensive innovation takes place within the factory and ancillary structures, whereas Poiesis-Intensive Innovation occurs in workshops. These different settings and structural characteristics affect the innovation and design processes, as those found within the second form (*poiesis*) allow the developer to think about aesthetics and functions before having to think about mass production implementation. He argues that this form of innovation lies at the base of the third industrial revolution, in which individuality and originality are production goals, much more so than the standardization,

---

[67] *The first Quaderni della Fondazione Giannino Bassetti*, entitled: "Innovazione, creatività e responsabilità. Formare gli imprenditori del futuro" is the result of the Foundation's participation in the "Innovazione e Creatività" module directed at students in the second year of the Master's Degree Course in Corporate Economics at the Carlo Cattaneo-LIUC University in Castellanza (academic year 2005-2006).

[68] The lecture in question took place in Baveni, Italy. Video of the event in Italian can be found on Vimeo: http://vimeo.com/album/2913716/video/94643512. Last accessed 24-08-2017

replicability and mass applicability of science-and-technology settings. According to Bassetti's logic, in the poiesis-intensive setting, creativity takes the lead in the innovation process with the problematization of mass production following.

Bassetti maintains that poiesis-innovation processes can be seen as representing the form of culture that lies behind the product. He argues that compared to industrial innovation, many production factors are different: beginning with the type of worker involved, following with the kind of design processes implemented, and ending with the types of contractual obligations, buying and distribution practices as well as credit and payment models. Many examples involve the use of high technology, but Bassetti argues that objects are not produced by machines (in one example he talks about the case of 3D printers) in the traditional understanding of the term. Rather, he still considered them as 'made by hand', using the technology as a tool much in the same way as any other hand tool. They are therefore the product of craftsmanship.

The following quote is taken from one of my recorded conversations. It provides an introduction to my argument that aesthetics is an integral part of the PII argument, a topic that I will return to in chapter 5.

> In all of this that I have said there is the assumption that innovation is science intensive episode. The knowledge that we are talking about is scientific or technological knowledge. But in reality, improbable changes come also from Picasso. But also your joiner. Or with 3D printing. People (who are) no longer following efficiency but in general beauty, driven by a logic of doing. Innovation that comes from someone who is driven by a logic of doing is different than from

someone who is driven by a logic of technology.

So the Greek verb poieo, that means 'doing' and also 'poetry', gives birth to the idea that we developed before going to San Francisco that there is a poiesis intensive innovation, that does not respond to a logic of ethics but if anything responds to a logic of aesthetics[69].

And here we must ask as we do with ethics, well what is aesthetics? For example if faced by an innovation such as the 3D printer, taking from doing and adding, in that the 3d printer is additive whereas the lathe is subtractive, faced with this kind of technology, the logic that regulates the program of doing responds to a logic that can be heavily influenced by aesthetics.

So here we meet all of the problematics of art. In which way is art innovative? Today in western thought innovation is the atomic bomb and not Michelangelo, but in reality, this impression is superficial because problematic change that is in thought can change history just as much as physical change.

As I argued above, the Foundation holds a slightly different standpoint from many of its partners regarding RI in that the concept here described does not necessarily fit into the technoscience fields that many other RI developments tend to be associated with. This leads to the broader drawing of practices involved that may be of interest for RI, but also represents the audience that the Foundation's work is aimed at. In the following quote, this position in sketched out in greater detail:

One of the things that the foundation has come across is the end of a limited audience, that is any person that innovates.

---

[69] I further develop this argument in chapter 5

And what comes from this is the birth of the problem of the difficulty of defining a border between newness and innovation. Because much of what is known as frugal innovation is more newness than innovation. And I think that this is a sector that we need to address because it is the other side of the initial argument.

If you start from the bomb you find atomic and quantum physics and extremely sophisticated problematics. But if you take the bike that is made easier to use on rocks, or the Vespa that uses small wheels instead of large wheels and creates the scooter, you no longer find sophisticated knowledge, but you meet all of the knowledge including those skills that come from the use and culture of the object. So, for example certain ways of sculpting wood that we find in artisanal furniture production don't come from equations or algorithms.

And in the middle we have this enormous problem of big data, the evolution of information that touches upon all of this argument, because it is obvious that the more information you have the more you bring the problem of responsibility to the fore. And the more information you have the more possibilities you have and so the more responsibility you have.

I argue that Bassetti's line can be seen in relationship to the situation within which the Foundation operates and has its roots. I now move on to examine the setting in further detail.

The Importance of the Milanese Socio-economic Context for the Conceptualization of Poiesis-Intensive Innovation (PII)

The Bassetti Foundation is based in Milan, and the interest in artisan working practices developed within arguments related to RI is directly related to the importance of this type of production in the Italian (and particularly Milanese) economy. I would argue that the Bassetti Foundation conception of responsible innovation has been developed as a result of being embedded within the working practices and everyday experiences that the presence *en mass* of artisanal working practices within its immediate geographical and socioeconomic surroundings afford (see Hankins, 2019 for an extended explanation).

The artisan sector is an important portion of the modern Italian economy, a fact that is particularly true of Milan and the surrounding Lombardy region. According to the 2014 Annual Confartigianato report[70] (the autonomous confederation of Italian artisan workers), there are 344,000 registered artisan businesses in Lombardy alone, of which approximately 27% are in manufacturing. They average 4 employees per firm, and even in a period of economic shrinkage and stagnation their economic output rose by 6.2% in 2014 (with export predominantly driving the increase), albeit after several years of sharp decline. In present day Lombardy 44% of all employees (excluding those in agriculture) work within artisan enterprises with less than 10 employees, with these companies representing 93% of all non-agricultural Lombard businesses.

Looking back to earlier times, before the enforced and involuntary restructuring brought about by the current economic crisis, artisan businesses were responsible for 33% of total industrial production in Lombardy, and 18% of total Italian production[71].

---

[70] Confartigianato is the professional association of Italian self-employed workers. They publish statistics and reports about their membership (in Italian). http://www.confartigianato-lombardia.it/upload/content/20201459161342354.pdf Last accessed 13-07-2017

[71] A document in Italian can be downloaded from the union of Trade groups at with a breakdown of economic categories in use in Italy at: http://www.unioncamerelombardia.it/images/File/OE%20-%20Dossier2009/DOSSIER%20ARTIGIANATO_aprile2009%20def.pdf Last accessed 13-07-2017

Living and working in the environment described above has led to the development of a concrete conception of responsible innovation - rather than the more theoretical or bureaucratic conception offered by policy-makers and sociologists of science. In these terms, responsibility is embedded in the beauty and functionality of the object produced. I would argue that this type of holistic conception makes sense when the artisan community of practice makes up such a large portion of the working population, leading to an *aesthetics of responsibility* that is grounded in a particular type of society, an argument related to the concept of communities of practice that forms the basis of this book and will be expanded upon in the two case studies.

To summarize, the Foundation is interested in the conceptualization and realization of a responsible system within which responsibility is not an abstract normative thought but rather lies within the actors, processes and objects of their design. To this embedded notion of responsibility, one should add the conditions surrounding production, such as norms, market dynamics etc. But norms and market regulations should not be the source of RI itself. It should be developed from within a system of practice.

In fact, the economic structure described above will present many problems to anyone wishing to implementing 'stewardship' of innovation following a top-down approach, precisely because it is such a diffused context. In this situation, 'skill' or 'poiesis' (or knowing how to do things) becomes the notion that allows the brokerage of ideas of responsible innovation.

A first Defining Moment: The Meeting in Alz

To better understand how the operating practices and underlying philosophy of the Bassetti Foundation came to be developed, I will now present documentation regarding how debates within the organization have evolved and how they relate to the current broader RI debate. I will demonstrate how the debates and decisions taken at and subsequent to the foundational meeting foresaw the development of arguments surrounding the nascent concept of RI, reflecting the visionary thinking developed within the Bassetti Foundation at that time.

I will begin with an often-discussed event with President Bassetti (cited above), a meeting at Alz in 1999, a meeting that was fundamental in laying the groundwork for the Foundation's philosophical and practical positioning over the following years. A transcription of parts of the meeting is available in the Foundation archives[72], a selection of which I have annotated below. The meeting was attended by Piero Bassetti, Francesco Alberoni[73], Claudio Carlone, Renato Ugo[74], Umberto Colombo[75], Ignazio Masulli[76] Adriano De Maio[77], Tomaso Quattrin[78] and Peter Goldmark[79].

The meeting in Alz was called by President Bassetti as a brainstorming, a reflection, with a group of entrepreneurs, scholars, and CEO's of leading industries and NGO's, with whom he wanted to address the idea of responsible innovation.

---

[72] http://www.fondazionebassetti.org/it/pagine/2009/02/workshop_sulla_fondazione_gian.html Last accessed 05/11/2019

[73] Francesco Alberoni is an Italian journalist and a professor of sociology. He was a board member and senior board member of RAI, the Italian state television network, from 2002 to 2005

[74] Renato Ugo is a renowned Chemist and Professor in General and inorganic Chemistry at the University of Milan.

[75] Umberto Colombo is a chemical engineer, a well known academic and former Italian Minister for Universities, Science and technology.

[76] Ignazio Masulli is a well known Historian and author

[77] Adriano De Maio is an engineer, former Rector of Luiss Guido Carli and delegate for Higher Education, Research and Innovation at the region of lombardy.

[78] Tomaso Quattrin served as the President of Altoprofilo SpA and was President of IBM Italy at the time

[79] Peter Goldmark is an environmentalist, has held several governance positions in the USA and former President of the Rockefeller Foundation.

As noted above, the people present were extremely diverse. Bassetti explained the concept of RI and that he wanted to lay the foundations to study the idea of the responsibility within innovation.

At this time (in 1999) this terminology was almost completely unheard of, innovation was generally seen and perceived as a good in itself, it was progress and unquestioned. The idea that it could be run in a more or less responsible way was a novelty. The meeting in Alz lasted 2 days, and many of the RI topics that have emerged over the following years were first raised at this meeting.

The following is a reconstruction based upon materials publicly available via the Foundation. As a turning point in the history of the Foundation, a keystone in thinking on RI, it warrants a fine detailed analysis.

The meeting minutes open with President Bassetti thanking the participants for having accepted his invitation, before describing the reasons for the meeting as the following:

a) The analysis of the original idea, the nature and the first steps of the Giannino Bassetti Foundation;

b) a contribution of ideas to the President and the Board of the Foundation on how to develop the study of innovation in entrepreneurial activity, with particular attention being devoted to the responsibility of innovation and the impact of new productive processes on economic and social conditions and on the ethics and politics of human society.

Here we see the mission of the Foundation succinctly distilled into its prime components, with a focus on the productive process that was later developed and redrawn as the innovation process, the physical and social effects on broader society and the influence of politics and ethics upon these developments.

In his opening presentation, Bassetti described how the Foundation originated in almost twenty years of thought connected to Giannino Bassetti's conviction that despite innovation's pervasive role, the responsibility for innovation is not clearly attributed in our society. He argued that this problem was not new.

Francesco Alberoni expressed his feeling that the issues Bassetti wished to address were the same as that which most modern philosophers (Heidegger, among others) had struggled with, being the result of the impossibility of foreseeing the long-term results of technological development. He described what is sometimes known in RI studies as the problem of many hands, not in terms of responsibility taking as such in terms of blaming someone for the consequences of her actions, but in terms of historical developments:

Alberoni described the problem as follows:

> M does something, N does something else, and the results of their action become common property, something that anybody can tap for whatever end they wish. Such separate actions generate effects which, beyond a certain threshold, in turn produce cultural, political, religious or ethical reactions. Action and reaction are always separated by a time lag: the reaction (panic, a movement, reformation) never runs in parallel with the process and cannot be conceptually foreseen or controlled.

He argues however that this problem has been amply studied by sociologists, calling for a new approach to the problem.

Claudio Carlone responded in arguing that the terms of the problem have changed from Heidegger's time. He argued that research had changed, no longer being an individual task or action but the result of the interactions within complex systems. He argued that the results are largely foreseen and aimed towards, and that there is little free research today.

Carlone followed with a comment drawn from the argument above that very much resonates with the development strategies of the Foundation:

> So far, in the footsteps of Heidegger, we have concerned ourselves with the responsibility of the scientist. Today we should instead start discussing the responsibility of the entrepreneur, arguing that the starting point of reflection can no longer be that research happens without any foresight about its results, but rather that the entrepreneur is the manager of research and its results.

I believe that this statement represents an early interest in innovation process management, an idea that went on to form the basis of the EU approach as described in chapter 3 (von Schomberg, 2011).

Carlone closed with a statement about the speed of modern innovation and the results that such rapid development provokes, raising the point that society no longer has control of innovation because questions arise regarding new developments quicker than they can be answered. This issue described in these terms can also be seen as reflected in development within RI. Debate around the need for the development of soft regulation due to the time restrictions necessary for the drawing of hard regulation has underpinned RI research in recent years (Bessant, 2013, Fisher and Rip 2013, Bosso, 2014, Reichow and Dorbeck-jung 2014).

Renato Ugo responded in arguing that the answer to Bassetti's question could be to distinguish separate levels. He addressed Bassetti's developing notion of how to approach responsibility arguing that he refers to social and political responsibility. He argued however that there is another level of responsibility that needs to be raised, although not of particular interest to the Foundation's goals:

> When you consider research results, though, a first level of responsibility is connected with the decision about whether such results can be used. It is a technical responsibility related to recognising that the discovery has some application and is therefore technically valid.

He argued that the Foundation is however concerned with a second level of responsibility that depends on the uncertainty surrounding the future development of innovation, a topic later developed by Bernd Stahl who described meta-responsibility (Stahl, 2013). Yet:

> If we consider the results of the innovation process as a whole, society is growing in statistical terms. Instead of concentrating solely on the point of responsibility, we perhaps should concern ourselves with estimating whether this kind of innovation is statistically an asset or a liability for society, without forgetting that an asset can be the result of an asset minus a smaller liability. Thirty years ago, life expectancy in Asia and Africa was 40 years, today it is 65-70. In the West, it was 65 years, today it is 82. This implies progress both in the West, where the innovation originated, and in Asia and Africa. The balance is positive all round. Even without precise political responsibility, innovation is so powerful that in spite of all our mistakes, society keeps developing. The problem is thus how to control such growth

and how to accelerate it.

This statement seems closely related to the developments in RI described in Chapter 1 and prevalent within the competing definitions of RI and the pillars of the EU and other funding bodies, in that it raises the point that innovation could work towards societal goals, although raising the question of how this could be measured. This is also an issue that appears in RI literature, particularly in terms of what the common good might be and how it might change in different settings and across different cultures (Macnaghten et.al., 2014).

Umberto Colombo argued that trying to inject an ethical dimension in the main motivation of the entrepreneur would be utopian, or even dangerous. He proposed the advancement of a new ethics, based on a global and intergenerational view of society since companies today tend to concentrate obsessively on short-term performance, the challenge could be to show them the compatibility between global and long-term goals and their interests.

He argued that the aim should be to create a new idea of entrepreneurship that includes an ethical dimension but without underscoring the ethical aspect too much, and focusing on the long-term future of the company in a global world.

Such proposals have been followed up within the RI community since this debate unfolded. One of the major operators working in this field is the think-tank Matter[80], based in London. Matter aim to bring the arguments of RI to the small and medium sized business table, operating very much in an action research settings.

---

[80] See the Matter website for further details http://www.matterforall.org/
Last accessed 05/11/2019

Ignazio Masulli responded that the problem goes beyond the responsibility of the entrepreneur. He argued that the responsibility of innovation concerns the future of our society and we can view it in two ways:

1. The responsibility for the consequences of innovation;
   2. The responsibility implied by the possibility of making free choices as to our future. For instance: since the gap between rich and poor countries is increasing, what kind of solutions can we find at a technological level? Which technologies are more easily exportable to less developed countries? In this sense innovation implies creating opportunities, making the improbable feasible, fostering economic, technological and social change.

From the archive notes it is apparent that he argued the need to study how innovation takes shape, under which conditions it asserts itself, which dynamics give rise to it. This is very much the scope and aim of this book, and has become a line of interest within academic publications as described in chapter 2 and within European policy-making as described in chapter 3.

He also raised the question of why innovations available in certain contexts is not applied, or applied only years after its discovery? Why is the innovation available in a given context not used in a similar context in the same country and time? He asked the following question that touches directly upon President Bassetti's political involvement and drives one of the lines of inquiry sponsored by the Foundation and recently present within the literature (van Oudheusden, 2014, Di Giulio et.al., 2016):

Moreover, are we satisfied with the fact that the responsibility of innovation has shifted from political institutions to the market, which is by definition irresponsible? Or do we believe that this poses a problem?

Adriano De Maio addressed the comment that Colombo had made about what he described as myopic research policy. He argued that in the face of industrial short termism regarding research, most innovation will be left to public institutions to carry out. This means a change in the division of responsibility, as decisions on types of research and their funding are increasingly taken by politicians. This statement should be seen in the context of the development of RI frameworks within funding institutions described in chapter 1. RI has become institutionalised through funding intervention across much of Europe.

This comment in fact seems to reflect many of the changes that have occurred since the time of this meeting, with many funding bodies taking on ideas born from RI in their funding processes (see chapter 2 for further description of large EU funded projects and chapter 1 for an overview of these developments.

De Maio continues by raising another issue that has become prevalent in RI discourse, that of the role of the media (Selin, 2014, Van der Burg, 2014, Withycombe and Foley, 2015):

> The mass-media also have an ethical responsibility in this respect, and so does government when it lets public opinion guide their decisions instead of fully analysing the problem of research. This is the paradox of democracy, since democracy should imply a deeper analysis of technical problems, but instead makes it impossible.

He also comments the issue of the speed of technological change arguing that

Up to a few decades ago the innovation process was slower and people had time to metabolize it. The advent of electricity, for instance, has revolutionized the behaviour of men, though in a very long-term perspective, which gave us the possibility of adjusting to it. Today, innovation comes faster and faster and we don't have time to adjust. I do not know who should be responsible for improving society to help it adjust to innovation, but I think this is a problem.

In his final comment De Maio argues that innovation is radically changing the cognitive process of humankind, pointing out that adolescents never read instructions on how to operate devices, they just try and make them work. This he argues implies that they never learn all of their functions; they just use them according to suggestions they receive from the outside. This implies that they do not learn to criticize innovation and new technologies.

He concludes that:

This will have an impact on our children's generation and should become the object of close study. If it doesn't, our capacity for critical analysis will be lost. This is a fundamental ethical responsibility, the most serious problem of our times.

Tomaso Quattrin raised two points that have featured heavily in the RI debate within the Bassetti Foundation: to whom are we responsible? He argued that:

It is not really very easy to create a connection between innovation and responsibility. Certainly, when research aims at foreseen results it could be easier to trace back who has done what and why, and who is responsible. But in many cases, things do not work that way.

He gives the example of the post-it and the IPad to demonstrate that many innovations are not born of planning.

Peter Goldmark spoke about his experience in running a foundation, the comparative advantages that different institutions possess and how they could be best used in the case of the development of the Bassetti Foundation. He agreed that

> There is indeed an ethical dimension in Bassetti's project. To make it effective, though, make the ethical dimension a performance test. If it is a performance test it will have a different time horizon and then it will be built into the system.

In the open debate that followed these opening remarks and discussions, Bassetti asked the participants to acknowledge that the idea of responsibility is very confused and to consider that we could find a niche in having in the courage to work on this assumption, rewarding someone who can theorise about the causes of irresponsibility. He raised a multi sided series of questions that resonate within the Foundation, the RI community and within the EU to this day:

> To whom is one responsible? For you cannot found any ethical system without having an end in mind. What I had in mind was a contribution to the improvement of society.

Continuing with the following set of statements and questions:

> The link between innovation and the improvement of living conditions is clear. But if the measure is not the GNP anymore, what will it be? Happiness? Is that too difficult to define? Harm reduction, as advocated by the Club of Rome? Thus the problem is not only to decide who is in charge of innovation, but also who is in charge of defining the lines along which innovation should be considered a factor for

improvement.

Alberoni responded to the questions above that Bassetti's main concern was responsibility, the responsibility of power. Who has the power? Who is responsible? Responsible not because one must answer to someone, but because one answers to one's self.

Ugo replied that Bassetti conceives the problem of responsibility in social terms, without limiting it to businesses. He argued that this view, though, does not allow for the concept of innovation. He raised one of the questions that has been amply debated in the RI debate (van den Hoven, 2013) related to the problem of responsibility as addressed above by Bassetti:

> can the entrepreneur manage the whole loop, after initiating it? Or, if he cannot, how can he make sure the loop is responsible?

Masulli responded that the ethics of responsibility could not be taught, developing a line however that could be seen as in parallel to that of von Schomberg (Von Schomberg, 2011).

> You cannot teach anybody to think in the interest of future generations and history tells us that man cannot be taught to be more responsible. Many innovations take shape in a totally contingent way, the industrial revolution being the most famous example. My point is: can we conceive a type of innovation with different scientific and social foundations than in the past? An innovation conceived and shaped in such a way that it only acts as a tool for change and nothing else?

Colombo responded that Bassetti demonstrated an ideological prejudice when he argued that certain categories are not responsible. From his point of view

The media, entrepreneurs etc. cannot be said to be irresponsible: they are responsible but in a different way, with another scale of values. We must be open and refrain from accusing others of irresponsibility, since that would be counterproductive.

Carlone concluded the discussion by arguing the need to distinguish between two fundamental concepts; the effect of innovation and its impact:

The impact of innovation is connected to the role of public opinion, which is basically guided by the mass media, exerting a major influence on the allocation of funds for research. The effect, on the other hand, concerns real society, the ways in which innovation can influence people's lives, by tackling problems like poverty, the North-South gap etc.

His suggestion very much mirrors the path of many academics working in the RI field in arguing that:

The Foundation should try and convince those who work in the most advanced fields of technology and innovation that they have to design their communication projects carefully, while recognizing the fundamental role of communication.

4.3 Some Conclusions

I argue from experience that this discussion above forms the basis of the philosophical drive behind the foundation, and that the issues raised have become the issues that the broader community addresses today, showing the visionary arguments that underlie the Foundation and its creation.

Literature can be seen across disciplines and the entire spectrum of RI fields that has further developed the ideas that were opened for discussion in 1999. The proposal to create the

Bassetti Foundation and to bring those present together can certainly be seen as visionary in hindsight, proven by the fact that the very questions raised on that day are those that continue to be asked today within RI literature.

The centrality of the questions reflects the centrality of the foundation to the development of the concept.

The geographical and political experiences that underpin the Foundation have led to its particular perspective on RI, leading to the development of Poiesis-Intensive innovation categorization as a research tool. The communities of practice (Lave, 1998) (both social and geographic) that the Foundation is immersed within has allowed the development of this concept which very much reflects the arguments about tacit knowledge that I will use in my case studies. This is a standpoint that I will expand upon in chapter 5 and implement in the case studies that follow.

In the following chapter I develop an argument about the concept of poiesis-intensive innovation and its relationship to responsible innovation.

Chapter 5

Poiesis-Intensive Innovation

Chapter 4 presented the background to the notion of Poiesis-Intensive Innovation, as conceptualized in the Bassetti Foundation. The concept grows out of the experience of being immersed within a particular community of practice (Lave and Wenger, 1991), a theme and central idea that runs through this book. The concept can be seen as developing as part of the narrative that the members of this community use to describe and steer their working practices. It reflects its surroundings as well as being part of them.

This chapter aims to expand upon the possibilities of applying such a framework of thinking in terms of its application for RI, to analyze the Poisis-Intensive Innovation concept further and to propose a relationship between Poisis-Intensive Innovation and RI; poiesis intensive responsible innovation (PIRI).

The fieldwork that underpins my analysis and development of the concept of Poiesis-Intensive Innovation as an analytical tool for the study of RI grows out of the daily practices seen and experienced through my work at and with the Giannino Bassetti Foundation in Milan, Italy over the last fifteen years and in particular throughout the duration of my PhD research.

The Foundation's characteristic interest in action-oriented research and policy as well as its historical grounding in the evolution of craft production processes - notably in the textile industry (Garruccio and Maifreda 2004) - has led to the development of this original concept of Poiesis-Intensive Innovation, as described by President Bassetti in chapter 4.

In this chapter, which serves as an introduction to the case studies and construction of an analytic framework using the concept, I will analyze and offer my own interpretation of Poiesis-Intensive Innovation, propose the category of Poiesis Intensive Responsible Innovation (PIRI), and describe the background to the case studies that follow.

For the purposes of this analysis I read poiesis as the addressing of ethical and aesthetic issues combined, through a production process. In broad terms, this is inspired by Plato's understanding of *poiein* as a form of making that addresses every aspect of being, namely not just producing things but making them as though growing out of an integral engagement with knowledge (as in music and poetry, but also artisan working practices). (Reale, 2003, p. 528).

As noted in the previous chapter, the earliest published use of the term Poiesis-Intensive Innovation on the Bassetti Foundation websites dates back to February 2006[81], with its development continuing over the coming years and culminating in Piero Bassetti's lecture held on April 2014 at ISTUD Foundation Business School, *Poiesis-Intensive Innovation: responsibility and culture for the third industrial revolution*[82].

In this lecture, Bassetti clarifies that innovation is the implementation of new knowledge in practice through the conscious exercise of power (thus more than invention or discovery, but also involving the means to produce and will to do so), adding that innovation processes can be divided within

---

[81] *The first Quaderni della Fondazione Giannino Bassetti*, entitled: "Innovazione, creatività e responsabilità. Formare gli imprenditori del futuro" is the result of the Foundation's participation in the "Innovazione e Creatività" module directed at students in the second year of the Master's Degree Course in Corporate Economics at the Carlo Cattaneo-LIUC University in Castellanza (academic year 2005-2006).

[82] The lecture in question took place in Baveno, Italy. Video of the event in Italian can be found on Vimeo: http://vimeo.com/album/2913716/video/94643512. Last accessed 24-08-2017

two broad categories, which he calls science-intensive and poiesis-intensive.

On other occasions Bassetti uses the term capital intensive innovation rather than science intensive, a further refinement of the argument. Capital intensive better represents the realities of high technology and high investment innovation, as science may be seen as (but should not be restricted to) laboratory work, and as I will later argue can be seen as displaying characteristics of artisan or craft work itself. The overarching focus for this book, and what connects the case studies mentioned, is that Poiesis-Intensive Innovation takes place in small groups in a restricted social setting, involving the participants working collaboratively within shared ideas of working norms and practices.

Poiesis-Intensive Innovation is led by soft forms of knowledge such as design, functional aesthetics, organizational and relational patterns, which are usually associated with social settings of learning such as artisanal workshops. Through apprenticeship and work experience, tacit knowledge is developed (Polanyi, 1966; Collins, 2010). For the purpose of this analysis, tacit knowledge can be understood as non-codified knowledge. It lives within bodies rather than on paper, and it is learned and distributed through bodily use. It is knowing how to do it.

In these social situations knowledge regarding how to do things is learned through membership within a community of practice (Lave, 1988) in a process that both requires and is based upon cooperation and shared understanding between its members. As a result, it does not always need to be formalized, and is characterized by working practices that are diverse, situated and fluid, as opposed to those developed in larger, capital-intensive settings, where following protocol and translating scientific innovation into mass production could be interpreted as aims. In short, Poiesis-Intensive Innovation develops out of a form of production that stems from knowing how to do things in practice[83].

Naturally, science always involves practice too. Lucy Suchman (Suchman 2007) and David Turnbull (Turnbull, 2009) (among others) show for example how 'muddling through', bricolage and relationality inhabit the practices of science as much as those of craftwork. Indeed, the argument of this thesis is that poiesis is a way of understanding all innovation processes through the lens of personal and practical, 'situated' knowledge. In the case I will argue, knowledge becomes embedded into specific qualities of certain material products for the market as argued in Callon et al (2002).

Callon et.al argue that an object has a life, and a career. They use the term product, as different from mere 'goods' in economic terms, and as seen from the point of view of its production, circulation and consumption. A product is a process whose characteristics change during this process, in a sequence of transformations. The authors argue that *the product describes, in both senses of the term, the different networks coordinating the actors involved in its design, distribution and consumption* (Callon et.al, 2002, p198).

For the purpose of my argument, I propose seeing poiesis-intensive innovation as occurring in sufficiently independent and intimate environments that the innovation and design processes are more typically than not bespoke procedures, allowing the developer to think about function through

---

[83] For further explanation of how the concept was conceived see the transcriptions in Chapter 4 on the Bassetti Foundationk.

aesthetics, before considering replicability and standardization. We might say that this form of innovation lies at the base of the so called third industrial revolution, with its use of 3D printing production techniques and promise of personalized procedures and products (Anderson, 2012).

5.1 Situated Learning

In the artisan sector, poiesis-intensive processes can be seen as representing a form of culture that can be described in terms of differences from larger scale working practices: The type of worker involved; the kind of design processes implemented; the types of contractual obligations; buying and distribution practices; and credit and payment models.

Contemporary examples involve the use of high technology, though objects are not necessarily seen as having been produced by machines but rather using technology as a tool much in the same way as any other hand tool - the product of craftsmanship. The second case study in this thesis follows the logic of this argument, describing how the tools themselves are manipulated towards an end goal within a University science lab, displaying many similarities to the first case study that takes place in a furniture restoration workshop and very much reflecting examples of other fieldwork experience carried out during this research period.

I argue however that it would be limiting to simply oppose craftsmanship to technology.

As Wiebe Bijker suggests, *technology comprises, first, artefacts and technical systems, second the knowledge about these and, third, the practices of handling these artefacts and systems* (Bijker, 2010, p64).

In order to contextualize my own understanding of poiesis and to introduce case studies related to the concept of Poiesis Intensive Responsible Innovation (PIRI), I borrow from an interdisciplinary scholarship on apprenticeship and practical knowledge.

Anthropologist Tim Ingold argues that the form of things arises within fields of force and flows of materials, so that the use of technology is *navigated*. He gives the example of a carpenter sawing a piece of wood, reacting to the way the wood responds to the use of the saw with different rhythms and body shaping (Ingold, 2010 p91). In this sense the carpenter navigates the materials in a similar way to that seen and described in the first case study described later in this book. This process is also visible in the science case study that follows, a biotechnologist who constructs 3D printers to form a production process that itself requires tool making, the tools being the machines themselves.

In a somewhat related argument, Trevor Pinch argues that intentionality can only be determined by context. In keeping with an Actor Network Theory framework, he proposes the notion of delegation to non-humans (tools) (Pinch, 2010). This is an important point for my argument if we see intentionality and not merely a technical action, but a goal that we could be described as responsibility based, or could be perceived and narrated as just or right. Could we find intentionality steered through social context delegated to a machine through it use?

Through this book I argue that the link between situated learning and related decision-making processes (including the delegation of work to both machines and tools) represents the opening of a new field of analysis within RI.

Jean Lave and Etienne Wenger develop the argument of situated learning within cultural contexts through their definition and use of the term *communities of practice* (Lave and Wenger, 1991). Their argument can be described in the following terms: Learning is brought about through the participation in routine activities that are often difficult to describe in verbal terms, but that involve important routine, material and bodily aspects; through the knowledge of and functional use of objects and instruments and spaces that guide actions, relationships and communication in a certain direction (and away from others) through the progressive taking on and delegation of responsibility through which the apprentice gains the role of legitimate peripheral participation, moving progressively towards the centre of the action. This movement represents the learning process with all of its tensions, hierarchy and complicit actions between the skilled and the apprentice in artisan working situations (Herzfeld, 2004) but can also be seen within science labs as the case study in this research seeks to demonstrate.

This approach sees knowledge as competence developing through a material and relational context, it is a practice of knowledge or for Grasseni and Ronzon the *pratica della conoscenza* (Grasseni e Ronzon, 2004) and is a transformative process. In her seminal and much celebrated Cognition in Practice argument, Lave also argues that learning is a practical activity demonstrating the practical use of mathematics in daily life (Lave, 1988).

In his book Craftsmen, and very much following this line, Richard Sennett underlines that *all skills, even the most abstract, begin as bodily practices* and that *technical understanding develops through the powers of imagination* (Sennett, 2008 p10), bringing in an argument that is fundamental for this research: the ambiguity of craftsmanship from an ethical point of view.

Sennett's example is that of Oppenheimer's approach to building the atomic bomb. He argues that the scientist's goal was to build the best bomb possible, pushing his own technical skills in crafting the best technical solutions for the problem at hand. He was searching for a solution to a physical problem, not a weapon. His work was that of seeking efficiency, or possibly as I will argue later, beauty within a process.

Edwin Hutchins also developed similar ideas working with US servicemen. Hutchins' aim was to investigate cognition in practice in context, developed through routine, developing the idea of a socially distributed knowledge through routine (Hutchins, 1995).

Through comparing these studies, I argue therefore that expert action can be seen as mediated, with every expert practice seen as situated. The action is mediated through coordination with external structures that offer support for the guide, description and the form of the action. These mediation structures are external and internal to the setting, being at once artifacts and tools, the availability of information brought by technology, and network connections.

The material learning process involves sharing an understanding of how a procedure should be correctly completed, which would seem to have implications for the conceptualization of RI. The sharing of a work space and the practices described above leads to the construction and sharing of a perspective on correct procedure, and the construction of what we might think of as a narrative that can be seen both in the process and as represented by product. In my case studies I will argue that the correct following of this narrative is appreciated by those involved in the process as beauty in the product, possible only through the acquisition and sharing of a skilled vision. The product is the codification of this narrative.

5.2 Skilled Visions

A central methodology and argument used for this thesis is that of skilled visions (Grasseni, 2007). A skilled vision is an example of a learned skill very much in line with the situated learning arguments made above, it is a learned vision. The vision is learned within a structured apprenticeship environment and is socially performed and inculcated as any other skill. It is seeing and knowing through a schooling of the eye.

I would like to expand upon the theme of skilled visions as developed by Grasseni, to argue that the apprentice experience not only allows the learner worker to learn to see quality in a finished produce in relation to its production process, but also that it allows a shared vision and understanding of the decision-making process that underlies the process, and more importantly the reasoning behind how decisions were actually made, and finally why according to the workplace narrative. To summarize this point: the skilled apprentice sees the narrative created within the workplace through the reasoning behind the decision-making process, represented in the beauty of both the finished product and the process itself.

he skilled visions approach relies on the concept of communities of practice (Lave and Wenger, 1991), membership of which allows for the development of a visual competence that is embodied and tacit, but also shared. A skilled vision is one that allows the viewer to interpret a range of factors within a process as represented within a final product or situation. It is an ability that is learned through enskillment (Ingold, 2000), via apprenticeship. The possessor of a skilled vision has the key to understanding the product as the codification of the workplace narrative, a judgement that can be shared through engagement in the narrative in work conversation.

Grasseni used the example of cattle breeders in Northern Italy to develop her concept. She describes a vision that a judge at a cattle fair performs, looking at the animals from certain angles, for different traits. The animal is a visual representation of the skills of the breeder, judged against an ideal type of form in what she describes as functional beauty (Grasseni, 2009). The ideal type takes into account the geographical and cultural environment within its judgement, representing markers of possibility. A cow bred in the mountains cannot look the same as one bred in the lowlands for example, her purpose and functions also affecting her aesthetic form. All of this can be understood through this form of professional visual analysis.

I myself possess a skilled vision that I use to demonstrate the argument of this book, as my first case study demonstrates. I served a four-year apprenticeship as a furniture restorer, learning to see both the qualities of the piece of furniture in question, but also the restoration work carried out on it. I wish to push the understanding of skilled visions to argue that I can also see, and share with my fellow workers, an understanding of the choices that were made during the restoration process and the reasoning behind them. I describe this as the ability to share a vision of the narration of the production process through a shared understanding of the moral imperatives that decisions taken during this process rely on.

The process of carrying out this research has also enskilled my vision when entering other types of workplaces, in particular manual restoration workshops. I am now more able to see the organization of the working process through the physical organization of the workshops in question. A skilled vision regarding workshop organization allows me to look for and see patterns found in other situations, home-made tools, the placing of artifacts on the walls, the use of several generations of technology side by side to give some examples that I will go on to highlight.

My skilled vision as a furniture restorer is the most developed however. I can look at a finished piece and understand how it has been technically constructed under the top-cover, hidden from a non-skilled viewers perspective. I can understand the choice of materials, not only in economic terms (some are cheaper than others), but also in terms of what should or should not be used in different contexts and more importantly why. I can see if the job has been done right according to my own particular workplace narrative. I can also make judgement upon the ability of the restorer and the quality of his or her work by looking at the organization of the workshop, the materials present and their layout. I will expand upon this argument through examples in the first of my case studies.

Following Grasseni's argument I argue that skilled visions are forms of tacit knowledge, that it is not a construction either of the viewer herself, nor the object, but of the complex relationship between attention, habit, representation, distributed cognition and a broad understanding of context. I refer to this as the narrative. I use an argument based upon a shared understanding of beauty, that a skilled vision sees an object as beautiful because the viewer sees the embodiment of the narrative within the product. The beauty lies within the narrative, it is constituted by this narrative, with its social actors, setting and processes. It is the beauty of the narrative, or how beauty is narrated within the workplace.

I argue that a skilled viewer sees (and shares the experience of) an object as beautiful because she understands the relationship between narrative and practice, and the decisions made within these practices. These decisions are reasoned, and the skilled viewer can see these reasons, they are aware of the underlying situations that underpin this reasoning such as cost, availability, quality, and more importantly something that we might think of as justice or a 'lay morality' of right and wrong, and as such the implications of these decisions. These concepts and understandings are negotiated and explicated through the work narrative every day in terms of the acceptance and delegation of responsibility. I argue therefore that they are able to see the responsibility that lies within the narrative within the beauty of the product. For the product to be beautiful from a skilled visions perspective, it must be responsible (however that is determined within the narrative). An object that is beautiful from a skilled visions perspective must be responsible.

This interpretation of Grasseni's skilled visions concept aims to build upon Goodwin's concept of professional vision (Goodwin, 1994). Goodwin describes how apparently evident states are discussed, debated and confirmed through different devices and mediations. These devices are multisensorial, and in the case that I will analyze of furniture restoration, involve stroking, hitting, pressing and lifting, leading to a judgement framed in terms of beauty. These forms of sharing judgements and supporting these expressions of beauty (or not) take place within structured and routine conversations and events that can be seen as forming part of the narrative of how to correctly address work in this workplace. These routines allow and create specific acts of looking, touching, and understanding.

It is not a long leap to argue that they also lead to the development of working practices and by extension standards, and therefore relate to responsible innovation.

Grasseni argues that the concept of skilled visions moves beyond Goodwin's earlier construction, as skilled visions are also moral visions. They inform the social circle within the community of practice, they build status and identities. This aesthetics view shapes an ecology of belonging (Grasseni, 2009), allowing membership within specific groups. This leads to the development of different forms of working networks, all of which is important for the development of the production process in terms of quality of materials, access to knowledge and funds. This argument can be made about both of the seemingly diverse extended case studies in this thesis, as well as the two shorter examples of fieldwork cited later in this chapter.

To pick up on Piero Bassetti's language once more, skilled visions allow the viewer to experience and share the poiesis element of the production process.

5.3 RI Definition and Poiesis Intensive Responsible Innovation (PIRI)

For the purpose of this analysis I re-propose an adaption to the Stilgoe defintion of Responsible Innovation described in chapter 1 (Hankins, 2019).

Responsible (research and) innovation means taking collective care for the future through a reflexive process within which all interested actors contribute to responsible choices within a "glocal" and topical context (Hankins, 2019, p396).

This definition aims to take into account the Poiesis-Intensive

Innovation concept via its application to the two case studies developed in this research and its relationship to Responsible Innovation, leading to the proposal of the concept of Poiesis Intensive Responsible Innovation (PIRI) (Hankins, 2019).

The glocal and topical context referred to in the definition, highlights the negotiation of accepted actions, but this negotiation must always take place within the context of the small-scale working relationship within broadly defined and accepted external norms. The responsible choices possible, therefore refer to a framework of external norms, although these are not the driving force for the process. The everyday narrative developed within the workplace is the driving force. This is important for the concept of RI as I argue that the framework that the process is judged by (internally) is constructed through these social (internal and external) relationships that exist within a global set of norms. As I will describe, the construction of beauty within the group (the production goal) as a measure of the job having been correctly carried out relies on the shared understanding of this narrative. I am not arguing that because the finished article or the working process is defined as beautiful it is necessarily correct from an outsider's perspective, but that it is correct from an insider perspective, according to the accepted norms of the group in question based upon the members' global understanding.

To explain this further I propose that we think about animal use in biology research. In my second case study described in Chapter 7, I follow a biologist who relies on animal use in experimental operations within his research. This use may well be criticised in terms of animal rights from an external perspective, but as an accepted process, if done correctly, within the working group, it is seen as not only justified but necessary.

As a result, it remains a parameter of working practices rather than a moral dilemma. Once accepted, the process of how the animals are used becomes the measure of correctness and how animal experiments are viewed and implemented into a research project, or what in other contexts we could refer to as the production or research process. These understandings form part of the narrative developed within the workplace through everyday conversation. This leads me to argue that the narrative and the possibilities it affords are constructed and shared in situ, through mutually understood and negotiated parameters.

Before moving on to the in-depth case studies that are presented in chapters 6 and 7 of this thesis, a brief description follows of how the PIRI concept was developed, with two mini case study examples taken from recent research sites that include my experience conducting fieldwork in Utrecht (Netherlands), described in further detail in my 2019 chapter in the International Handbook on Responsible Innovation (Hankins, 2019).

Following Randles and Laredo (Randles and Laredo, 2013) and Deblonde (Deblonde, 2015) the short cases here presented were analyzed as examples of what has previously referred to as grass-roots Responsible Innovation (Hankins and Grasseni, 2014). The analysis builds upon the notion of 'rri' versus 'RRI', as developed by Randles et.al. (Randles et.al. 2016). Randles and her fellow authors argue that 'rri' (little rri) processes are de-facto (Rip, 2010) in that they represent the responsibilities that the actors themselves feel and act upon within the innovation process.

Borrowing from Sayer on 'lay normativity', the authors argue that a variety of normativities reflect societal values, cares and concerns (Sayer, 2011). Societal cares and concerns become embedded in practices, structures, and governance instruments which then steer and orient organizational business models towards specific normative goals. Following the skilled visions argument described above I argue that in the examples offered here these factors are visible to the trained eye, embodied within the beauty of the product or process.

Grass-roots Responsible Innovation (Hankins and Grasseni 2014) also takes as its starting point the worldview of concrete societal actors grappling (in the case of the article here cited), with dilemmas about food procurement and sustainable provisioning. In the case described, the construction of the concept that is parallel to that of beauty used in the furniture workshop lies within the organization structure of those provisioning food as much as within the foodstuffs themselves, a theme that is also visible in the case studies described in this chapter.

The article describes the workings of the Italian GAS movement (gruppi di acquisto solidale), describing how the members engineer a short chain procurement system that allows them to trace the entire production line of the goods (mainly food) that they purchase.

In the article the authors argue that, faced by the environmental, financial, and social non-sustainability of current food provisioning practices (demonstrated by food insecurity, environmental concerns, malnutrition and increasing health issues in industrialized countries), grassroots networks are rethinking the core elements of contemporary society: the market, the commons, and the role of the individual: citizen, consumer, and producer, leading to the creation of a system that offers several similarities to those described in the RI literature by *Randles et.al. (Randles et.al. 2016) and Deblonde (Deblonde, 2015)* as de-facto forms of RI. I will not expand further on this argument here, but conclude by making the point that production processes need not only produce goods, they can be organizationally beautiful and responsible to those participating within their shared and negotiated definition and narrative.

The following examples display many similarities with the two case studies that were expanded later in this book, offering an abbreviated overview of how such concepts could be applied in further depth. I present them here as an introduction to the methodological basis of the argument for this book. The subsequent case studies described in chapters 6 and 7 build upon these examples and were specifically developed for my PhD research following this earlier investigation.

PIRI Case Study 1:

Roadrunner Engineering

Roadrunner engineering[84] is a small-scale industrial engineering company based in Milan. The business produces artificial legs and feet for both running and walking. It has a research arm whose aim is to develop the means to produce fully made to measure bespoke products using high technology. The company was founded by Daniele Bonacina, who lost a leg in a motorcycle accident in his youth. This led him to experiment with artificial walking solutions and eventually to start his own company to continue this research and put his findings into production.

---

[84] The Roadrunner Engineering website contains further details of their research and current products. http://www.roadrunnerfoot.com/

At the time of writing Roadrunner produces three types of running feet alongside their line for walking, and have developed and patented an artificial knee joint. They use an innovative approach totally based on digital data to optimize lower-limb socket prosthesis design[85]. The approach involves using 3D imaging and printing techniques to improve the fit of the prosthetic attachment, replacing the standard plaster cast methodology in use today.

The company carries out research and publishes papers in collaboration with external researchers. Alongside Bonacina, Giorgio Colombo, Massimiliano Bertetti and Grazia Magrassi (2006)[86] describe how their Rapid Prototyping technologies approach is based on generating a stump's 3D detailed geometric model using laser, CT and MRI imaging.

The laser technique provides bone structure and surface geometrical modeling, while the CT and MRI techniques depict soft tissue and muscle structure. The authors argue that they can improve fit, comfort and functionality through these techniques and are currently attempting to define a protocol procedure with improved accuracy.

I argue that the poiesis element is present both in terms of Bonacina's embedded experience and of the team's technical skills to develop a made-to-measure model of the artificial limb, and reflected in their use of high technology alongside a mechanical weighting system. This use of high technology can be seen as a tool, used thanks to both their technical but also their poietic skills and approaches. Their choice to publish their

---

[85] An overview of current research and techniques used is offered in this downloadable poster. *http://www.roadrunnerfoot.com/eng/attivita/Poster_TMOLLPD.pdf*. Last accessed 24-08-2017

[86] A Professional publication article describing the approach is available for download: http://www.roadrunnerfoot.com/eng/attivita/RE_RPTech_Inn_Prosthetic_Socket.pdf. Last accessed 24-08-2017

findings through open access platforms with collaborations with Universities and aim to improve user experience displays several characteristics of the RI models described in chapter 1, allowing me to argue that this type of development and production model could represent a form of Poiesis Intensive Responsible Innovation.

PIRI Case Study 2:

Officina Corpuscoli

The second case of craft-based Poiesis Intensive RI comes directly from the communities of practice of a science laboratory.

Maurizio Montalti runs the Officina Corpuscoli project[87]. Montalti has a background in Industrial engineering and design, with a particular interest in developing conceptual design in context. Within this particular design field, the emphasis is not only on the product itself but also upon everything that the product represents and can incorporate, taking into account layers of meaning and the storytelling capacity that are integral to the object, rather reflecting my own ideas on craft practices and workplace narrative already outlined. Montalti has a particular interest in connecting design to microbiology, his chosen medium being bacterial fungi.

Through his project, Montalti has managed the difficult task of coupling design with science.

One of his most interesting lines of research is 'System Synthetics'. Developed in collaboration with the Kluyver Centre for Industrial Fermentation in the context of the DA4GA (Designers & Artists for genomics Award, 2011), the project

---

[87] The Corpuscoli Project website offers an overview of current and past research: www.corpuscoli.com. Last accessed 24-08-2017

deals with plastic decomposition. The objective is to try to stimulate symbiosis in a short time-frame, with the aim of degrading plastic in order to turn it into an energy source, namely a biofuel. Given the scientific difficulties involved, Montalti explains that the project's parallel aim is to stimulate public discussion about synthetic biology.

Supporting many of the lines investigated in the current RI debate, Montalti argues that the public should participate in a debate about the potentials that certain tools could provide, and how certain technologies should be seen (see Spruit, 2014 and Wynne, 2006 for further discussion on this topic). He believes that the wider public should be involved, so that decision-making processes do not remain confined within the lab, an aim that involves addressing problems of language used as well as what he calls the 'democratization of science'. He summarizes this point by stating that *we should provide the public with questions, not answers or judgements*[88].

A large portion of the laboratory's research is dedicated to using fungi to create matter. In the process of what Montalti describes as *collaborating with fungal microorganisms to create new matter,* the researchers use waste materials from the food industry and agriculture, colonizing different bio-types to produce different materials. Given his undoubted abilities, vision and funding success, Montalti's experiments have become a core business for Utrecht University, leading him into full integration into academic research life.

The Corpuscoli research project has also made a move towards operating on an industrial scale. This research aims to produce biodegradable packaging materials that can replace polystyrene

---

[88] This quote is taken from recorded and transcribed interview material, collected as part of this PhD research.

and other petroleum-based materials currently in use. The pilot project that is currently operational under the name MOGU[89] required the purchase of an abandoned textile factory in Northern Italy and its conversion to produce fungal materials on a larger scale. The factory produces pellets and sheets of materials that can be layered and treated to determine their properties, including their strength, elasticity and water resistance.

Montalti consistently refers to his work as a craft. He began as a bio-hacker, learning his skills as an amateur with help from other enthusiasts, and maintains a large network of this type of collaborator in his field. He argues that his approach differs from those who are trained in science as actions are not guided by learned procedures, rather relying on the experience of both the researcher herself but also of other fungi growers present in her network. He argues that the results are different precisely because the process is not guided by conventions, which leads him into a more reflexive but less guided approach, while remaining within established laboratory protocols. He constantly maintains that in order to understand something he has to touch it, to experience its growth and the effects of his interventions upon the organism.

I would argue that the moral intentions that underpin his work, the reflexive nature of his approach, and the intention to bring in broader actors within the decision-making process, coupled with his hands-on approach, would seem to show similarities to a model of craft based PIRI as proposed above. A further important factor is that the objects produced are often displayed in art galleries as pieces of art, and are perceived as beautiful by

---

[89] MOGU http://www.madeinitalylab.it/2018/06/25/mogu-biomateriale-che-nasce-dai-funghi/
Last accessed 08/11/2019

those involved in their production and showing[90].

Both of the brief examples cited above display poiesis-intensive traits as described earlier, and also display elements of RI models as described in chapter 1, leading me to argue that the processes described could be seen as offering a model worthy of investigation for a form of Poiesis Intensive Responsible Innovation (PIRI).

5.4 Some Conclusions

Poiesis-Intensive Innovation is led by soft forms of knowledge such as design, functional aesthetics, organizational and relational patters and include forms of tacit knowledge that are usually found within forms of socialized learning, typical of apprenticeship. In these social situations, knowledge regarding *how to do things* is learned through participation within a community of practice, resulting in a shared understanding between its members that is dependent on relations of trust and cooperation beyond and above functional transactions and hierarchical interactions. As a result, Poiesis-Intensive Innovation in general is difficult to formalize and is found in diverse, situated and fluid working practices.

The most obvious way in which these case studies fit the PIRI model is their leaning towards moralized forms of aesthetics and bespoke functions over and above anonymous and abstract formalized efficiency. Both of the examples clearly display the producers' wishes to develop tailor made solutions to individual situations. In the case of Roadrunner, a bespoke product for an individual situation, crafted to the needs of an individual person and developed through a process that views the end product in

---

[90] For example see the Fungal Futures exhibition
  https://www.fondazionebassetti.org/tags/Maurizio%20Montalti
Last accessed 08/11/2019

terms of its functional beauty, but also of the design and developmental choices made during that process and which are very much lived by the chief engineer. In the case of Corpuscoli, we once more find a bespoke production process that involves the creation (through DNA modification) of a specific material for a specific piece of work. The finished pieces are very much seen as artistic creations as demonstrated by their appearance in art installations, demonstrating the philosophies that underpin the approaches.

Both of these examples could be categorized as displaying similarities to frameworks used in RI approaches, and move towards a characterization of a form of PIRI. I argue that these forms of innovation, if framed within an individual's concept of responsible behaviour, can be critiqued from an RI perspective. The decision-making processes are negotiated within a narrative, that is itself negotiated, and if this negotiation process is informed by the ideas proposed for RI as described in chapter 1 of this thesis, this could lead to the development of a model of this particular form of Poiesis Intensive Responsible Innovation.

In the following chapters I present two case studies. The first case study describes the experience of conducting research in a workplace that I know very well as it takes place in a furniture restoration workshop, the trade that I trained into upon leaving school. I use my personal experience and skills to analyze recorded conversation transcriptions with a fellow upholsterer to test my thesis; a skilled vision can be shared that sees beauty as a representation of the correctness of the decision-making process for each individual piece of work as understood through the workplace narrative.

The second case study relates to similar conversational

transcriptions from a bio-technology laboratory in Utrecht, describing similarities and differences in approach in an analysis of possible PIRI working practices.

175

Chapter 6

Apprenticeship: Learning to See, Learning to Do: The Upholsterer's narrative

Background to the Fieldwork

The chapter that follows is based upon ethnographic experience and conversation that took place within an upholstery workshop that I know very well. Although this may seem far removed from the typical fieldwork sites chosen within RI (see Fisher 2007 for a more typical setting), I feel that the data gained during this fieldwork experience provides me with the grounding and evidence to comment upon the RI debate precisely because it is a workplace with working practices that I know so well.

This extensive first-hand knowledge requires and allows a nuanced explanation and description of the context, something that I am able to do based upon 17 years of work experience and using audio recordings and photos made during my fieldwork. The recordings are conversational rather than interviews, they form part of a co-constructed narrative produced internally within the process and workplace, whose analysis could be described as taking a narrative approach to the analysis of working practices.

This extensive working experience allows me to describe the local production of a process from an intimate perspective. In this case the process involves upholstery within furniture restoration, but my argument is that the narrative mechanism through which the process is developed could easily be applied to other settings, something that I will demonstrate in Chapter 7.

I believe that a narrative approach could be used across a broad collection of workplaces if they can be seen as being structurally similar. How similar are the structures between a small craft-based workshop setting and that of a high technology science laboratory? Can we see similar structures in play? I hope to answer some of these questions in Chapter 7. I will argue that language used may be different but that the model that refers to the internal organization of working practices with reference to external norms as described in the previous chapter and the construction of a workplace narrative can be applied across these and many other contexts.

If, as I believe, the conversations analyzed and working and narration practices discussed in this chapter can be applied to other contexts, it is precisely knowing this particular context so well that will allow me to understand and explicate the narrative from an insider perspective and make comparison to contexts that I am less familiar with. The type of in-depth analysis of the recorded conversations that follows is only made possible by the participants' (including my own) shared understanding of the context.

The recording of these conversations allows me to attempt to understand and describe the narrative that affords such a process within such a social setting (Gibson, 1979). If the social setting affords process construction (the basis of my argument), can my understanding of how this may work in a craft workshop be applied to a science laboratory? Can patterns and similarities be found? If so, what are the implications for the governance of science in terms of responsibility and governance, or investigation into the de-facto or grass-roots models of RI previously described, or being able to visualize such a mechanism?

The Working Experience

Over the winter between 1982 and 1983 I was preparing to leave school in Manchester UK, and looking for a job. I was interested in working in furniture making or restoration, so I sent dozens of letters to local cabinet makers, French polishers and upholsterers. I also applied for and was offered a highly coveted place at the Manchester Building School for a 3-year course in furniture making.

At that time the country was in an economic crisis, and jobs were not easy to come by. I received a call from a local upholsterer (a restorer of furniture using textiles), who invited me to go and meet him. I called in the workshop after school, in my Altrincham Grammar School uniform, by coincidence the same school that my prospective employer had attended. We met for a few minutes, and he asked me if I would like to start working Saturdays with a view to starting as apprentice in the following September.

I became the new boy at Gordon Stewart Upholstery, served my 4-year apprenticeship and have maintained both a working and social relationship with my boss Gordon and the other older apprentice Adam to this day.

This apprenticeship period turned out to be one of the most important in my life. I was brought into a world of craftsmanship, small business entrepreneurship, beer drinking and the appreciation of beauty and correctness. Correctness in working practices, in workshop maintenance, and in customer services.

I came to know all of the other upholsterers in the city, and to understand their particular approaches to the problems related to both running a business and making and recovering furniture. The workshops were all very different. I worked in a clean well-ordered workshop, where every tool had its place and the floor was swept clean regularly, waste was taken to the dump once a week and the pattern books were hung neatly from the walls.

Other workshops I visited were nothing like that however. Some had piles of used textiles and stuffing materials in the corners or under the bench. Others were damp and scruffy garages with piles of foam strewn over half-finished or stripped-down pieces of furniture. Gordon was the butt of jokes about his cleanliness and organization mania, but it was part of a narrative, a larger scheme of organization related to working practices as much as presentation. The preparation of the piece to be covered had to be clean and orderly, as not only was that important for the quality of the finished work but also for the apprenticeship experience and clarity of learning. The photos below show the organization of G C Stewart's workshop.

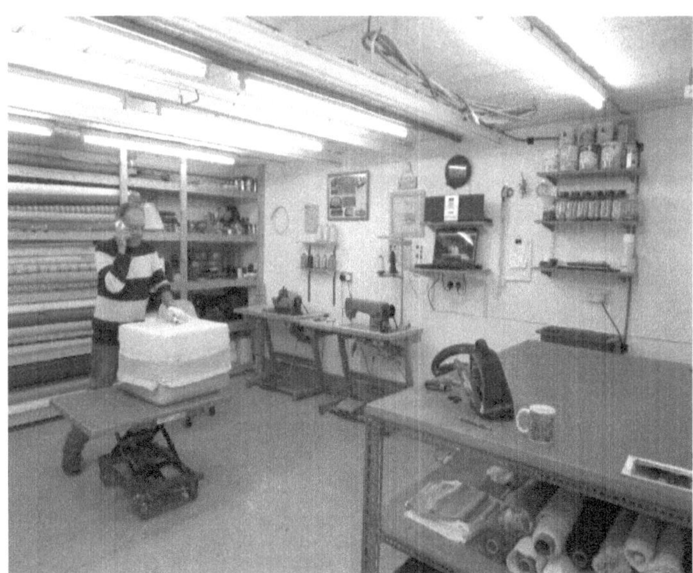

Figure 1. An overview of the workshop with Gordon at work

Photo: Jonathan Hankins

As I came to know all of the other small businesses in the field, I witnessed many workshops, but the order and presentation of the one I worked in was unparalleled. The quality of work was too (skill), as (for my own eyes) was the beauty of the work produced. There seemed to be a relationship between the production of beauty and the cleanliness of the working area, a feature that has become more apparent as I carried out the research for this book.

The experience of learning to be an upholsterer begins with a period of stripping out old furniture, long before a newcomer to the trade can attach his or her first piece of fabric to a frame. This process is structurally the most important in learning the process, as if done correctly it teaches the new worker how the chair has been made. As the piece is undone it reveals the order in which the different cut textiles were prepared and attached. The first piece to come off is the bottom, then the back, the outsides and inward. An orderly approach makes this apparent, as the chair remains untouched apart from the piece that is being removed, each time revealing one more piece that can then be removed once again without disturbing the rest, offering a reverse model of the order in which the piece was constructed from the frame up.

This is not however the only way a piece can be stripped out. The cloth can be cut with a knife along the staple line and pulled off, leaving the staples in place. This not only leaves a rough finish on the frame, but also negates the possibility of learning through dissection of the process. It is a sign of lower quality work, and would certainly be seen as not the right way to do the job in a high-quality furniture restoration business.

Once correctly stripped, the textile coverings can then be laid down in order and used as patterns for the new fabric, but also represent the order that the piece of furniture has to be covered in order to make it look exactly as it did when it was first done. If a piece is taken apart in a disorderly manner this pattern making and process viewing feature is lost, and an important part of the learning process is missed for the apprentice. Using this technique, a worker learns to tackle pieces that are different from each other. A technique or approach is learned, that when integrated into a skilled and stylized manuality leads to a signature piece. The orderly stacking of these used textiles is a form of mapping, an eye into the processes used during its manufacturing, and I would argue that the orderly nature of the workshop plays a similar role. The orderly organization of the surroundings is reflected in the orderly approach to the work, and talked about as such, the relationship easy to see for those who possess the right skilled vision (Grasseni, 2007).

On the day that I took the photo above I spent several hours in the workshop discussing our shared experiences working within the trade, with Gordon, the man who had trained me. He claimed that myself and Adam, the other apprentice and case study informant for this thesis, had learned the trade on our own, that he had never taught us anything. Following on from the arguments outlined in chapter 5 on situated learning, Gordon argued that we learned from watching others within context, both himself and each other, and that the practicalities are not taught in terms of ever explicitly being demonstrated. The learner copies in some way what they see the others do. It is a learning process through experiencing the situation that you must then apply, supported through the constant engagement with the constructed narrative through everyday conversation.

Gordon also believed that this narrative should also involve, and does involve, learning about how to run a business. I was taught a few harsh lessons involving money, as Gordon played a role in which exploitation was also justified as a learning experience. On one occasion I was docked part of my wages as I cut the fabric upside down for a series of dining chairs. The fabric could not be used and more was ordered, the costs publicly deducted from my wages on the following Friday afternoon. On another occasion I gave a price for a chair that was too low, Gordon upping the price and keeping the difference. I was learning the trade, but it was a trade that involved taking responsibility and paying for mistakes.

However harsh this seems it was seen as justified in terms of learning. If as a craftsperson you make a mistake with raw materials and have to order more you cannot ask the customer to cover the difference, the business has to take the loss, and this rule was applied to apprentices within the structure, invited to share the experience of losing money.

Following these examples and many more to follow, I argue in this chapter that the apprenticeship experience is a learning process through experience, an experience narrated through working within a particular social group in a particular social area and organizational structure.

The point of departure is that of Polanyi's tacit knowledge (Polanyi, 1958), further developed by several others (see Collins, 2010 for an overview of the argument).

Tacit Knowledge

Tacit knowledge or understanding is the way that humans perceive objects and processes despite not being conscious of the neural processes that create this perception. In other words, we know more than we can say, as every aspect of conscious thought contains subsidiary components that we are only conscious of at the moment in which we focus upon the principal content of the thought or its synthetic objective of action.

For example, in the case in question, I can learn to restore a piece of furniture by working alongside Gordon, but he cannot explain to me how to do it. I can learn to know how a process is to be undertaken according to context, which materials to choose and techniques to adopt, and I also learn why.

A classic example given to demonstrate this phenomenon is that of face recognition. We are able to recognize a single face within thousands of other faces, but we are not capable of describing how and why we can. This can be applied to science equally as easily as it can to enskillment within an apprenticeship setting. It may be impossible to describe all aspects of a process of furniture restoration through words, even with the help of images, as the description will never be exhaustive, thus Gordon's explanation that we as apprentices taught ourselves can be framed within a narrow conception of teaching and learning; things were not explained, but this does not mean that they are not learned or taught. Techniques are taught and learned through imitation, the movement of the body and learning both what to look at and for, much of which may not be intentional or conscious to all parties involved. The approach is learned both through action and through sharing in the workplace narrative.

The carrying out of a complex action therefore involves the use of knowledge that is not fully brought to consciousness by the actor. It is impossible for that person to offer a full and exhaustive explanation of the reasons underlying the motivations and skills brought into play, but it can be demonstrated and learned, and following Grasseni and as argued in chapter 5, it can be seen and appreciated through a skilled vision (Grasseni, 2007).

Importantly for this argument, Polanyi argued that values can be introduced tacitly, in other words by implication. These values are not followed as rules might be, but absorbed in the same way as knowledge, so thought and creativity as well as values can be seen as anchored within a reality within which they can be shared. Polanyi argues that the ability to learn and teach depends on intelligent cooperation, in which the learner must not only follow, but synthetically capture the meaning (within the contextual narration) of a demonstration (Polanyi, 1966).

Tacit knowledge in a skilled setting such as the workshop is made up of bodily action that the practitioner is not able to exhaustively explain, and their activation according to relational patterns, that he or she can also not exhaustively describe or explain. The effects of the ability to carry out the work can be seen and felt, leading to knowledge of how to do things. It is a working knowledge that is personal, situation specific and fluid, and learned through a structured experience of apprenticeship.

Much of the narration in this chapter is born through my own personal experience, as I knew the workplaces that I entered during fieldwork very well. I had been trained myself in one of them, and worked in another, albeit between 20 and 30 years earlier.

The workshops tell the history of the work completed, as well as narrating the present processes in action. Every saw cut in the trestle top. Every line of over-sprayed glue on the cutting bench, every piece of left-over fabric represents a completed piece of work that is now sitting in someone's house, in daily use. I am myself part of that history. I still see some of the pieces I worked upon many years ago, in the houses of friends who became customers or returning to the workshop to be maintained or restored once more[91].

The workshop in which I trained and that later became one of my research sites is situated in Hale, a wealthy suburb of Manchester, and an ideal situation for someone with a passion for high quality furniture. I trained there between 1983 and 1987, and maintained a working relationship with the owner for the following ten years. The clientele for this particular business was quite particular. Many of the customers were retired, had owned their furniture since the 1960's or before, and had enough money and understanding of quality to commission restoration works of high quality.

The appearance of a highly ordered workspace and the quality that such an orderly approach afforded to the finished work led to a successful small business that was well known and appreciated in the surrounding towns. The orderly presentation and approach was also reflected in the style that the workshop produced, a recognizable stylistic choice of straight lines with sharply defined borders, the use of high quality textiles and combinations of traditional skills with modern manufacturing techniques. I argue that this represents an aesthetics that

---

[91] During my research time I entered Adam's workshop to see a piece that I had myself worked on some 20 years before. I can recognize pieces through their style, but also through the materials used. My father supplied the workshop with flat woven cotton samples from his work in the textile industry, and we used it as platform and bottom cloth. This would have been a very expensive solution if we had bought it at retail price, and gave a touch of class to the work, but was purely incidental. To us it was cheap, but also of high quality.

reflected the organization as a whole, a representation of its working practices and narrative through its style.

Each of the different self-employed upholsterers in the area has their own style. My trainer Gordon's style was orderly, clean and demonstrated a mix of techniques. ABCD Upholstery, run by Adam Black (the second workshop in this case study and main interview participant), has a more designer style. This can be seen in the choice of fabrics and finishing techniques, as well as business card presentation. Adam was the senior apprentice during my period of training and several traits (tidiness the most apparent) can be seen to have been shared from our time as apprentices.

Within the small geographical area of Altrincham that serves as a single customer catchment area (a satellite town to the South of Manchester), there are three small upholstery companies. The clientele of each is different. ABCD have a young designer clientele, G C Stewart's a slightly older clientele, but both working at the top end of the market. The third is a lower end upholsterer, a fact that can be seen in the presentation of the workshop in many ways. The workshop space is not well organized, clean or orderly, underpinning my argument that the beauty of the finished piece is an embodiment of the process, including the organization of the social space in which it is produced. An orderly workshop is capable of producing high quality pieces, a disorderly workshop reflects lower quality work.

In the lower end example that I will refer to as TC, the workshop is not as well kept as the other two, and is not so well positioned. The other two are on the outskirts of a wealthy village within a larger urban area, and can be seen to have a kind of village tradesman attraction. TC is based in a residential area, has less passing trade and does not present such a craft-person feel. At TC they do more industrial or less glamorous domestic work, and the technical quality is not as high (which raises an interesting question related to lay normativity as TC trained with Gordon).

I argue that the orderly presentation and maintenance of the workshop and the techniques that it reflects reflect the underlying values that the individual upholsterers hold about how a restoration should be carried out. The approach should be seen as a whole, the process of running the business and not just restoring furniture, and that it reflects what Sayer describes as 'lay normativity', or *what matters to people and why* (Sayer, 2011).

The theory that Sayer proposes argues that individuals have an evaluative standpoint or orientation, or a relationship of caring about and reacting to the world around them. The influence of personally held ideas of dignity and fairness in what he describes as a fundamentally evaluative world can be seen in practices, daily interaction and everyday life. I argue that what we see in these daily practices of stripping and recovering furniture, the differences in technique used and approaches to waste storage and removal, tidiness and even choices of which pattern books to stock, represent individual orientations to the world on show and in action.

I clarify my position however that processes based upon ideas of lay normativity find themselves socially situated, as the geographical positioning of a small business and the social relationships within it (and what the positioning affords) influence the type and quality of work that can be carried out and the expectations of all parties in the transaction. It is what we might describe as *the job being right* according to possibilities and the narrative.

The geographical and social positioning that framed my training led to me learning traditional restoration techniques that are now being lost, not only because they do not suit modern furnishing techniques, but also because they are extremely time consuming and require a certain type of customer who can pay more to restore a piece than it would cost to replace it. Expectations of how a finished piece should look also change, a topic that I will address later in this chapter as I analyze some of my recorded conversations with Adam made during my fieldwork. During my time working in this trade expectations were high from both customers and my boss, as were prices. The work completed was the highest quality in greater Manchester, with norms and expectations from all sides under fine scrutiny.

The relationship within the workshop was not always easy however. The sharing of such intimacy and understanding does lead to friction, arguments about how to proceed and of course errors must be paid for both in economic and emotional terms. But the skills shared create a lifelong feeling of brotherhood, the shared knowledge being the tie. It is to be noted that in a small business the employer is reliant on the worker in the way the worker is reliant on the employer. The work must be done to the correct standard, so the employer is reliant on the employee to maintain standards, but the employee is needed to carry the article into the customer's house once it is finished, in the evening after work, on Christmas Eve, or whenever necessary. Thus, the relationship within the workspace is constantly negotiated and reaffirmed.

I would argue that in this negotiation the underlying idea of *for the good for all parties involved* plays an important role. The negotiation takes place within a social setting that is characterized by expectations as described above, but that is infused with the characteristics of the normativity practiced within the setting. The shared understanding of doing the job right, from start to finish, informs the process, norms and expectations are known to all parties, and most importantly the reasons that underlie them are also known even if not stated. They are learned through the practice of apprenticeship in that particular setting, and as such are specific and non-generalizable. They make up part of the everyday narrative that is shared and developed through everyday conversation. Expectations vary between settings, being responsibility but at the same time aesthetically based, as I hope the following example will demonstrate.

As a finished piece is inspected, stroked and the cushions arranged in a display of beauty, the fact that it has been done to a high standard is noted and celebrated. In this social setting, mutual appreciation of ability is expressed, strengthening the social relationships, and reaffirming the argument that the sharing of a skilled vision allows responsibility to be seen and shared within beauty.

During my period of training I worked alongside a French polisher's apprentice, within a rather antagonistic relationship. I have documented much about this experience in my Master's Thesis[92] and will not go into detail once more, but a single taunt from the polishers towards the upholsterers holds a key argument for this thesis. The taunt was that upholstery is a semi-

---

[92] Master in Applied Social Research, University of Manchester 2001. *Upholsterers in Ethnography,* unpublished

skilled trade, unlike polishing (of wood), because with wood all of the work is on show when the piece is finished, but with upholstery most of the work is hidden. The top layer of textile covers and hides the work below, which therefore can be of varying quality.

There is some truth to this taunt, wooden frames are hidden by stuffing so are made to be strong and not pretty, they are not seen so the joinery is not fine. Shortcuts in the stuffing can be hidden, and this means that an upholsterer has many choices in how to proceed while restoring a piece of furniture. This fact is extremely important for the argument of this book, as it implies that the restorer makes choices, both economic, stylistic and for ease, that are hidden from the public. They can only be detected by another skilled worker who possesses a skilled vision.

In the case that the upholsterer chooses a long process of traditional methods over what we might call a quick fix, he or she does so because of personal values. Following Sayer (Sayer, 2011) I argue that they practice a form of lay normativity in the choices made during the restoration process. They practice what they believe is morally correct to do, because of their own particular beliefs in fairness, what is right to do and how something should be done as afforded by the narrative developed in that particular setting. Much of this argument can be seen in the recorded utterances that make up the second half of this chapter, and are related to the argument of skilled visions (Grasseni 2007), but I would like to argue that an upholsterer who puts in days of work to do a traditional job when he or she could take an easier route does so because it is perceived as the right way to do it, and because they can do it both technically and economically. These are ethical choices, as they are hidden from the customer. They could of course always take the higher charges and cut corners, but working within a narrative that is socially constructed both constrains and affords such choices.

The situated learning experience of the apprenticeship with a trainer that is at once a learning example and a boss involves the sharing, understanding, discussion and negotiation of these ethical positions, which are then extended to the outside world. These are after all value judgements that are learned through the apprenticeship experience and that are only visible to other experts with whom they share a skilled vision, forming part of the narrative developed within the workplace.

Skilled Vision in the Workshop

Before moving on to the analysis of the recorded conversations, I here offer a short recap:

One central argument to this chapter is that the apprenticeship process trains individuals into a skilled vision (Grasseni 2007), allowing participants to share a moral judgement through aesthetics. My argument is that skilled participants in the restoration process are apprenticed into seeing the quality of the work carried out by looking at a finished piece, into sharing an aesthetic judgement that includes an understanding and appreciation of the qualities of the process in question, including the choices that underpin them.

For Grasseni, the skilling of vision, or ability of learning to see, takes place within a structured social environment, and is cognitive, relational and social at the same time. Communities of practice (Lave and Wenger 1991) engage differently with the capacity to see and to know, the common ground being that a sensibility is learned and reinforced through repeated acts of looking. Grasseni argues that skilled visions are aesthetic, moral, functional and normative, and I forward the argument that a skilled vision can be seen as an appreciation of poiesis within the workplace narrative, as described above and used within Bassetti Foundation discourse.

Visual skills are learnt within specific communities of practice through processes of enskilment (Ingold 2000). Enskillment can be seen as a matter of apprenticeship, with specific ways of mastering professional and relational domains through distinct visual skills that are not identical for different places, people, practices and periods.

Ingold's approach builds on studies of situated learning and distributed condition. Charles Goodwin, a linguistic anthropologist, used techniques of discourse analysis to study *professional vision* (Goodwin, 1994), or an apprenticeship of standards. This research aims to develop the idea of a professional vision with the inclusion of lay morality through aesthetics as part of a greater narrative.

As outlined above Grasseni developed her concept of skilled visions during fieldwork in the Italian Alps (Grasseni 2009). Her interest was in studying the capacity of breed inspectors, working breeders and cattle-fair judges who visualize the animal body in terms of *functional* beauty. In the case of cows, the functional beauty represents practical functionality and is standardized into internationally recognized traits and models.

These traits are represented in artefacts such as plastic or china models, photos and ways of viewing the animals, are part of everyday conversation and play roles in public events. I argue that in furniture restoration aesthetics also represent a functional beauty, partially but not entirely based on durability, beauty and an openness towards ideas of trust and fairness, often described as responsibility (also in terms of not hiding shortcuts that are easy to hide and only detectable through expert vision).

Grasseni argues that *Aesthetic apprenticeship shapes and articulates an entire 'ecology of belonging', namely the environment - both social and material - that allows, encourages, and confirms membership of a specific community of lookers*[93], and I will argue that this can also be seen in the small business re-upholstery relationships I have been involved in and studied. The visions are multi sensorial, and can also involve touch and sound, occurring within a multi sensorial apprenticeship.

As outlined above I wish to push Grasseni's argument to argue that the skilled vision of an upholsterer not only takes into account an appreciation of the process enacted in the workplace and the social setting, but that for the skilled apprentice the shared aesthetic experience involves an appreciation into an understanding of why the decisions taken during this process were taken. The social setting allows a shared aesthetic understanding of the practical but also the ethical decision-making process that created the finished piece, and as therefore the poiesis element as described in Chapter 4 can be appreciated through the beauty of the finished piece.

The shared understanding of the process hidden under the textile, the understanding of how that process was chosen and why, informs the value and status given to the piece and the worker. A beautiful piece hides many techniques that could have easily been simplified or substituted, but the fact that they have been included even though they are hidden creates the beauty for the expert eye. I argue that these can be seen as moral choices, as they are not immediately visible to the general

---

[93] Taken from the Forthcoming Wiley Encyclopedia of Cultural Anthropology

public, but may be time consuming or expensive. They are often described as doing the job right, an issue that I constantly return to in this chapter.

The typical viewing of the piece is multi sensorial as noted above. Typical actions that accompany the viewing involve stroking the fabric on the seat forward to test the tension (if it is not correct the seat will sag once sat on), the pushing down of the front edge to test if it has been sprung and stitched or replaced with a fixed article (typically a cut up piece of broom handle or cotton rolled into a rope), and the lifting of a single leg off the floor to test the strength of the frame. These are typical actions that are computed multiple times each day without thought, they are learned through exposure, but they are just checking what is already visible, if it is a correctly done piece.

The choice of textiles and techniques is also set within a particular social setting. A furniture restorer working in a wealthy area will have greater possibilities in terms of prices and materials used. Time restraints caused by lack of money will make structural choices necessary, which are fully justifiable in terms of an individual piece. This is also a topic that I address later in this chapter through my recorded conversation with Adam. A skilled vision therefore sees quality and technique within a social context.

After serving my time I worked in a self-employed capacity[94] for Gordon for many years, before becoming Adam's employee on a part time basis as I made the decision to go back to school and eventually on to university.

As noted above though, the apprenticeship experience and

---

[94] Workers are paid under the self-employed regime as it avoids many of the health and safety and insurance issues associated with employment.

ability to work with my hands and produce beauty remained with me, and as I came to write my MA thesis at Manchester University, I returned to the place of work to write an ethnography about self-employed furniture restorers and their networks of collaboration and cooperation.

As I moved into my collaboration with the Bassetti Foundation and their mission of promoting responsible innovation, my focus was drawn to these working practices in terms of how to *do the job right*. Doing the job right is a complex category, difficult to pin down, and different in every case. The parameters may be drawn by financial constraints; physical possibility of doing what the customer wants, time constraints, suitability and many other reasons, but taking all of these things into account there is a shared understanding of the correct way to do the job, each job, and each part of each job, developed through the workplace narrative. The narrative is developed through everyday conversation at work.

6.1 Methodology for the Recorded Conversations

During my PhD period I returned to the workshop in South Manchester where I had worked between 1997 and 2000. During that period I was an employee of ABCD Upholstery, a small business owned by Adam Black. Adam had been the senior apprentice at G C Stewart Upholsterery when I had served my apprenticeship. I have known Adam since those days and had maintained a working relationship in terms of collaboration in times of (mutual) need throughout this time.

Adam works for himself in collaboration with Louise his wife. Louise is a trained clothes designer and tailor, and cuts and prepares the fabrics on a part time basis. In order to carry out this research I returned to the workshop with camera and audio recorder, spending long periods of time during the working day recording conversation within the workplace. The resulting recordings should be seen as co-produced.

Although I had prepared open ended questions, the conversations were very broad and unstructured, very much examples of the everyday conversations that had taken place throughout my working relationships over the years. They included talking about work, customers, working relationships between different businesses and the broader community. The setting is important in this case, as the conversations were very close to being the natural types of discussion in that particular social setting. The workshop is a place that we both know well, it is full of tools that we both know how to use and that become a spark for conversation. As apprentices we both bought our own set of tools, an upholsterer's tack hammer, a pair of scissors, a ripper and mallet, and they are important for our identity. We made our own pair of trestles on our first day at work, Adam still uses his today. As I write my hammer and scissors are sitting here in my office, having travelled the world with me, but I feel that the work setting is the only natural place to carry out our discussion. Anywhere else would be forced. (Edwards and Holland, 2013)

The recordings were then transcribed and ordered and analyzed. The transcriptions were sent to Adam so that he could check meaning, and followed up with further meetings in order to deepen understanding through further conversation on certain topics. Agreement for their use was given, while certain sections were asked to be excluded. I am aware that this co-construction of data will lead to a selective representation of these working experiences, as we are selecting what do discuss and then what to publish (Stanley and Wise, 1993), but argue that this methodology allows myself as researcher to probe a setting that I know well. I am therefore not reporting the results as sociological or anthropological ethnography, but as a co-constructed case study.

The conversations reported in this chapter were recorded and are used with the consent of those involved. They are open ended discussions on topics that were steered (from both participants), rather that question answer format interviews. I would argue that this allows the re-creation of a coherent description of a shared understanding, in this case of the mechanisms necessary to lead to a shared understanding of the beauty of a finished piece of furniture and its appreciation as acceptance of the work process. Therefore, following Dillard I am not arguing that the recorded conversations *offer a mirror or window into the inner life of a person*, but offer insight into shared experiences of apprenticeship in a single environment (Dillard, 1982).

The conversation is a simulacrum, *a perfectly miniature and coherent world in its own right* (Dillard, 1982, p.152). Seen in this way, the conversation plays the role of offering a narrative device that allows the participants to tell the story of their shared experiences; to discuss and demonstrate the shared experiences and emotions of a shared history (Porter, 2000). A narrative device to describe a workplace narrative.

The interaction in question is not an interview, it is a discussion. It is fully interactional and relies on the participants' mutual trust, understanding and reflexivity.

Following Jennifer Mason, I argue that meaning and understanding is created within the interaction, effectively a co-production involving the construction or reconstruction of knowledge (Adapted from Mason 2002, p62), within what

Atkinson and Silverman describe as a confessional situation (Atkinson and Silverman, 1997).

Following ethnomethodological approaches (Garfinkel, 1996) this approach aims to understand social phenomena from the perspectives of those involved, but is particular in that the researcher is one of those participating in co-producing the description. The objective is the same as other ethnomethodological and interactional approaches therefore, within which knowledge takes the form of explanations of how individuals interpret and make sense of their day-to-day life and interactions (Yanow and Schwartz-Shea 2006).

I argue that following Ann Oakley, in the context of an interview or conversation that involves any discussion on shared understandings or experiences (be that family practices or skilled manufacturing or craft techniques), arguments that interviews or conversations could be uncontaminated by the presence and participation of the interviewer are flawed, and therefore accept that my presence forms an integral part of the data and its creation (Oakley, 1981 p.41).

Oakley argued that there can be no intimacy without reciprocity (p.49), and that researchers give something of themselves to the interaction and to the participants. This notion is particularly present in the case of a recorded conversation such as those I analyze in this chapter, and should not be seen as a point of criticism but as a methodological tool that is openly used by both participants and understood by both as such.

Following Barbara Sherman Heyl's interpretist understanding of interview and conversation as methodological tools, this technique aims to empower interviewees within the conversation, to give them control over the topics covered in the conversations, the ways these topics are addressed, the relevance of underlying meanings and worldviews of the individuals participating and discussed, and champion reflexivity as a methodological tool for all participants (Sherman Heyl, 2000, p.368).

The aim is to construct a life history of the setting in question, rather than an oral history of the individuals (Thompson, 2008, Thompson et al. 1983), with events as well as relationships recounted that cover a broad spectrum of aspects related to the social setting in question. These conversations are interpretive devices through which the participants represent themselves, both to themselves and to others, in order to describe not only events and their meanings but life-long relationships of trust and interdependency. For a fuller description of narrative research methodologies see Riessman (1993), and Cussins (1998).

6.2 An Analysis of the Recordings: Conversations with the Village Upholsterer.

The following analysis is conducted on transcribed interview data, collected in autumn 2015 using the methodology described above. The conversations took place between myself and Adam Black in his workplace, the context within which the interviews took place being described in greater detail above. The analysis aims to elicit the fullest description possible of Adam's relationship to his work and network, taking the concept of responsibility to the workplace narrative as its core analytic principle.

One of the arguments that prevails in the Bassetti Foundation and described in Chapter 4 is that responsibility is something that is felt differently by artisan workers than by those working in large organizations. The owner of a small business finds him or herself within a community. They work but also live within that community, their waste treatment and the way they run their business in terms of the local and wider environment is tied to this position, they are in some ways personally answerable to the local community in a way that larger organizations are not.

I argue that these relationships lead to the artisan holding a different conception of responsibility than an employee within a large organization, a conception that could be described as more organic and less rules or regulation based.

In the following exchange we discuss the small business relationship with the local community. Throughout the conversation reported Adam's comments are indented, while my part in the conversation appears in bold.

If you work for yourself, do you feel you have a different relationship to the local community than if you are a large organization? Large organizations do have a relationship with the city that they are in, but is it a different relationship, and maybe not the same as your relationship?

Yes, because I am the village upholsterer, and I am part of the local community like the local baker or butcher, and I do feel that. And it is funny that you should say that because they are having a whip round for the Christmas lights and even though I won't personally benefit from contribution you do feel obliged, because a lot of the shop keepers and businesses have furniture covered by me, and the customers generally own businesses and even though I am not going to benefit (from the Christmas decorations) I can see the point. You cannot just put that burden on the shop keepers because there are not enough shops to pay for the lights so everyone has to participate, but if you work for a big organization you would not really consider that. So you do feel obliged to contribute, and I suppose the people who live in Hale Village are supporting you, and you support them back.

Above we can see the description of how the working situation of the artisan worker changes their outlook. Adam is talking about how his personal view and his actions (in this case contributing to the Christmas decorations that will run down the village main street) is affected by his position in the community, a situation that is not shared by an employee in a larger institution. He justifies the expense of participation in terms of customers as well as in terms of belonging and solidarity with other businesses. The choice is expressed in terms not only of good will, but also in terms of responsibility, a sharing of the load between the different small businesses. These are decisions of course that an employee of a large organization would not typically make, and would play a part in only very few job descriptions, but it displays a process of thinking about responsibility in terms of the immediate surroundings that the particular social position affords.

I almost have friendly relationships with the customers, I feel part of the community, even if I don't actually live here.

Adam goes on to differentiate between being part of a community through living there or through work, I would question whether you would find this in an employee however, particularly one who worked in a large building with a large number of other employees. In this case I would argue that the feeling of community would be that within the organization more than with the local community. The tie with those working within a small business is easier to see in relation to the response above however. Following the argument made above that the employees in a small artisan workshop live within a relationship of interdependence with their boss and the business as a whole, their likelihood to be exposed to the reasoning behind the choices made within the business are higher as a result of their sharing through the situated working experience.

As a result, the question of whether the choice of belonging is tied to economic necessity, and obligation felt as owner is also blurred, as the economic situation can be seen as having a much closer tie to the employee's well-being. There is a smaller distance between the accounting and banking procedures and the relationship towards the good of the business can be counted on a daily basis. I carried the cash to the bank myself as an apprentice while working for Adam, and financial stability was a regular topic of conversation. Although the responsibility to maintain the business is on the boss, the employees live the experience too, they are not cut out of the interaction and they feel the importance of sustaining good customer relations, quality and impressions in the broader sense. If something goes wrong within the business, the employees suffer directly, in prima persona, and are not shielded by a bureaucracy or formalized hierarchy. The threat is not only to lose their job, but to see the business that they have worked within suffer.

I argue that the attachment to the business is also tied to the apprentice experience through the learning of how the business is run as a whole. From experience I know that the two companies that I worked within were run differently in terms of what was acceptable treatment for customers and how work was completed. The rules were understood within the differing situations however, but were at the same time the subject of criticism (see the discussion on lay normativity in chapter 5 for further debate).

This can also be seen within the following utterance from Adam, after a conversation with a customer:

> This customer on the phone is buying some furniture from Wesley Barrett and he was just telling me that dealing with a company is a different thing altogether. It is because companies just have a policy, but whereas I would come up with suggestion, half the time you are just talking to a salesman with them, and they don't really know the trade, they are just salesmen really, following company policy. And there is flexibility as well, because you think on the hoof, you deal with customers in different ways and you tailor your relationship. As you are giving them a bespoke upholstery experience the way you deal with them has to be bespoke as well, as it has to adapt to what they want, whereas a company like Wesley Barrett would just say 'well this is just the way we do it and that it that'. And that it why they are loaded and I am not!

Here we find a reference to money and standardization. The argument made is that offering a bespoke service inhibits capacity to make large sums of money. The value of the service is not therefore in how much money it makes, but in the service itself. The importance of the service and the work completed can therefore be expressed in terms of an ethical choice, the choice to offer a better service than a larger business but at personal cost, that of making less money.

Another issue of skilling is raised here however. In order to maintain a relationship such as the one described above as bespoke, the customer has to deal with the person that is at least capable of doing the job, if not that does the work themselves. In the example above, at Wesley Barrett (a high-quality furniture supplier), the person that the customer has contact with is not an upholsterer. The argument is made that there is a need to know how to do the job, to have the experience of working in the trade and of making the choices involved, in order to maintain or produce that type of relationship.

This is important because here we draw the line between those that can do the job and those who sell, one of the defining borders in the identity of an artisan worker. The relationship can only exist if the person who deals with the customer is the person who does the job, because that allows a move in the relationship from selling to co-production, and as such a relationship of trust. The customer becomes part of the narrative, rather than subject to it.

Adam also highlights the one-off nature of customer interaction, leading me to argue that the relationship between himself and his customers is not standardized, but is based upon the negotiation between the business and the individual customer. The negotiation involved is also an element of job satisfaction as it relates to a concept of correct practices.

> As far as I am concerned, I am not a business person, although I run a business. It just goes with knowing how to do it, in order to make a living, whereas say Wesley Barrett, the salesman could just as easily work in a toy shop or a shoe shop. It doesn't matter what the product is, they are just making sales. Whereas me, I don't know how well I could sell other products. I could sell them just from the experience with people I have had over the years, but money is not the motivation. I just want to get the job right. Years ago I used to do repairs, but I try to knock them back these days, because you want some job satisfaction.

Here Adam continues to speak about job satisfaction and the importance of making money. The conversation regards abilities, such as selling versus actually doing the skilled work of restoring furniture, with the argument returning to money.

The argument about repairs refers to doing a job for money, and not for the pleasure of producing a piece of beauty. Repairs can be lucrative and are often quick ways to make cash, but they are structural and return the piece to function rather than producing something beautiful. The implication is that if a job is taken on for the money it produces, the result does not contain artistic value, it may be functional but it does not give the same feeling of satisfaction.

Adam also brings in the concept of doing the job right, and the fact that it is more important than financial considerations. This is important also in that it raises the issue of pricing up bespoke work of an innovative type. If a designer requires something that is completely new it cannot be priced in terms of time, as the time needed is not known. It can be guessed, but the price is not the time it will take, but the artistic value that the finished product possesses.

The conversation on job satisfaction continues with a section on reasons behind the choice of which work to accept (it is of note that the small businesses involved in this research project have large backlogs of work to complete, customers must wait sometimes up to 6 months and not all work is accepted).

> Well sometimes if you are working on a nice job it is almost like doing a work of art. But then again you also have to look for different goals, because sometimes you cannot get that in a job. I had a stage when I was doing Costa coffee shop chairs, well if you have 40 of the same chairs it is like

cracking rocks in the sun, so you look for a different goal for satisfaction like just trying to do them quickly, and that gives satisfaction, so you change your goals. But generally what motives me is to do a job and the client be surprised how good it looks, and often it looks better than when they bought it new.

When talking about job satisfaction we find almost contradictory statements about artistic quality. This is inherent to the trade, as not all work can be artistic in nature. The production of chairs for a contract as in this case cannot be seen by the artisan as artistic work. It is factory production on a small scale. But satisfaction can be gained from such work if the goals are changed. The motivations however for running the business are said to be satisfying the client in terms of beauty, with other aspects occurring much less throughout our recorded conversations.

In the example below Adam goes on to talk about the skill involved in manufacturing, a field that he worked in shortly after finishing his apprenticeship. This is very unusual for an upholsterer who runs a small business, as manufacturing requires different skills. There is less of a requirement for flexibility and problem solving as the frames, fabrics and stuffing is pre-prepared, techniques used are modern and would not suit re-upholstery, and as a result the trade is seen as less skillful. Furniture manufacturing is an assembly line process, the more you do it the faster you get. A single upholsterer may do 6 sofas a day, whereas an upholsterer recovering the same sofa would require 1.5 days to complete one.

That was actually a better experience than you would imagine. The goals were different, you had to make something that someone would buy on the shop floor. When we were training we were told that they are not proper upholsterers and they cannot do a good job like we can, but the fact of the matter was that I almost had to retrain to get the speed up so you got satisfaction from doing the job quickly, but also from producing something that was saleable on the floor. Because quite often you know something has been reupholstered wouldn't pass the shop floor credit controls. So it was satisfying.

The above reflects another conversation that I did not record in which Adam also talked about gaining the ability to make things look as they had been mass produced, because the shop floor look for new furniture is a mass-produced look. I remember an example in my work of how we recovered a sectional suite from the 1970's that had been done using elasticated cushions. It looked like poorly fitting bags to us as restorers; it was the product of a manufacturing process that had only been used to cut time and to allow a machinist to sew a cushion quickly without attaching a border or pleats on the corner. It was a short cut. We pleated the borders beautifully and regularly so that they were regular and defined, and the customer complained that it was no longer 'bleuson', a term that we translated as 'looking like a bag of shit'.

The shortcut of using elastic and making the seat look baggy, which was to the skilled eye merely to save time, had been translated into a style, our perfect pleats were not right. We did not pass the factory test! These manufacturing techniques actually led to a change of style in furniture in the 1980's due to the fact that machinists were predominantly low paid women, while upholsterers were higher paid. This meant that from a production cost point of view the more machining the better as it made the furniture cheaper to manufacture. This meant that the upholsterers ended up just tacking on pre sewn and foamed gloves onto frames, dramatically cutting down on their time, but also effecting the styles that became popular. The production of modular seating in the 1970's offers another example of how large pieces of furniture can be assembled in pieces and screwed together once in place. Built as self-standing units the pieces were easy to transport (many of the producers were in Scandinavia and the products had to be shipped), the modular solution became a style in itself, incorporating the transport advantages with those of machining large sections as described above.

The following interaction introduces the topic of traditional techniques as craft, the problems of maintaining such traditions and the importance of passing them down. This is of particular personal interest to myself, as these techniques played a part in my apprenticeship. I have not however passed these skills on, and have left the trade, bringing an end to a long line of passed down skills. As noted above the ability to learn these skills is geographical as well as social in nature. The artisan who wishes to hone and practice such skills must have access to suitable antique furniture, owned by people who are willing and able to pay the high prices that a traditional restoration requires. The position within the business is also important, as noted below the chance to practice is based upon the hierarchy in terms of skill sets within the business at the time. I never fully developed my skills because this type of work was handed to Adam who was more equipped to tackle it at the time of my apprenticeship.

I have been thinking about training. I have been searching the internet looking for photos of traditional stitched in horsehair seats, but since people have started posting things

on the internet, so in the last 15 years or so let's say, since people started posting photos of work on the internet, nobody can do a good stitched in horsehair seat.

Well I do them now you know. Remember in the past, in the early days with Gordon, we would always look for the short cut, well I have stopped doing that. You spend almost as long trying to do something that is going to be less successful. I did one recently, with a sprung edge, cane etc, and I just told them it was going to cost a lot of money and I took photos of the stages. But there is hardly anyone that can do it, and I tell people that. And the reason I do it is that the more you put it off the more difficult it becomes. And you know people will pay to do a course to learn to do it, they do it for fun.

Yes, but they will not get the quality. You can find 100 photos on the internet but not one has the quality. And the difference between you and me is that you started your training a couple of years before me, and you learned to do it properly. But because you were learning to do it properly, I never really learned to do it properly. I did not get the practice (I trained alongside Adam, he had started 2 years before myself and so was constantly ahead in ability. If horsehair work came in, he did the stitching work. Only after he left did I start to pick up from where he had left off). **In theory I can do it, I can do it, and I can show you how to do it, but mine won't look like yours, I do not have the ability to do one that looks as good as yours.**

Yes it took me a long time though; even working here on my own, it is experience.

Most of our descriptions above are about what something looks like, and not technique. The practicalities of how to do the seat are not mentioned, we both know how to make such a seat (although to differing degrees) but our abilities are constantly judged in terms of how our work looks. Mine will work just as well but it will not look the same. We refer to neatness more than structure. Of particular note here is that we are talking about the neatness and structure of the piece under the textiles, not the finished cover! This is an example of our shared skilled vision. The finished piece may look the same to the customer, but the stitching is not so neat underneath, and the skilled practitioner can deduce what it looks like underneath from the overall look and the context. The quality is measured in terms of aesthetics and not functionality, in other words the quality of the process is appreciated as beauty.

There is also a position for tradition in the aesthetics of the presentation of the workshop. It is tidy, tools are grouped as are materials, and both traditional techniques as well as modern are on show, grouped for function and passing through different techniques and time-spans.

Figure 2. Diverse generations of springing techniques

Photo: Jonathan Hankins

Figure 3. A series of planes on display

Photo Jonathan Hankins

Above, a series of planes spanning different periods over the last century and the development of spring techniques, from circular springs from the 1500's, plastic or nylon coated lateral coil springing typical of the 1930's and zig-zag springing from the 1970's.

Figure 4. Modern finishing techniques

Photos: Jonathan Hankins

In the figures above we see modern fixing methods and

Figure 5. Traditional finishing techniques

traditional sewing tools. The zinc pieces are pli-grip, explained later in this chapter. Interestingly the traditional forms of curved and straight needles are on display but the modern techniques hidden. Traditional techniques rank higher in status due to their difficulty and scarcity of use.

The discussion of traditional techniques continues, with the narration of how a traditional piece came to be done in the workshop. The discussion also touches upon the need to practice such skills in order not to lose them, and refers to our times as apprentices. It also demonstrates an understanding of the type of work each business is capable of and interested in doing. The discussion carries an unvoiced criticism, in that the person that we are talking about undoubtedly has the ability to do a fully traditional piece of work but chooses not to. Customer-relations is also criticized and the nature of Adam's relationship with the customer is discussed. He narrates reasons that the other companies might not have done the work based on his experience and understanding of the positions adopted towards such type of work by the other companies.

Yes, I can do it all. I have photos, in fact I have one to do now. It is another upholster who has let the customer down, he should have done it for months and months, and when I saw the job I told her that he wouldn't have done it anyway, when is the last time that he did something like that anyway? You know when you talk about me doing the stitched in work while we were training, well he never did it while I was training. He could do it, he has the ability, or certainly had, but you need to do it, you need to practice, and that is why at every opportunity I will do it, because otherwise you get rusty and you can't do it.

Adam shows me the photos taken in stages. It is a superbly finished piece of work, carried out exactly 'to the book'.

You wouldn't get that anywhere though would you? Because Plumb's came and gave them a price, saying they would strip it down to the frame, and do it, I think they were actually a bit cheaper than me, but I said they will not be able to do it. I said you know I'm not blowing my own trumpet but there is hardly anyone around that can do this, so they are not going to do it. They would just approach me or any upholsterer and again they operate on a salesman basis. And the woman she wanted me to do it. And that is the thing they trust you as well, they trust you because they are dealing with just one guy, rather than an organization where you are going to have to call a call centre or whatever it is. And the other thing is that they will want the money up front before they do anything, so they have got you over a barrel. So you pay for it, and then in about 3 months' time they will do it, and if you don't like it you have got a load of agro.

During my time as an apprentice there were two other upholsterers in the village. They shared a workshop. It was the small untidy musty type, with one of the upholsterers specializing in low quality recovering work, headboards and industrial supply. The other was Fred. Fred was a traditional upholsterer. He refused to adapt to new techniques, never used staples or a gun but only a hammer and tacks as was the tradition before 1950, and used only traditional stuffing techniques. His work was robust, extremely heavy duty (including choice of fabrics), but rather without flair.

Fred continued to work in this way well into the 1990's before these techniques became unprofitable and he closed his business. Shortly after Adam himself rented his old workshop, redecorated and cleaned it and set up his own business.

Fred's approach would have to be defined as the most traditional, but also the most environmentally friendly.

> Yes he could do it all traditionally, but he didn't have any flair as such. So he could do all the practicalities but it didn't necessarily look very nice. I have a sofa. Everyone who had covered it had signed it except Fred

Upholsterers used to sign the frame inside, visible only to the next person to take the fabric off, so many chairs contain the history of recovers that only the upholsterers ever see. It is a signature piece of art. I once found a piece that was probably Dutch, an antique, and it had been signed Jonathan Hankins (possibly Hankinson) 1892, a surreal experience that resulted in a photo in the local paper. The comment above carries an implicit criticism of Fred's choice not to sign his work, my interpretation of which is that he feels Fred did not hold the same feeling that his work was an art form, but much more functional as in the description, an argument that runs through the discussion about the style of his work and its functionality rather than its beauty. This relates to the discussion below.

> If you are doing something that is like a craft, or an art as this is you want to do the best you can if you are interested or you care. I don't want to mention any names but some people just don't seem to care about it, and I certainly don't understand that.

> I take a lot of pride in that, round here the people in the community kind of give me a bit of respect. You know it is mutual; I treat them the same way. When I worked for someone he was always falling out with people and I used to think oh I don't want to work for myself because I am not up for that, but I never fall out with people because I get on well with people. And it is a two-way thing, they don't want a row, they want the whole experience to be pleasurable, and so you try to deal with them nicely and give them what they want and generally 99 percent of the time it works all right.

Here Adam again reiterates the co-production and shared understanding involved in the transaction of restoring someone's furniture. He talks about mutual respect, not just between himself and his customers but also between himself and the local community. Once more the description is laden with ideas of responsibility, mutual understanding and fulfilling expectations.

This interpretation can also be seen in the following description of life for the self-employed. Adam describes how his interest has changed over the years that he has run his business from going to work in order to build up the business into making a good start to the day doing a job that he loves. He also describes his motivation once more, to make the job look as good as possible, once more raising the issue of the importance of beauty over that of strictly function.

> Yes you motivate yourself to go in, like I say I come in at 7.30 in the morning, now no-one is kicking you out of bed telling you to get into work at that time so you must enjoy what you are doing to get in early to make a bright start. It is not just about turning up. And I probably feel that even more so now than in previous years, when I was setting up the business it was all about getting up and going in so that people will come to you and now you feel that you have established yourself and I used to do anything. But now there are certain jobs and I think Oh I have done it a million times. I have been going now for 18 years.

> Regarding flair and art I think a lot of it has to do with working on your own, because if you have someone working with you then the jobs are different, two people doing a chair each make a different job, so it is just that some people want to just do it and make the money, while others just want to make it look as good as they can in the home, that is what motivates them. And I don't know whether you have either got it or not. Because you can cover a chair and it just be functional, all the insides are going to do the job etc, and not really be aesthetically bothered about finishing touches. So I think that is where you make it precious.

As noted above Adam talks about motivation driven through the aim to make the furniture look as good in the home as possible. This once more alludes to the idea of co-production of the work production, but I would argue in this case more specifically to the co-production of a situated beauty. The beauty is said to be in the home, in the surroundings of the customer's house, the added value of the work is in its situated beauty, and this is where Adam finds his motivation. This is an example of the main tenant of this chapter; Adam and I share a concept of beauty that embodies an appreciation of the choices made during the process of restoring the furniture.

This raises the issue of style, as beauty is defined by the viewer and personal taste. Styles can be promoted as described above through the use of techniques that are introduced and promoted for economic or practical reasons (the example of the modular or elasticated furniture) but they are also created through the availability of materials, both through price constraints related to the social setting and through ready availability.

To give an example; when I was learning the trade my employer had a passion for straight lines and the use of antique copy studs to finish non sealed borders. Much of his furniture was studded, it produced a defined line to borders and added an idea of expense to a piece of work. It is labour intensive to stud a chair and there are many easier and cheaper options. The stud passion was born however from the fact that my employer had bought a huge stock of studs from an auction of a bankrupt upholstery supplier some years ago. So in effect the materials were free, or had already been paid for anyway, readily available and added a classical touch. The style was not so much by design but by accident. These examples clearly show how production techniques and broad interests, as well as almost accidental factors of instant availability shape the design of the finished product.

Adam addresses the issue of creating and maintaining a style below. He describes how he sometimes does not accept work because he *cannot bring himself to do it*, and describes in further detail how some work is not to his taste, but as described above may be suitable for the setting in the house that it will be returned to. The description below describes the process of choosing which textiles to carry in stock and why these decisions are made. I argue that other upholsterers such as myself and close colleagues can see these choices in the finished piece, and understand the social setting that allows them to come into reality. They are not so much made but once again co-produced within the particular social setting for that particular piece of work at that moment. I feel that this part of our discussions encapsulates the Bassetti Foundation argument of poiesis perfectly.

In the following statements Adam talks about the relationship between style and vision and the idea of how something should look in order to allow a full appreciation of the process.

Yes I think you have got to keep on top of it though, I think I have got a style, I don't like to over frill it up, and I suppose sometimes when someone really wants ultra-frilly kind of work I don't do it, I can't make myself do it. And that is what happens, you have to like what you are working on, it is almost like you say well this is what I am going to do and you enjoy doing it, but if it is something that is so way off you lose that sort of what you would want to do. And there is some furniture that you wouldn't have in your house, you can like it but everything in its place. Sometimes what I have got wouldn't suit a client's house. But I love some fabrics, I have got this type of fabric on my sofa, and I will have a range of fabrics, I pick the ranges of fabrics, and sometimes some of them I have because I know that people will like them, but generally I try to choose something that is tasteful, and I would put on my furniture. You know like we used to just get the Singleton's books for free but I wouldn't want any of that stuff on my furniture. And again, that is part of providing the service, sourcing a range is important, the right materials for the job.

Singleton's was a fabric supplier based in Manchester. They merged with another supplier at the end of the 1980's. The local suppliers gave pattern books for free, but they were unimaginative and extremely traditional, even though some of the fabrics were expensive and they were all of high quality. Other companies that specialize in certain types of fabric sell their pattern books, with costs up to several hundred pounds for a book. These are much more stylized in both presentation and content, and sometimes are only supplied to certain upholsterers in an area, depending on their clientele, so that they can remain prestigious. If you have to buy a book you generally choose something that you think you can sell, but also that you like, which leads to a certain style. Adam likes plain finishes and high-quality wool tweeds, and this is reflected in the range on sale in his workshop. His house is also full of furniture that he has covered in these same materials. As he has noted above his work is linear, he has no frills and little piping, and this type of fabric suits that style, and is often geometric in design. This suits certain types of furniture, and so the choice of pattern books to show the customer is already a stylized choice, both in terms of what he has purchased and which fabrics are right for a certain job in terms of texture and durability as well as design. Something frilly that he cannot bring himself to do does not fit within this narrative.

You have to enjoy doing it and that means producing something that you yourself find beautiful.

I would argue that flair (and by extension shared conceptions of beauty) are tied to the types of choices available as described above. Beauty does not merely reside in the ability to cover the furniture but in the much more holistic approach, in stylistic, technical and moral choices. It involves the technical capability to do the work in a certain way and to a certain quality but also the vision to buy the suitable pattern books, know how to apply stylistic choices and to be able to maintain a relationship with the (right) customer in order to end up with the right job.

The importance of this approach is not merely between Adam and his customers however. As noted, he uses the fabrics he stocks in his own house, and as with many small businesses, household life runs parallel to business life. Family life is important also because Adam shares a professional understanding and skill with his wife Louise.

It (family involvement and understanding) is important, it is very high on the agenda. Priorities. I don't have any responsibilities in the morning, I just have to get here in the morning because Louise looks after family duties at home, so I can get on with it, but yes it is taken very seriously. And Louise is a trades person as well, she actually works here cutting the fabrics and certainly the cushions. So she understands the textile part of it all, and she is keen on interiors so it is something that she can relate to.

And is it important for your family that she can understand technically what you are doing?

Well maybe yes, because we can talk about it and she also supports and tells you how good you are and appreciates what you do. I suppose.... I am not sure that if you did the job and your partner wasn't interested whether you would be as interested. I play the guitar and she is not interested in that and I can feel the difference I feel in doing that.

Once again in this conversation and as mirrored in the Avanti Artigiani film produced by the Bassetti Foundation[95], family involvement is not only practical in terms of helping in the workshop but also in terms of discussion in the home. The work to family borderline is fluid. Adam goes on to describe how his home relationship supports and strengthens the moral underpinning of his approach to work. Conversation at home is also influential in terms of supporting working norms and normativity. The work narrative carries over to home life, which is not surprising given Louise's working experience and involvement in the business.

> As I say I get home at dinner time and we talk about work, and if I have to go out somewhere for a job and it is a bit of a distance she will understand, and we sometimes tailor the weekend to it, you know we go out for a walk and take the dog out there sometimes we will make a weekend around seeing a job. And I suppose if you didn't share interest in the job, that would be out of the question I think she understands the importance. They always say you shouldn't define yourself by your work but I probably do.

I would argue that the statement about identification above is more important than it at first seems. Adam is talking about defining himself through his work, but he does not simply mean that he defines himself through his job. He defines himself through the way he approaches his work, in the sense of the choices he makes during his working life. Doing the job right, being prepared, being able to maintain a good relationship with

---

[95] Avanti Artigiani is a documentary film constructed of interviews conducted with small and medium sized business owners in Milan, commissioned by the Foundation in 2014.

the customers and create something of beauty, both morally and aesthetically, play into his definition.

This self-definition and family involvement however is not always treated as ideal, particularly in terms of making money. Talking about the Italian small business model that prevails in Milan in which children follow their parents into the family business and which very much provided the basis for much of the impetus for many aspects within this book, Adam says the following:

> I don't think people would do that here in UK, they want their kids to do better than them, it's like when people do well on the markets and make money, they don't want their kids to follow them they want them to get a profession, for example if I had kids and you asked me, I would say that I wouldn't want my child to train to be an upholsterer. Well..... I suppose you could train them yourself, but I wouldn't want them to do it the way I did it. Then you could train them the way you would want them trained, so under the umbrella of working for the family business yes, but not working for somebody else. It just took too long to earn a living, it was a long training process really.

The conversation above revolves around the question of how the artisan position affects lifestyle choices and possibilities. The advantage is always stated that those who have a trade are not so dependent on third parties in that they can work for themselves. In the case of upholstery, the artisan has the ability to make a piece of furniture in order to try and sell it, and the shortage of skilled workers in this field means that an upholsterer can always find a job if she or he needs one. Neither Adam nor myself have ever been out of work. This form of work carries a reasonable salary as a skilled job, but the artisan can make considerably more money working for him or herself. The possibilities of making large sums of money however are very small, particularly if the artisan wishes to control and maintain the quality of the work done and pass on her lay normativity.

Adam is however going beyond this, he envisages training as training to work in the way that I do, not training to technically do a job. He says 'the way you would want them trained' in referring to the business, the embodiment of the entire narrative that drives his work. He would think about training a son or daughter into the business and its particular approach and narrative rather than into the trade.

As in other non-recorded conversations with members of this small community, money is always one of the main talking points. The conclusion of these discussions is one of paradox; a self-employed person who works with his or her hands will never make large sums of money, and the higher the quality of their work the less chance they have, but at the same time the more it will be appreciated as a form of art or beauty. This is felt because the time required to do a high-quality job restricts the possible income, as the maximum prices that can be charged are capped. If an upholsterer wishes to restore an antique using traditional methods, he or she will have to invest a certain amount of time if the work is to be done well. There are no short cuts to doing the job right. The flexibility is minimal in terms of time but also of cost. A customer will only pay so much for a piece, regardless of the quality, restricting the amount of profit possible.

With smaller jobs or more modern techniques however there is more flexibility on all sides. The techniques can be modified and done quicker, leading to more flexibility on pricing, and a piece of ingenious thinking on the part of the artisan can make a piece more profitable without compromising quality or the relationship of trust between the customer and the upholsterer.

In the case of the antique, not doing the job right in order to make more money risks damaging this relationship of trust, leaving the worker with the moral imperative to spend the time necessary on the work, almost regardless of the effect that these choices have on the amount of money made. To take on such a job and to do it correctly, to the peak of an upholsterer's ability, is therefore a choice that involves a long series of decisions during the process: Regardless of how long it will take it will be done right. A skilled appreciation of the beauty of the finished piece is a shared appreciation of the process.

In the following quote Adam addresses the learning process in terms of the importance of the apprentice period in relation to how much he has learned through his work once qualified.

> When you look at the way we trained though, I don't think I would do that again. We could have gone to college and we would have done it a lot quicker, worked in a bigger environment.

Yes, but we would not have got the skills we got; you would not be able to turn out work of this kind of quality

> Yes, you are right, but this is home though, we are more or less self-taught. You are given a framework of how to do the job, and then you hone it over the years. I have been doing this job for 34 years, so I suppose no kind of training is going to match up to 34 years of experience.

Here Adam returns to his learning through work idea, after posing the thought that maybe college would have been a better way to learn the trade (at least in the beginning). I feel that this argument comes about because we have begun to talk about money, and other ideas for work. The training issue is about how long it took to make a living, rather than quality of work, an argument that is related to the idea that you learn as you work for yourself, so learning the basic skills earlier means an artisan can make a living earlier but still learn the job properly.

I am not convinced by this argument however because I believe that a trainee needs to live the work experience by seeing other people doing it, which would be lacking without the apprentice structure as it might not lead to the shared understanding of doing the job correctly. Adam earlier stated that Gordon, his employer during his time as an apprentice, did not do the work that required traditional horsehair methods himself, so Adam in effect taught himself. During conversations with the upholsterer in question he made the same argument himself, that we (Adam and myself) had taught ourselves, that he had never showed us what to do. This is not entirely true of course. We were shown how to stitch in horsehair, the different stitches used and the order to proceed, but we then had to put these techniques into practice. We were in effect being taught a system, or more precisely a systematic approach and an idea about correctness, which as I have argued above ran through the workspace and business organization.

I would argue however that as apprentices we gained access to such work as a direct result of working in that particular social setting, which would not have arisen if we had worked on our own. A customer will only entrust the restoration of such a piece to someone they think can do it. See Adam's comments above about telling the customer that the other upholstery company would not be able to do the work themselves for a concrete example of the negotiation of the relationship of trust, a relationship that is two way, the customer trusts the artisan to do a good job, and the artisan trusts the customer to pay for a piece that they first deliver to the house.

The advantage of being an apprentice in this situation is two-fold: the expert negotiates the relationship of trust with the customer, giving the apprentice the chance to work on the job while supervising him or her during the process; the apprentice is given the time necessary to do the work right, as he or she is on a fixed salary so has no incentive to rush the job.

Apprentice salaries are low, so the employee has the flexibility to allow the apprentice time to perfect the restoration skills, even to the point of possibly doing the same piece twice. I saw this happen when I was an apprentice and Adam was learning to stitch in horsehair backs on a pair of antique chairs. We came in to work one morning and our employer had written "EMPTY" and "NOT MUCH BETTER" in large chalk letters on the inside canvas backs of the chairs. No explanation was offered of how to rectify the situation other than to re-do them from scratch. That is what had to be done and it was done.

The apprentice situation allows the learning of these techniques as an art. If we take the example above, the furniture was finished to a high standard. Adam was paid his salary to re-do the backs, in effect paid to have another attempt and perfect his skills. I experienced the mechanism of how the apprenticeship system allows the flexibility for the trainee to learn these time consuming and specialist techniques. The employer had to pay a day's wages for the backs to be re-done, but this is accounted for in the fact that the apprentice wages were low enough to incorporate what we might describe as learning time. I would argue that this would not have happened in any other situation than within an apprenticeship relation, the quality would not have been improved and the lesson of making the job better rather than trying to deliver a substandard piece not shared, so the learning experience would not be so rounded.

In the following piece of conversation Adam describes how he builds his relationships of trust with his customers. Once more the language reflects ideas of fairness and doing the job right, the co-production of the transaction can once more be seen as can the poiesis element, the finished article has been done correctly, through a just and upstanding process that is visible in the beauty of the finished piece. It also summarizes how working practices relate to responsibility not only to the customers, but also to the artisan herself.

> Another thing I find important, apart from job satisfaction, is supplying a job that I am quite happy with. Because some people will just do a job, charge as much as they can, and if it is good or not means nothing to them, but for me I want the price to be a fair price and to know that they are happy with what they have got. I can proudly say that they have got a piece of furniture in their house that if someone says 'who did your chair?' I wouldn't be embarrassed about it. And another thing is the reliability of the service. So there might be a long waiting list but I am pretty accurate, I do it when I say I am going to do it, and quickly so it is not a long drawn out process. And I have a small place here so it has to be in and out but still for the client it is a better experience. They are not messed around, they know when it will be ready, and that is the service. It is the way you run it and that is equally important.

Techniques have changed over the years that Adam has been working in the trade. He embraces these changes, and follows the line that each individual piece should be restored according how it was meant to be done. An antique should not be done using modern techniques, although the staple gun is one exception, (using hammer and tacks is extremely time consuming and much more invasive for an old piece, the holes made are much larger and the action possibly damaging), but equally a modern piece should not be done using traditional methods.

Techniques are different, for example remember the glue? You had to spread it on with a knife. Now we have instant glue for sticking foam together, the dacron, no more hand sewing, instant tack with that glue. And cushions, we used to get standard sizes but now any density of foam you want, you can get them made to size with a dome finish, I wrap them. They replicate the rounded look. All that comes, delivery service any time. Years ago we had to drive up to Singletons and wait for ages, all that is gone. Instant service. And that just takes away so much time wasting and makes your life so much easier. Pli-grip, although I do still hand slip a lot, it depends on the fabric and the job, tartan is no good for pli-grip. And certain textiles look better sewn and certain look better with pli-grip, it was designed for leather.

Pli-grip is a blind finish that replaces the need to hand slip outsides on to furniture. It is a zinc strip that is stapled on that looks a bit like a line of Venus fly trap leaves, which you can hammer over the cloth to make a blind finish. It makes a very clean line with some textiles, but with others that are stretchy it does not look as good. It does however, if used correctly give the factory look, as it was primarily designed for manufacturing.

Here Adam brings in the idea of shop floor testing from his manufacturing experience. His argument is that he can recover a piece of furniture and hand sew it, so it looks like an antique or a recovered piece, or use pli-grip so that it looks as if it has been manufactured. These different looks will be more or less desirable depending on the job. Pli-grip was designed for leather but as manufacturers started using it on stiffer fire-retardant fabric the manufacturers realized that there was a market, and now make a lighter gauge version for use with lighter materials. The 'incorrect' use has been institutionalized, and in some way makes it easier to provide a mass-produced finish on a bespoke product, creating what Adam describes as the correct newly manufactured look. The justification for the use of such a piece of technology has been embodied in beauty by becoming 'a look'.

Adam is arguing that what might be seen as the use of a short cut or the incorrect use of a product that was designed for another role is perfectly justified, in fact it would be incorrect not to use them, in the case of working on a piece that would aesthetically and functionally benefit from it.

> So years ago we did everything hand sewn but none of it would look like something that you bought in a shop really, but now if the jobs you are doing might be a pair of sofas, you try to make it look as if it had been bought in a showroom. In a showroom they are not doing hand sewing. There are no curved needles, so if you want to get the job right you have to do it as they do it.

As we see, this aesthetic judgement once again refers to having followed the correct procedures, having used the right materials and having understood and had the capability to carry out what is needed in order to do the job right. It is the correct way to do that type of work. This judgement continues when working on antiques pieces:

> Even with the antiques I do I don't want them to look like anyone's touched them. I mean I don't want them to look tatty, but I don't want them to look new. The absolute perfection is if the chair has always looked like that, rather than something with new fabric and bright studs.

During his career Adam has pushed the boundaries both of his own capabilities and of what can be done in terms of upholstery as design. For an artisan every piece is different, so the business proceeds through applying known skills to sometimes unknown situations (very much like a scientist). In this case prices are given and contracts are taken without the artisan fully understanding how his or her skills will be applied. This is a high-risk strategy however, as Adam explains:

> Yes. But to do a one off and not know if it is even going to work is not something that I would do these days. And they did work, but I was always pushing the boundaries and I always thought that it was going to end in tears one day.... And the last job I did for that company was Motorola offices. Doors covered in leather, and I told them that I wouldn't do the job if I had to wait, so they paid me immediately, but Motorola never paid, and the company went bankrupt. If you work through another company you work to a brief that someone else tells you what to do. You cannot tell them that something is not going to work, or 'I wouldn't have taken it on if I had known that was what you wanted', and you have lost that control. That is why I don't do it, work through interior designers that want something that you would not

have done it that way.

There are of course the problems with payment too, because everything you do is on credit, and so the last job you ever do for them they don't pay.

In this, Adam's final statement in this chapter, he raises the issue of the possibility the artisan maintains of making his or her own choices in how to proceed with a job. In the context above, these rights and possibilities are sacrificed, and he or she finds herself working to order, following other people's orders and the poiesis element is lost and correctness cannot be maintained. The art and aesthetics is not lost, but control over the decision-making procedure is, and without that the justice element is compromised, and as a result, also the beauty of the piece. I argue that both of these aspects are fundamental if an understanding of poiesis and trust is to be shared, and now that Adam has a choice, he no longer takes on work under these restrictions.

6.3 Concluding Remarks: The death of our mentor

In mid-2016 as I was carrying out the research for this case study, Gordon Stewart, the man who had first employed both Adam and myself and trained us into the upholstery trade suddenly died. I travelled to the UK, met up with Adam and we went to the funeral together. It was an emotional day. Gordon's wife spoke about the passing down of Gordon's trade to the next generation, citing both Adam and myself as recipients of this craft. There were four upholsterers and a French polisher at the funeral, we had all collaborated over many years, worked together in various different settings, and socialized as colleagues, albeit from different self-employed standpoints.

As I was making the editorial updates to this book I learned that

Fred, the traditional upholsterer had also died. I had last seen him at Gordon's funeral.

In my Masters thesis I recount these relationships in more detail, we held an annual Christmas party and when I left the trade to move to Italy a party was held for me in the workshop where I had trained and we had 'the official firing of the last staple'. We shared a skill-set that we had learned from each other.

Speaking to Adam on the day of the funeral it became apparent to us both that we both felt a great deal of fondness for Gordon as our mentor. He had, as Adam noted, introduced us to the trade, given us the possibility to learn and practice it and we had collaborated for almost 35 years. When I started playing the drums and formed a band with Adam, Gordon's upholstery workshop became our rehearsal room.

The quote 'Just pull it front to back and lay it down the sides' is taken from Gordon. It was oft used during my apprenticeship, and epitomizes what Sennett describes as the inability of the artisan to explain what she can show (Sennett, 2008). Following a similar line, in this chapter I argue that poiesis can be shown and appreciated through the acquisition and sharing of a skilled vision, but it cannot de described.

The analysis of the conversation with Adam demonstrates the importance of such a skilled vision in relation to ideas of beauty, as I argue that the appreciation of beauty experienced through such skilled visions is an appreciation of the correctness of the process involved in its production.

The appreciation and sharing of this acceptance of beauty is narrated through everyday working conversation and practices. The capacity to understand the relationship between the narration and the ascription of beauty could be seen as the codification of the unwritten knowledge that has formed the production process, allowing those who have worked within it to share their judgement through a shared language.

This language used in the narrative is much broader than that of beauty, but I argue that the responsibility and right and wrong juxtaposition elements are all represented within its appreciation. The construction of this category of beautiful and how the piece is perceived as beautiful or not is socially generated on a daily basis, and represented in style. Certain correct procedures lead to the adoption and creation of certain aesthetic styles becoming identity markers, that represent the following of the narrative.

The link to RI lies here. The codification of the narrative here refers to furniture restoration, but it could easily represent a working narrative in a science laboratory or innovation department in a technology company. The issues of decision-making procedures and the negotiation between all of the parties involved might look very similar. The training of the eye to read the process in terms of correct procedure and the sharing and celebration of such may also be found elsewhere. I believe that the local, glocal, and social construction of the narrative and its effect on decision-making can be seen across the spectrum of workplaces in which small groups work on bespoke production or research techniques.

In the following chapter I describe my second case study that took place in a bio-technology laboratory in Utrecht. I draw similarities and differences between the two settings raising the question of how the arguments demonstrated in this first case study could be applied to further and diverse settings.

The photo of Gordon in his workshop in this chapter is the last in a long series dating back to my teens when I started my apprenticeship. The apprenticeship experience guides my work today as it did then.

234

Chapter 7

The Scientist's Narrative

During my PhD I was fortunate enough to spend 18 months in the Netherlands affiliated to Utrecht University Anthropology Department. During this period, I studied Dutch, attended Departmental seminars and followed several lines of inquiry in order to investigate forms of Poiesis-Intensive Innovation within the Netherlands, with particular interest in the scientific community based within Utrecht University. This period included both the extended case study that I describe in this chapter, and the time spent with Ufficina Corpuscoli, the smaller case study described in chapter 5 that became a test bed for this in-depth study.

This is the setting that allows me to draw some very tentative comparative conclusions with respect to my previous case study on artisanal Knowledge.

The case study that I will present in this narrative is one of scientists working in a biology lab attached to the University of Utrecht. The lab sits within the campus, and represents the cutting edge of research in this particular field. The case study looks at the work and working practices of Prof. Jos Malda, based in the Hubrecht Institute.

My understanding of the working practices in this case study does not allow an analysis that can go into such depth as that in the previous chapter. My methodology is identical, based upon recorded conversation and subsequent clarifications and analysis, but I do not know the techniques applied on a daily basis within the research setting nor fully understand the science underpinning the work. My aim is to highlight what we may describe as structural similarities in practices, in order to test the hypothesis of a guiding narrative that is shared, tacit, glocal, language and practice based and steers working practices, in a similar way as that described in the previous chapter.

The case study grows out of a working relationship that has developed between the Bassetti Foundation and Professor Jos Malda.

7.1 Jos Malda

In this section I will first outline Professor Malda's approach, describe his work, working practices and experiences based on field notes taken within his workplace, before concluding with an analysis and transcriptions of conversations recorded in the institute that hosts his lab and materials gained through several subsequent meetings in other working environments.

Prof. Jos Malda heads a research group that focuses on biofabrication and biomaterials design, in particular for the regeneration of (osteo) chondral defects. The team is investigating regenerative means for repairing damaged joints in humans and animals, with particular interest in the knee. The team works alongside and within both the medical and veterinary facilities at Utrecht University, studying wear on both animal and human joints and have designed and built a production facility that allows for the 3D printing of living cells to make live repair implants that can be surgically implanted.

The team has very much become the focus of different 3D printing needs for the University and beyond, having the capability to manufacture medical pieces as well as other bespoke objects as required by different departments. The best-known example of this side of their work is the plastic skull that was successfully implanted in 2014, and functioning perfectly at the time of writing[96]. The main focus of their work however involves the use of live cells in 3D printing techniques. The team also use their printing technology to make copies of joints in order to test how materials react when they are put under natural movement stress, such as when a joint is naturally used. This capability offers several advantages in that it allows the developers to test their products in simulated lifelike environments, giving data not just about resistance to pressure stress but also demonstrating other forms of stress that the implants would be under if placed within a live animal.

A related specialty involves the printing of 3D organs for toxicity testing but also for use in preparing surgeons for difficult tasks. The team can produce a replica of an organ that may have to be operated upon in order to allow the surgeons to develop a technique and strategy in the laboratory before commencing the operation. They can in effect practice on the replica to see if the operation that they are proposing is likely to work.

A further application is in making patient specific guides for surgery. The guides are prepared for a particular cut and can be put in place during the operation. The guides work very much like a miter saw works in woodworking. Once in place the cut is more precise as the guides aid the work of the operator. This is an example of tools being made for a one-off procedure, a topic that I return to repeatedly in this publication. It is a technique that runs through all of the examples given, an example of Poiesis-Intensive Innovation in action across my fieldwork sites, and a characteristic of the many different processes described in this book. It is the art of knowing how to build a necessary tool

---

[96] Further details are available through the university website:
   http://www.umcutrecht.nl/en/Research/News/3D-printed-skull-implanted-in-patient last accessed 13-11-2019

using a pre-determined collection of different implements in what anthropologist Levi Strauss calls 'bricolage' (Strauss, 1962).

The team describe these as novel biofabriaction strategies, and the living materials that the printer uses as *bioinks for 3D printing*. These hydrogel-based 'inks' are both designed to drive specific differentiation of the embedded and/or endogenous cells, as well as to allow fabrication with high shape fidelity in order to generate constructs that are a blueprint of the real tissue.

3D Printing techniques as we know them today however are not suitable for living cell use because they require high temperature, often involve laser use and sometimes organic solvents, so the team have built a 3D printing machine that works at human body temperature, using pressure to force the bio inks through the nozzle, and eliminated the use of solvents and lasers, basing the entire system predominantly on water (Malda et.al. 2013).

These bio inks are cells held in a hydrogel solution, a substance akin to gelatin. They can contain different types of cells, according to how they are needed to develop, or stem cells, that can develop into any type of cell needed. A layer of water-based gel is printed between each cell layer, allowing the researchers to combine strong bio materials with biodegradable plastics that have been approved for medical use and integrate it all into their printing process. Malda informally describes the resulting materials as resembling reinforced concrete[97].

Prof. Malda's main line of research involves using these bio-inks alongside a plastic scaffold to create an implant that will grow

---

[97] Quote taken from BBC Click Online 27 May 2014 http://www.bbc.co.uk/programmes/p01zvv3k
Last accessed 13/11/2019

into position and regenerate damaged tissue, offering a durable and fully integrated repair that is self-sustaining and therefore (unlike a prosthesis) does not require maintenance.

The implant is designed in strata, with a crisscross mesh of plastic filled with living cells built up across several layers. The types of cells vary between layers, so that (for example) the lower cells may develop into bone, with middle layers developing into cartilage and the upper layers into a surface tissue. The plastic offers protection for the cells as they grow into place, cushioning them from wear, allowing them to grow whilst minimizing the risk of damage. The plastic scaffolds can be produced in different densities and with different flexibility properties, allowing the team to design a suitable implant for each particular application. The team also produce plastic replica bones with their machines in order to test the different properties of the scaffolds, modelling the effect of real wear in a laboratory environment, in order to discover the different effects of crushing, rubbing and tearing on their product.

The process is described below in a diagram taken from an article in 3DIndustry.com that describes the team's work[98].

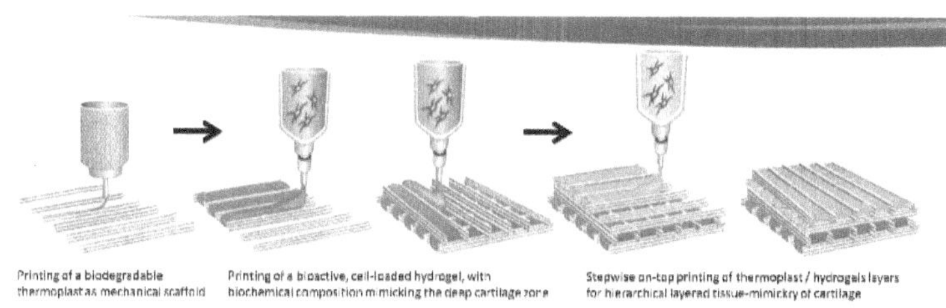

Figure 6. 3D cell printing technique

---

[98] The article speaks about Malda's work https://3dprintingindustry.com/news/utrecht-set-become-global-center-3d-bioprinting-30110/ last accessed 27/01/2020

Figure taken from 3DIndustry.com

Of particular interest for my argument is that Malda and his team are designing and building the entire process required for the production and testing of their product. Several of the 3D printing machines that they use have been built by the team using parts made by other commercially bought 3D printing machines. These commercial machines can be seen as the3DIndustry.com ir tools, with which they build their bespoke machine that allows them to carry out their research. What we find is a process of making that is very much craft based, the team builds a machine that they can use to complete their process, but they build it using the tools that lie at their disposal, namely their 3D machines, programming skills, engineering know-how, technical understanding of how cells can be treated and used and manual capacities to build a finely engineered machine.

I believe that in the same way as the processes described in the previous chapter can be described as a poiesis intensive processes, those witnessed within this science laboratory can also be described as such. The system that has been constructed in order to carry out this research relies on craftsmanship and imagination, as much as it relies on technical expertise and experience.

I argue that this process and these (varied) embodied skills (held within individuals that are collected into a team) can be seen as very similar to the skilled processes that were described in the previous chapter. The team is immersed in a bricolage process as described by Levi Strauss (Strauss, 1962), using a set of tools to produce pieces for a different tool to make another machine that is integral to the process of production that they are engaged with.

Returning to Grasseni's skilled visions approach (Grasseni, 2007) I argue that the members of the team are apprenticed into this engineering work, learning to see and do very much as the furniture restorer described in the previous case study. I also argue that in the final product, in this case the prepared scaffold, primed and ready to implant, they see the process of production in terms of the decision making process that has led to its creation and the underlying reasoning behind the decisions taken in the same way as the skilled craftsperson in the workshop through the same mechanism of situated learning described above (Grasseni, 2007, Polanyi, 1966, Collins, 2010). I believe that they see the correctness of the choices made through their view of technical innovation, both in terms of the functional beauty and capabilities that the machines exhibit and in the process as an entity itself.

As I argued in the previous case study, the members of the team see functional beauty in the machines they build, the development process and the final implantable product, and within that beauty they see and appreciate the correctness and responsibility within the decision-making process in terms of why decisions were taken and how they even came to the table, as well as their technical capabilities as a group. I will try to show this in the ethnographic description of the laboratory that now follows.

7.2 The Laboratory

Prof. Malda's laboratory is hosted in the Hubrecht Instituut, within the University of Utrecht Uithof Campus. At the time of my research the Institute building was newly built and beautifully designed, open, light and minimal. Professor Malda's group had been one of the first teams to take up residence, just 3 months before my visit in 2015, and found itself still in a transnational period with several white boxes of unpacked equipment still awaiting placing. Prof Malda is very happy with his new host building, a fact that is easy to see on his face and in his body movements as he moves around the building.

The new positioning of the group offers several advantages over their previous placing, as the team was somewhat spread across the university hospital buildings. In the new building the team is housed together, with the culture labs all together and with the 3D printing technology sitting adjacent to each other, avoiding the long walks between different sections of the research project previously necessary.

In the new building they layout is orderly, with a clear division of labour and process visible and practiced. A single room houses the 3D technology, with a series of machines that are used to produce parts for the bio-printer lined up in something that reflects a production line, also displaying the capacities of the team to produce what we might call regular 3D printed objects (see below).

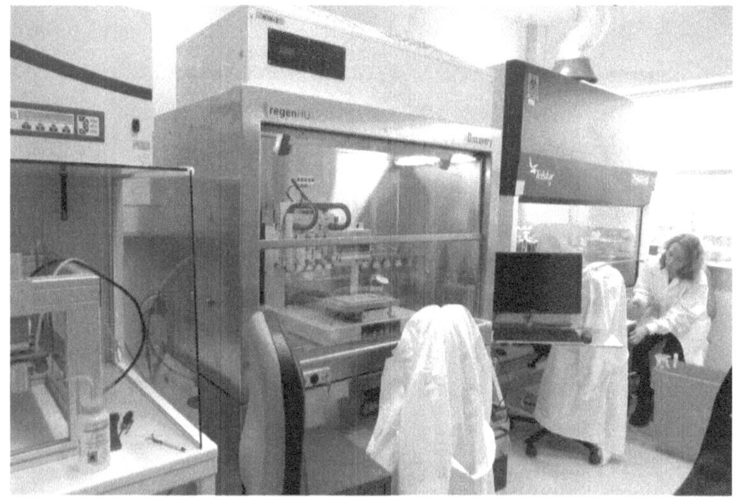

Figure 7. A series of 3D printers in a row in Prof. Malda's laboratory

Photo: Jonathan Hankins

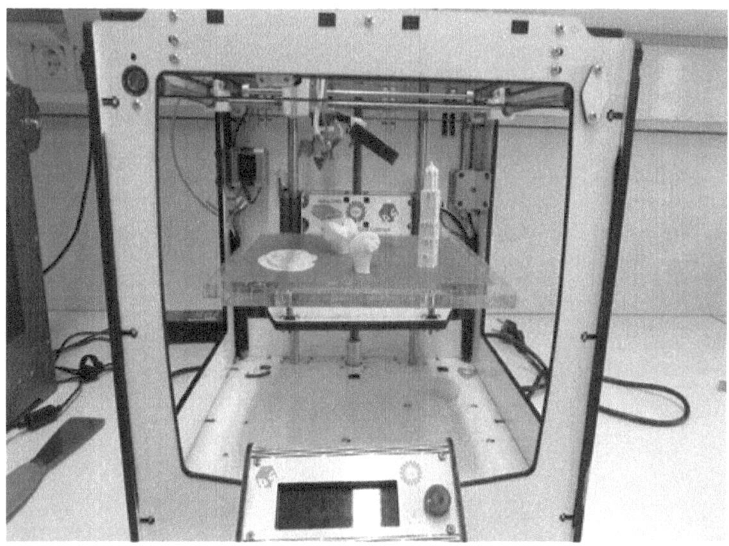

Figure 8. 3D printed objects sitting on display

Photo: Jonathan Hankins

A closer look at the printers reveals their craft-produced nature. As the photos show, the laboratory created machines do not share the aesthetics of the industrially produced machines that we are accustomed to seeing. They have been built by the team, technicians from the university have cut the plexi-glass boxes that they sit in, wires are not hidden within the structure and they are designed to have easily changeable parts. The boxes themselves are built by PhD students. The beauty of the machine lies in its construction, not its styling. They possess a functional beauty, in the same way as the cows described in the cattle fairs in Grasseni's account of how skilled visions are learned and shared (Grasseni, 2009)

The laboratory also has several 3D printed objects on display. Following Grasseni I argue that the placing of the small 3D plastic models that the machines have produced implies the sharing of a skilled vision, a shared appreciation of beauty constituted by an appreciation of a production process through the apprenticeship of vision (Grasseni, 2009). To the untrained eye the models look like trinkets, but to the skilled viewer they demonstrate the capabilities of the machine and its operators and designers, very much in the same way as the plastic and porcelain models of cows described by Grasseni in her study of cow breeders, a theme that I address below (Grasseni, 2007).

In the photos that follow we can clearly see the development process on display, alongside the continual evidence of the poiesis nature of the production process.

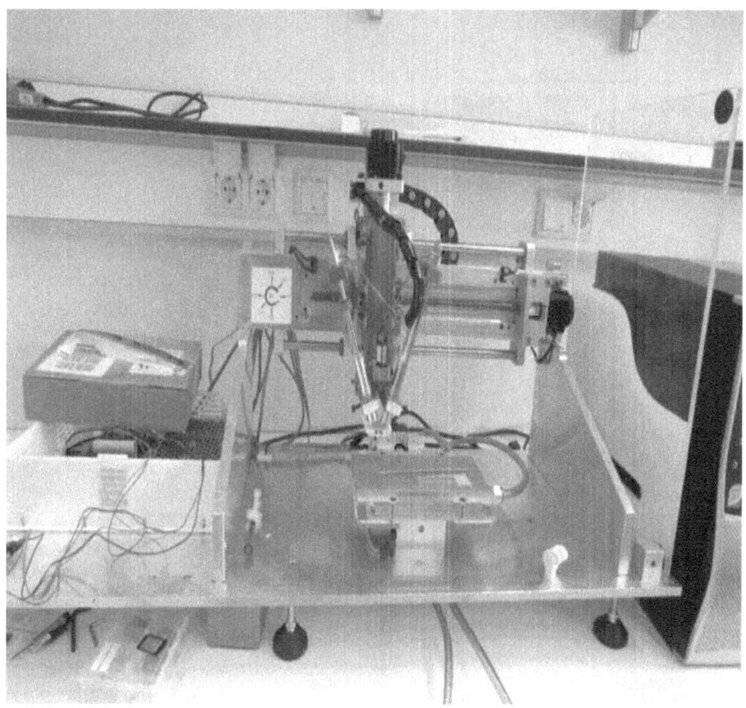

Figure 9. An early printer with wires and tools

Photo: Jonathan Hankins

In both photos (above and below), tools and other sundries are visible, as are the wires and electronics that are usually hidden in commercial machines. The computer that controls the machine sits by the side of the printing machine in a plastic box. In photo 1 we clearly see the development of the live cell printing process described earlier in this chapter, with the pressure method of forcing the cells through the nozzle clearly visible. In the second photo above we see how this process has been further developed in a machine that operates with different heads and nozzles, allowing different materials to be used within the same piece.

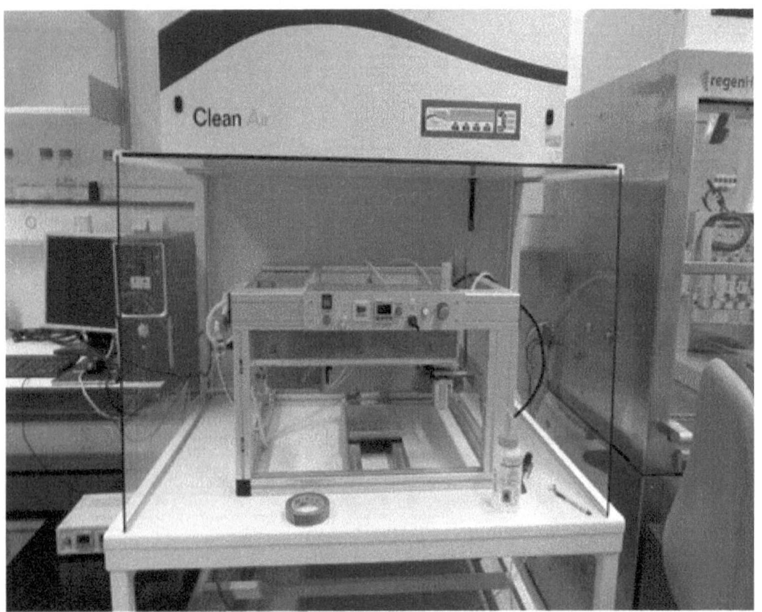

Figure 10. A further developed version, still with associated tools

Photo: Jonathan Hankins

Also on view are several tools that are necessary for the adjustment of the machine. There are parallels here too with the furniture workshop, where machines (the sewing machine primarily) have their own dedicated set of tools. The sewing machine has its own screwdriver that is housed in a drawer under the machine. Although merely a screwdriver it is only used to adjust the sewing machine, and never for other purposes, and as a result is housed separately. Malda's machines above also have a dedicated set of tools as can be seen in the photos. For the skilled operator these tools are seen as part of the machine, an understanding that is shared within the workspace if never expressed. It is learned through experience, from a sharing of the space, even in the case that an individual does not use the machine in question, they see it.

Below the latest version of the printer.

Figure 11. Prof. Malda with his latest printing technology

Photo: Jonathan Hankins

As the photo shows, this version of the printer is much more industrial looking. It was built in Germany as part of collaboration with the commercial 3D Printing company RegenHU. Malda explains that during his collaboration with the company he and his staff had received training in how to adapt the printer towards their own needs and wishes reflecting the fact that the machine has been purpose built for their needs.

7.3 Skilled vision: The Development of the Process on Display

Malda describes the machine as extremely precise, but inflexible. He argues that his own machines are more flexible than this commercial machine, even though it has multiple heads, because he can easily produce and substitute the nozzles on his own machines. The nozzles can be made to allow the strands to be produced in different thicknesses and shapes so that their properties can then be tested. Different patterns can be made on dishes and their capabilities tested. The craftsman techniques are clearly visible here once more, as the tools can be adapted readily and trialed. The process also leads to broader collaboration possibilities as different researchers develop different techniques and capabilities that can then be shared within collaboration projects.

The importance of network relations in terms of affording instruments and information is also visible here, mirroring the position of the furniture restorers in the previous chapter. Here once more the sharing of mutual understandings of capacities and capabilities allows the research line to develop as its operators gain access to the cutting-edge technology they require, and the industrial 3D printer producers gain valuable insight and information regarding the capabilities of their machines. As in the pattern book example given in the previous chapter, what we see on display is a process of mutual investment and interest.

There is also a certain similarity present in the layout of this (the printer) room in the laboratory to the workshop in the UK from the first case study. The printers are arranged in a line from least technically developed to most technically developed, very much as are the planes in the photo in the previous case study. This is not due to the times at which they were acquired or developed in either case however, it is by design. The planes in the restorer's workshop are lined up in order of their age and technical capacities, almost as a display of technical or technological improvement, as are the 3D printers. The printers have been recently moved and placed in-situ, their placing is not the result of an ad-hoc approach, they are in this position by design, a display of progress.

I argue that in both cases the presentation in some way represents the passage of time and technological development, but also a specialization that leads to a narrowing of the use of the tools. The upholsterer does not discard old tools as they not only represent the past, presenting their skills at a time honoured tradition, but that on occasion the tools may be used as they offer a versatility that newer tools may not offer. The wooden block plane offers the possibility to change the angle of the cutting blade manually, making it difficult to regulate for a fine cut but easier to use for a broader rougher cut. The blades are manually interchangeable; they are held in with a wedge of wood and can be removed with the tap of a hammer. Newer planes are regulated using a screw, making them much more precise but less flexible.

Each plane can still be used however and each has different characteristics. One might be better adapted to a particular job, very much in the way the 3D printers are better adapted (or adaptable) to specific types of work, but I argue that the display represents technical capacity, in the one case the capacity to use traditional restoration techniques, and in the other the capacity to construct ever more precise tools for research purposes.

The machines that Malda's team has produced are easier to regulate than the new industrial machine, as the placing of the tools required and visible in the photos testify. The nozzles can be easily removed and changed, the team members understand how the machines work internally and more importantly how they have been designed and for which purpose. These machines are flexible because of this know-how; the team understands how to adapt them for different uses through what we could describe as their poiesis knowledge and craftsmanship.

A further similarity can be seen in the display of objects that have been produced using the two sets of technology in use, 3D printing and furniture restoration. As noted above Malda has several objects on show that he has produced using his commercial 3D printing machine. Interestingly however, although some of the parts are objects that have been (or at least could have been) produced in relation to the work carried out, such as plastic copies of bones that are used to enact stress testing for his products, several others are ornamental pieces that can only have been made to demonstrate the capacities of the machines. One such object is a copy of the local church bell tower, the well-known Utrecht Dom Tor, see the figure above[99].

The furniture workshop also has its products on display, both in photo form but also in physical form. For many years the workshop walls were lined with headboards that had been made as examples of a possible sales-line, traditional work was presented half finished, deliberately left open in order to allow customers to see the work entailed in such techniques, work carried out in downtime or in the evenings as much for passion

---

[99] Over the years the furniture restoration workshop had several pieces on display. A series of headboards made in the 1980's adorned the walls for many years, alongside traditional pieces left in a semi-completed state as a display of worker capabilities.

as any other reason.

The picture below is such an example. The photo was taken of a picture frame that hangs in G Stewart's Upholstery workshop. It documents the restoration of a suite of chairs that the upholsterer himself had bought in France in 2003 and restored. The stripped photo is taken in the back garden of his house, as the work was carried out at home. The chairs now sit in the house beautifully restored. The picture frame also contains a piece of the textile removed and the old braid, a demonstration of the restorer's capacities but also of the historical significance of the pieces and the work carried out.

This photo serves to demonstrate these capacities, but it is small and would have to be narrated to be understood. It stands as a symbol of capabilities very much like the Dom Tor in the 3D lab. Both representations require a skilled vision to understand their significance as a demonstration of a skilled process, one shared by the experts in the respective expertise and learned in a situated and social environment (Grasseni 2009). It creates status for visitors from the trade who share an understanding of the process involved, allowing them to share the experience upon meeting through discussion of the techniques and choices involved. This is a valuable tool when dealing with fabric supply representatives as it allows a display of quality and expertise, leading to the expansion of the network into higher quality material procurement and the related information offered within such a relationship.

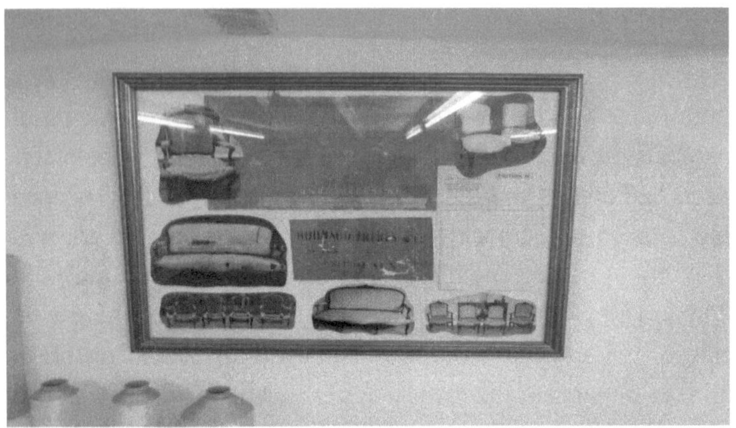

Figure 12. Photo of antique restoration process

Photo: Jonathan Hankins

7.4 Similarities in Problem Solving Techniques

During several conversations between Prof Malda and myself the topic of problem solving within our different working environments was raised in terms of similarities in approaches rather than difference. In this section I would like to describe some of these interactions in order to offer examples of how different forms of knowledge interact within a single project. Malda describes his project as multidisciplinary in nature (see the interview in this chapter) but I feel that the following examples show how the working practice and decision-making processes are closely related between the two geographic situations, leading me to argue that the poiesis analysis can be used within the science laboratory setting, blurring the line between science and scientific approaches and craft approaches (Van der Burg and Swierstra, 2013).

One of the main problems with the implant that Prof Malda is developing is its ability to resist the stress that it is put under once transplanted into position. In one conversation he was describing how he tries to model the movement of a knee joint by producing exact replicas of the system using 3D printing techniques. The resulting models and mathematical modelling however cannot replicate the stresses that the actual transplanted pieces are subjected to. He described how the sheering effect of stresses running from side to side and across the top of the implant leads to its total collapse, describing how his team were aiming to resolve this problem.

The team was experimenting with placing ties between the framework and the base structure in order to give it strength, in effect pegging each side wall to the base, rather like a tent, and with giving the material a type of pile, rather like velvet, in order to strengthen the structure, exactly as in fabric manufacturing for furniture. He described how the experiments were going, that they strengthened the structure but not enough to avoid damage completely.

Malda used the description of the tent himself, describing how the members of his team look around to see how similar problems are addressed in different structures in the outside world. As we discussed this problem, I followed his example by explaining how the problem is found in furniture making and how we resolve it.

In furniture design and manufacturing we also find the problem of sheering. Springs within the seat are the most affected by this problem. Conical springs (the traditional spring also found in beds) are designed to soak up stress vertically. They compress and return to their original position if pushed from above, but if pushed from the side they become deformed and eventually break.

If these springs are set into a seat and always used correctly, with the weight only applied from above they will function correctly for many years. They are however subject to pressure from the front, as people sit on a seat from the front and not from above. The strain applied comes from the front of the spring at a 45% angle, pushing the springs backwards and damaging them.

In order to resolve this issue, the springs are tied together in their centre, as well as the tops and bottoms held in position. This central cord is left flexible allowing a small sideways movement preventing damage, being wrapped around the springs rather than tied to them, holding them upright regardless of where the pressure is applied.

I described and drew the solution for Prof Malda to see and we discussed it further. He explained that he could not make a spring with a 3D printer as it could not print objects that were not set to a base, but I argued that it was not the spring structure itself that was so important, rather the fact that they were tied together and not individually to the base. Malda explained that this technique of using approaches gained from other problem solving techniques is invaluable within his research, bringing a broader idea of cross-disciplinarity into play than we might imagine.

A further element can also be seen as running through the two production techniques and philosophies. Prof Malda is designing and building an implant that must grow, his product is not a finished product in terms of a good, but a part of a process. The process in question involves the implanting and growth of the 3D object, it is to become something more than it is when it is finished. This is similar to a piece of furniture, in that a piece of furniture is also designed with its use in mind, although in this case it is its wear and destruction and not its growth.

To clarify, a furniture designer can foresee possible problems of wear on a piece before it is produced. Particular areas are more susceptible to dirt and wear, and techniques can be used to minimize this wear. A simple example is on the arm tops. A hard arm top with fabric on top of it will wear very quickly, while springing on the very front of the arm will lead to the piece lasting much longer. The choice of fabric is also important as we would imagine, but the placing of decoration such as piping (chord) or ruche (frills) also has an effect upon the longevity of the piece. A design can not only be aesthetically functional therefore at time of completion, but design choice also affects the life of the piece. The design is drawn with the life of the object in mind in both cases.

The artefact can therefore be seen as produced within an imaginary life cycle, with decisions made within the design process based upon this imaginary cycle. The product does not therefore represent an end product as such, but part of a process that continues autonomously as it moves into use with its new user. This life cycle view is perceived by all of those working within the development process, and also shared and negotiated, reflecting many of the issues of futures and foresight present in the RI literature (Robinson, 2009, Stahl et.al, 2013, Selin, 2014, Grunwald, 2014, Groves et.al. 2016,).

History

The drive for Prof Malda's interest in following his particular path of regenerative medicine is to solve the problems of metal joint implants, reflecting a wish to improve the lives of those needing such surgery and the goal of improving efficiency within the health service (social improvement goals that are very tied to the grand Challenges argument outlined in Chapter 3). The prosthetic joints currently in general use only last 10 to 15 years, then requiring further surgery to adjust and repair them. This is often a larger and more expensive operation that the original fitting, raising the question of how suitable such treatment is in both younger people, and even those much older as they expect to live ever longer lives. He argues that the replacement of such surgery with a regeneration repair that grows in-situ and requires no maintenance would offer a solution to some of these questions. Cells from the patient to be treated could be used to avoid the problem of rejection, meaning that the operation can be concluded in a single sitting. Stem cells can be used that develop at different speeds, and patients are not required to return for the collection of further specimens.

The development of Malda's first 3D bio-printer came about via a study trip to Australia in order to visit old friends and ex colleagues. Malda had been Research Fellow in Tissue Bio-regeneration at the Institute of Health and Biomedical Innovation, Queensland University of Technology between 2004 and 2007, taking an adjunct position at the same university in 2010. Malda took a PhD student and Masters student over for a short trip, and during this time they began experimenting an idea of how to use live cells with 3D printing technology. The first attempt involved fabricating a sort of printer using hypodermic syringes as printing nozzles, experimenting with delivering materials using pressure. These developments were conducted without major funding but a collaboration team was born that moved forward following something that looks like a poiesis intensive approach, as described above.

Malda explains that his interest was developed during his PhD (2000-2004 Doctor of Philosophy in Tissue Engineering at the

University of Twente), where he worked alongside a small 3D printing company that had an agreement with the University. These are described as the very early days of this technology, but Malda took a great interest. He explains that his father was an artist, and that maybe his interest in this particular form of development of techniques owes a debt to his influence. As his team's experimental capacity grew, Malda took a particular interest in how thinner fibres could be developed.

He described the realities of what the printer does as trying to write your name on the floor in honey drizzling from a tube at arm's length while standing, with one of his early aims to produce as fine a fibre as possible. During his description of this process he speaks about trial and error processes, incrementing to find the limits of the technology and pushing them ever further. He explains that many factors play a part, but that the only way to really proceed is through physical experimentation, rather mirroring the sentiments expressed by Maurizio Montalti in my shorter case study into Officina Corpuscoli cited earlier. He gives the example of how static makes the fibres stick together at a certain point, leading to new parts being made for the printing technology and more trials to see if the problem can be overcome.

This description seems very much to reflect an artisanal approach to research. Malda is producing single bespoke made to measure articles, his concept of functional beauty includes categories of strength, precision and size, with experimentation and adjustment common. Practical judgement prevails, physical testing and visual data coming to the fore.

Malda explains that in the early days of his research his goals were quite contained. He explained that he just wanted to see if a printer could be used to build an implant that would be stronger and resist damage from being placed between bones. The results were astounding both for his own research team and his colleagues, as the resulting implants were much stronger and cell growth much more efficient. He explains that his colleagues insisted that they must have made a mistake with their calculations, and that they should try the process again. Once repeated the results were the same, leading to interest in the process that led to the scaling up of the project to the position that it finds itself in today, a world leader.

The strength of the implant can be modified depending on how soft or hard the materials are made, which can be changed according to the particular needs to be addressed. He warns however that the process of making an operational and versatile machine was long and arduous, and that they have to work extremely slowly to attain the necessary precision. They often leave the machine running overnight as the production process currently takes so long. Experience and investigation has led to the team developing solutions for these problems which have been shared through their collaborations within their network, a process of collaboration that has sped up the research and manufacturing process very much reflecting the RI philosophy in relation to data sharing and trans-disciplinarity.

Today Malda works as part of a large international network, and has won several large grants to pursue his work, including a 2015 ERC Consolidator grant. Collaboration projects include the aim to build a much larger machine on a marble base (in order to make it more stable) with the 3D printing collaborators RegenHU, and the creation of a larger lab in Germany.

In the following section I analyze transcriptions of recorded conversations between myself and Prof. Malda. The methodology used in creating this data is similar to that described in chapter 6, although my involvement in the co-production element of the data is greatly restricted due to my lack of competence in the field. As a result, the conversation is more descriptive, resembling an open-ended interview more than the conversation between experts of the previous chapter and my analysis should be read bearing this in mind.

Interestingly my first interview was conducted before beginning my fieldwork in Manchester, very much providing a springboard for the approach used within the furniture workshop. My own relationship, alongside that between Malda and the Bassetti Foundation, has continued up to the present day, including working towards the preparation of a large Horizon 2020 project and invited lecture in Milan[100].

7.5 Professor Jos Malda in his Own Words

This open ended semi-structured interview was carried out in Professor Malda's laboratory, recorded and transcribed using the methodology and following the protocols described in chapter 6.

The conversation opened with a description of the breakthrough that allowed the implantation of a plastic skull noted above.

> We had the implantable skull, the skull replacement that we did here in the hospital about 2 years ago. This was a patient with a bone disease, the bone kept growing and started to compress the brain and so she had major issues and complaints. Based on 3D printing technology they created a replacement of the skull and implanted it successfully. It was a 24-hour operation, a major thing, but what is important to

---

[100] Video of a 2017 lecture and event held at the Bassetti Foundation is available here:
https://www.fondazionebassetti.org/en/focus/2017/10/3d_printing_an_overview_a_dial.html
Last accessed 13/11/2019

note here is that the 3D printing industry is really becoming hyped and expectations are high. And that can be illustrated by the fact that I got a phone call from a journalist just after that saying oh wow, so you in the hospital can print a cranial skull. Next year can you also print a heart?

Well these are two completely different things, and that is what we have to bring to the general public. The technology of 3D bio printing is very promising and has enormous potential, but it will be a long time until we see all the potential that we envisage at this stage.

For example we can already create little 3D liver models on which we can do toxicity tests, but before you can really use these as a replacement for a liver of someone who has liver disease there are a number of steps to be taken so to be realistic about it is one of our academic tasks, to be realistic about the real expectations but also be realistic about the real potential, which is a great potential with these technologies.

In this description Malda touches upon a topic that has been addressed several times in the RI literature and described in chapter 2 of this thesis, that of the depictions of the future and the opportunities that new technological development really offers (Grunwald, 2014, Groves et.al. 2016, Stahl et.al, 2013, Nordman, 2014, von Schomberg 2019). Malda address the problem of scientists presenting realistic goals and possibilities to the press and funding bodies, raising the issue of hype and expectation and the importance of scientific and ethics education for the general public as well as within technical fields (Robaey, 2014, Raman, 2015, Nordmann, 2019).

Malda then moves on to addressing a second topic related to RI and addressed in the literature, that of human enhancement and the line between repair and improvement (Eggleson and Berry, 2015).

> One of the things too about bio fabrication is that you can create living objects, living objects that can replace or regenerate parts of diseased tissues or degenerated tissues, but it also touches upon the aspect of human enhancement. Can we then create organs that we could not have had before? So we have a close relationship with the ethics people here in Utrecht and we also look at the societal impact of this technology and we also try to create that awareness, not only for society of course and the outside world but also the people that we educate, the PhD students and researchers, it is an integral part of the conception of the topic, of the field.

> With regards to that field, one thing is that it is bringing together many different disciplines. The technology is based on stem cell biology, on material science, on robotics, on engineering and software development, and that is why we aim to create a multidisciplinary team. Not only here in our group where we have members from all of these disciplines and fields working together on different aspects of the same technology but also in our broader collaborations, in our European projects. We work with mathematicians, with polymer chemists, stem cell biologists, who all have their specific tasks and we try to converge these different fields and technologies, and through this we believe that we can take larger steps in the field of regenerative medicine.

In the description above Malda talks about the networks he requires in order to carry out his research. As noted in the first case study, the network allows the production process to function by providing expertise and materials to support the process. In the case of the furniture restorer, this network is built up through reputation. A high-quality worker will gain access to higher quality materials that may be selectively distributed. In the case in question here, I would argue that the innovative capacities and technical capabilities that Malda displays allow him to build a network of similarly high-quality collaborators. As in the first case study the implication here is that responsibility becomes distributed and shared across the network. Mutual support is required not merely technically but also in terms of the sharing and promotion of the vision behind the research and also the narrative within its working practices.

The creation and maintenance of such a network is important for those in the research community, not only in terms of finding the necessary expertise, but also because it forms one of the bases for recognition from funding bodies. As noted in chapter 3, RI is currently a cross cutting feature of EU funding, and a shared recognition both within the network and between network members and funding bodies is imperative if funding is to be procured.

The German 3D printer manufacturing company RegenHU that works alongside Malda is one example, they invest their time in training Malda's team so that they can use the machinery as they wish, all of which adds to the development of both projects. The 3D printer manufacturer gains a new form of expertise and innovation and feedback from the group, and the group gains input to the development of the machinery. The appreciation of technical ability is demonstrated through collaborative actions, as it is with the furniture restorer in her relationship to exclusive fabric producers who in turn recognize their ability and social positioning, but also with designers who look to push boundaries of what can be achieved in practice relying on expertise and the poiesis knowledge of the highest quality but most inventive furniture makers and restorers (see Adam's comments on pricing work without fully understanding the process required in Chapter 6 for further discussion). Innovation in furniture design is reliant on such skills and abilities procured through such networks in the same way as science is.

Malda goes on to discuss the importance of this network in terms of how mathematicians play a part in his research and what they offer his project.

> The mathematical models give us a simplification of the real world. And if we simplify things, we can actually look at the governing processes which actually are the real things at stake. You shouldn't make them too simple, because then they don't make sense any more, but if you have a number of parameters that are influencing the specific process that you are studying you can develop models that tell you which parameters are the most sensitive to change, which is the real governing parameter. And this can help you then in the design of your experiments. And this can save you a lot of time in your experiments too. I have been working with applied mathematicians for a long time, in Australia and Oxford and Southampton, to connect our research to theirs. So we have had a number of mathematicians actually spending time on our lab to get an idea of what the problems are that we are actually working with, what are the things you are dealing with? Rather than just supplying a set of data in an excel file and saying well let's go and model them.

The influence of a broad spectrum of expertise is noted by Malda, reflecting a broader interest in RI literature related not only to non-expert but also multidisciplinary participation within science and the organizational effect of current EU funding structures[101], the influence of broader publics in research direction and its possible effect upon responsibility (Li et.al, 2015).

> And that has been interesting not only for them but also for people of our own team, working with these cells and looking from a different perspective, which is a good arrangement I think, besides the advantages of international activities and input from different cultures.

In the following section, Malda explains the rationale of his work, expanding upon the problem noted above with metal implants. This part of the discussion very much reflects the discussion in RI in the health system, as promoted through the EC pillar system described in Chapter 1 (EC, 2012, EC, 2013, Chalmers et.al, 2014, Demers – Payet et.al, 2016, Fisher et.al, 2015).

> Our main vision is that with regenerative medicine we can help the body to repair itself, to regenerate itself. So from the point of view of regenerative medicine it is the patient in the end that is our driving force. We are here in a hospital environment and it is the patient we need to help. It is patient centred progress. In this there are some essential questions, some essential and challenging translational and basic science questions. We try to address these, especially through the focus of translational medicine but we are not afraid of basic science questions too. So our research is focusing on 3D printing technologies. We call them bio fabrication

---

[101] Current structure typically leads to the creation of multidisciplinary teams to conduct scientific research. In the case of Malda's team this includes computer programmers, mathematicians and robotice engineers who work alongside biologists.

technologies because there are cells and bio electrical components involved, and we use these to create models and potentially implants for patients with specific diseases. One of our main spearhead programs is focusing on the development of the inks. How can we develop materials that have attractive physical properties on the one hand, biological properties on the other hand that are suitable for the bio fabrication process. So we can then create 3D structures with high shape fidelity in which cells can differentiate a positive specific matrix that you would like to have them create depending on the purpose that you are focusing on. The research focus problem that we really look at is joint disease. We know that joints can be treated with metal implants, so if you have a worn down joint you can put a metal implant in there, but still they only survive for about 10 to 15 years, so you then need to have a revision which is a more costly surgery and they do not survive as long as the first or primary implant. So if you look at our society with increasing age and in which we are getting more and more active and want to keep active and expect more quality of life then these metal implants, even though they are probably the most successful medical treatment, might not be the right solution for us any more, especially for younger patients, so therefore with the approach to recreate biological implants, we can either postpone or maybe even get rid of the need for these metal implants, and therefore improve the quality of life, and that is the basic focus.

Also related to EC and wider EU aims addressed through the RI project of improving research for economic and social betterment of EU citizens (Treaty of Lisbon, 2007), but that also sits within the RI goal of working for the good of society and the EU goal of conducting research to address the problem of an aging population[102], Malda talks about his sharing of information and technical ability both within the academic and industrial worlds, and how working together provides advantages across a range of fields.

> That is an interesting thing, because we were initially focused on the regeneration of the joint with the investment of the University and hospital. Here we have been able to set up a facility that facilitates access to the equipment for other researchers and other companies and other people in the field too. This has boosted the portfolio of ongoing research products so there is a range now, from heart tissue to liver tissue and kidney so on all focusing on the 3D biological living construction, either for model development or testing or for replacement of those living tissues. So yes there are definitely implications there but I think on a wider scale that 3D printing is really changing the way we perceive manufacturing and how we are moving towards the mass personalization of a lot of things such as tools, implants and products, so I think in that sense it is a very important aspect. And our challenges faced are often the same as those seen in general additive manufacturing with regards to data management or data translation from imaging to 3D file that can actually then be processed by the printer and result in a 3D object which incorporates not just one material in a specific shape, but incorporates multiple materials in a single shape. I think that is the primary outreach of how that integrates with many of the different challenges that are out there.

---

[102] One of the Key Research Areas for Horizon 2020 funding in health research is Human development and ageing. https://ec.europa.eu/research/health/index.cfm?pg=area&areaname=ageing

A further issue touched upon in this discussion and within RI literature is that of standardization and regulation within science (Wickson and Carew, 2014, Tuma, 2014).

> We have recently stressed that there is a need for standards and standardization in our field because there are currently standards for additive manufacturing but there are not for bio manufacturing yet. The main driving force or aspect for that is that what you design in the end is what you get. That is where regulation has to and will fulfil its role. Because we work with machines that can be programmed, so we know what the output should be, but the inputs should be certified as well. A good example is the personalized metal implants that companies like Materialize are developing, and they have their certified software to create these implants. These are complex hip provision surgeries where there is a lot of bone loss and you have to look at the strength of the bone and where it can fit in, it is a mechanically driven process. But for a biological part there is one other challenge because it is not just one material or one material at different densities, we need imaging modalities that can predict or visualize where the tissue boundaries are. Where is the boundary between cartilage and bone for example if you want to create a joint implant, and that is going to be a challenging aspect for the standardization of how that can be done. But the good thing is that we can do it more or less in a closed system, where the machine does its work and is reproducible etc. and you don't have to do a lot of handling steps, so that is really important if you compare it to traditional cell engineering technologies where you seat cells on a scaffold, I think that is a real step forward in science.

The broader and well documented arguments surrounding the

direction and governance of innovation is also discussed (Li et.al, 2015, Asantea et.al, 2015, Stilgoe et.al, 2013, Randles and laasch, 2015), which directly relates to the argument that underpins this chapter, the proposal that Malda's working practices could form the basis upon which a possible PIRI model could be founded.

It is interesting to note that we had a large European project with the FP7 program that focuses on the 3D printing of cartilage implants, and the first thing we did in that multinational collaboration was to set protocols, so we agreed on the way that we would harvest the cells, how we would isolate and culture them how we would then put them in the printer and so on. And that is essential in order to come and discuss the end results, because if we don't know how these things are done then it is impossible to communicate about them. Some are internally created within the project, some are standard procedures because that is how these things are best done, they are best practice because we know that if we isolate the cells in this way we get the best performing cells. But generally a lot of these protocols are just developed by the researchers themselves based on research to find out what gives the best outcome.

These protocols are public, and the results of the project are disseminated and these outcomes become available. With the new funding rules too within the EU I think it is very good that these also require open source open access publication and that is how we disseminate our results to an ever-broader audience.

In terms of language you are often limited to your own language or to English. The scientific community uses only

English of course, but the lay public, well in NL they are relatively proficient in English and we do a lot of outreach to primary and secondary schools where we bring our printers and tell the story of how bio printing can affect daily life. Of course, scientific language and lay language are completely different ball parks, so we have a different form of communication for these kids and we get completely different questions that are often a lot cooler than you get with adults and then of course we have scientific meetings. So we do travel a lot to different conferences to meet with our peers and to discuss our work with our peers and share our results. But that is all in English. But we also have close connections with patient societies, like the Dutch Arthritis Association that we discuss the directions of our research with and the impact that it may have, and we use them as a sounding board for the actions that we take.

Malda once more addresses the multidisciplinary nature of his work and possibility of working with a designer, bringing in the debate of beauty and that of the importance of the influence of a broad spectrum of experts as described above (see Van den Hoven, 2013 for further discussion on the importance of design for responsibility).

Well in general, multidisciplinarity gives different views on a problem and issue and for us that has been extremely important. For example the mathematicians who don't know anything about biology ask questions that are based on logic, they ask the most obvious questions sometimes, but we cannot give them an answer, and that makes us feel stupid because we say well it is just because it is. But why? Well does this happen first or this first...well no, it just happens. And that makes you think in a different way about your problems or your research and that is a very valuable aspect. I think that with a designer that would be a similar relationship, and especially if you look at 3D design, working with these software issues is sometimes quite complex and so we have a number of people that can work with it but not from an industrial design point of view. So we have not tried to incorporate that yet but it may be a good idea.

This description matches the arguments made within the RI literature about the influence of experts in different fields upon scientific development (Stilgoe et.al, 2011, Foley et.al. 2016, Fisher et.al, 2015, Sunderland et.al, 2014, Balmer et.al, 2016) and is further developed below, before he concludes with a description of how different techniques and different forms of poiesis knowledge could be combined in future research.

The truth is that you cannot do it alone, you need those specialties, you cannot be everything. And the great thing is that if you have the opportunity to bring these people together in a team you can really make it reality and get this research moving.

And the future research is looking at the convergence of different bio fabrication technologies, and this reflects the whole field of research and its multidisciplinarity and with biofabrication the same thing happens within the field. So if you have one particular technology that is based on, for example, fuse deposition modelling for example where you have thick fibres, you would want to be able to combine it with an electro spinning system where you can make much thinner fibres, or a cell spray technology where you can deposit single cells or multiple cells in a surrounding hydrogel or matrix, because a tissue is very complex and so you need these different possibilities in order to re-capitulate the structure and that is really where the research is moving towards and the translation of this technology to those predictive models. So there are a number of these models under development and they have to demonstrate their value and predictive ability.

7.6 Some Conclusions

Throughout the research process I found Professor Malda extremely helpful and open to discussing both his work and arguments surrounding Responsible Innovation approaches. He is very knowledgeable on the RI argument, and maintains a position that ethics must be an integral part of education within all of the fields that he is involved in. He is reflexive about his work and open to speaking about it publicly to diverse audiences. His interest in public education and participation puts him very much in line with current RI approaches

Much of his focus on 3D printing is aimed at improving clinical efficiency for surgical techniques, while also cutting costs, putting him in line with the EU grand challenges model of responsible scientific approaches. His continued work on the use of 3D techniques to minimize animal use in science is laudable, and although RI and RRI has not really touched upon this debate (see literature review), it is an argument that I believe could be addressed from an RI perspective. He also consistently calls for the standardization of working practices whilst referring to global norms, reflecting the glocal element of the definition of PIRI offered in Chapter 5.

Malda places high importance on education models - from his work travelling around schools to present his work - to his development of the techniques that allow the creation of 3D printed organs for surgical operative planning and proposed development of training regimes for future surgeons and doctors, an idea that also bears important similarity to RI models.

As I describe above, the process that Malda's team have developed and the structures they have built rely on poiesis forms of knowledge and practice. Problems (and the ways solutions are sought) that are typical of artisan working practices are visible within this science laboratory. The process can be described as poiesis-intensive, and would fit the description of Poiesis-Intensive Innovation as used within the Bassetti Foundation. Given that Malda's approach to the way he conducts his scientific research and his understanding of the RI related issues, I take the step of arguing that the working practices described above could form the basis for a Poiesis Intensive Responsible Innovation model (PIRI).

Throughout my time both within Prof Malda's laboratory and in conversation with him outside the laboratory, I noted many similarities between his approach to decision-making and problem solving and those of the small business artisan workers that I followed during my research. The geographical similarities in terms of the organization of space, the importance of a network and the organization of collaborators through a relationship of respect and understanding of needs run through all of the examples touched upon in this book. The importance of the delegation of responsibilities to those collaborators best qualified for the particular task in hand is a product and also constructor of these networks and relationships, with risk negation and information sharing making up important sub categories for analysis.

One of the most striking similarities is in the way both the scientists and artisan workers relate to their particular tool sets. Both groups rely on knowing exactly what they can 'make' their sets of tools do, the limitations and possibilities that each individual tool offers. They both rely on producing bespoke tools for individual roles or pieces, and understand and experiment with the modification of accepted techniques for particular purposes.

This use of a particular set of tools used to produce a further more specialized set of tools can be seen as the building of a process, within which the artisan or scientist is the architect and the maker. They create a process that reflects their individual perspectives, visions and standpoints in relation to their work, a process that they are then able to see and share in both the artefact produced and the process itself through reference to a shared narrative.

All of the actors involved in these case studies have visions that are projected over longer time frames than those of just the production process itself. These could be thought of as future visions of the uses of their products that guide the development of the process. These visions are constructed within the workplace in the form of a narrative, referring to personally held beliefs as well as external norms. They are negotiated within a discussion that is not only based on the vision but also on know-how, technical experience and that of those in the broader network. And these visions are also bodily learned, held, appreciated and shared.

The understanding of this bodily knowledge is necessary for the construction of the projects in question and the working practices within them. There is an inter-reliance between all of those in the network through a sharing of an understanding of the narrative constructed. This supply of materials, knowledge and network and information sharing leads to the sharing of responsibilities and the construction of a type of language that allows this sharing to be discussed and shared. Quality is judged and shared using abstract ideas such as beauty, cleanliness, precision and suitability, through the acquisition of skilled visions and understandings. The workplace narrative can be seen as a shared construction that frames such understandings.

In summary, I suggest there seem to be many similarities between the two case studies presented. As I explained in Chapter 5, the production process in the upholstery workshop had a goal, that goal being what Grasseni describes as functional beauty (Grasseni, 2007).

This functional beauty encapsulates the function that the product should fulfil. In the case of a piece of furniture this means a piece that looks good in the owner's house. It must be suitable for its placing. But by extension it must also look good in Adam's workshop, in the fabrics that he chooses to stock and has access to, and in the style that he prefers and choses to produce.

It is a co-constructed beauty, with the aim of the restoration process this co-constucted form.

For Professor Malda his goals are not the same in that he is not aiming for beauty. Malda talks about precision and function as goals, with what he describes as 'fascination' as one of his driving forces. Function relies on precision, whereas for Adam it relies on style. But I would argue that Malda also has an aim that is guided by his workplace narrative, a multifaceted narrative that addresses the different issues of responsibility that he faces, guided by his own values.

He shares a language with his collaborators that allows the construction of the workplace narrative, a narrative is built through practice. In the case of the high-quality craftsman when doing a piece that he has chosen to do (which includes stamping his style and using fabrics that he has chosen to source), the goal is the production of functional beauty.

Returning to the science lab, Professor Malda talks about fascination, and precision, the need watch something in order to understand how it will develop, to trial approaches in order to discover variables that models cannot predict (static making the threads stick together for example), pursuing the aim of making them as thin as possible before they are no longer workable.

The language used may not be that of beauty, but we can see a clear narrative guiding this approach, shared in the same way as the workshop narrative, built upon watching, waiting, practicing, network, experimentation and the experience and flexibility of all those working within the process. All of the team share an understanding of the narrative, it's aims, what it affords, how each challenge should be addressed.

Professor Malda does not say that his goal is beauty, but function, which is also the aim of the upholsterer's narrative, it's just that in the case of furniture, beauty can be used as a shared measure of function.

Chapter 8

Concluding Remarks

As noted in the introduction to this book, its aim was to open a field of study within RI that sees narration and aesthetics as playing central analytical roles within daily decision-making practices in small scale production processes, be those artisanal working or scientific working situations.

The argument presented here is that people working in such environments learn not only the technicalities of their work, but also co-construct the narrative through which decisions are made and possibilities are granted or excluded (Ingold, 2000, Lave and Wenger, 1991, Herzfeld, 2004, Collins, 2010, Polanyi, 1958). This could be described as the narrative of doing things right, or correctly, a concept that is socially constructed within the place of work through daily work talk. It is negotiated and fluid, refers to a shared understanding of a narrative framework and is recognized and codified through the appreciation of the values intrinsic to either the finished product, its production process or both. The narrative affords the framing of the decision-making process and the sharing of a language that allows the sharing and expression of judgement in terms of correctness.

In the case of craftwork, the shared understanding can be seen as expressed through an appreciation of the functional beauty that such an object or process possesses and demonstrates (Grasseni, 2009). Each object has its own functional beauty, defined by different criteria and affected by the amount of resources available, objectives and resources, meaning that the appreciation of beauty cannot be transferred from one to another without modification. No two processes are the same, as resources are different, meaning that the construction of their aesthetic appreciation must also be different, although the framework through which it is drawn in terms of the narrative is similar.

I argue that within this form of poiesis intensive production, this shared understanding of aesthetics is a driving force within the decision-making process, as social status production through its appreciation leads to the construction of networks of both colleagues and suppliers of both materials, technology and tools, ideas and information, that are necessary for the production process. Beauty is intrinsic to function, and I feel that these conclusions may be applicable to research in the laboratory setting.

To summarize; ideas of responsibility, narrative and the aim of the process (beauty in this case) may be related, I would say intertwined, and can both be seen and appreciated through an educated vision via the appreciation of abstract and unmeasurable categories (such as but not restricted to aesthetic beauty) ascribed to the product or process possesses.

Although in the science lab the language may be different, precision is discussed more than beauty, there are similarities in that precision is functional precision, as beauty is functional beauty. Functional precision relates to purpose and function. It is one facet of a functional goal, very much as beauty is for the upholsterer.

I argue that the considerations here described can play a part in the development of scholastic and practical work surrounding the concept of RI. The concept of getting it right (product), or doing it right (process) is a fundamental idea for artisan working practices as well as in scientific research (Herzfeld, 2004, Bijker, 2010), as well as being a fundamental argument that sits at the core of RI. Following Paul Bohannan, I summarize this relationship with the argument that what he describes as morality (or for my purposes responsibility) is culture, and as such working culture should be seen as an important field for study within RI (Bohannan, 1995).

RI literature at the point of writing however has not developed this concept in terms of how innovation operators view their work, but has tended to focus on governance and the development of such principles using means that could be seen as external to the feelings and motivations of these operatives. The approach outlined here aims to bridge that gap by investigating the motivations and understandings shared through the narratives present in the workplace, via the analysis of recorded conversations and interviews between myself and a furniture restorer, bio-medical surgeon and synthetic biologist, and field visits to many other artisan workshops both in the high technology sector and those that we might describe as more traditional.

The methodology of recording, transcribing and analyzing recorded interviews and conversations is carried through to the different subjects involved in this thesis (Mason 2002). Much of the chapter referring to the work of the Bassetti Foundation is based upon documentary evidence that is backed up and strengthened through the use of this technique with several interviews conducted with President Piero Bassetti. The European perspective is also drawn through an analysis of published documents (de Saille, 2015), with the personal account given by René von Schomberg offering a much deeper understanding of these developments through cross reference and comparison.

As noted throughout this thesis these arguments have been prevalent throughout the years of operation of the Bassetti Foundation, the sponsor of this research and my host workplace over the last three years. This publication demonstrates the forward thinking of those present at its inception and displayed through the Foundation's leadership over the following twenty years, an inception that can be seen as one of the foundation stones upon which the development of the concept of RI rests.

The book is divided into seven self-standing chapters, each representing a narrative from a particular perspective. It can be broadly seen as divided into two larger sections. The first section offers a representation of the current state of the art in RI research. Chapters 1, 2, 3, and 4 are all related to this construction, narrating the development of the concept of RI from different perspectives. The construction of this broader narrative (my own RI narrative) leads to the second section of this thesis, based upon an argument (outlined above) that sees the sharing of a concept of functional beauty in terms of its position within a workplace narrative and its relevance to decision-making processes.

The second section is split into three chapters, the first offering an overview of methodology and argument, followed by two case studies. The first case study involves a furniture restorer in South Manchester (UK) and the second a surgeon developing 3D bio-printing techniques in Utrecht (NL). Other fieldwork experiences that constituted my research period are also recounted as they underpin both the methodology and the theory applied to the two in-depth case studies.

In the following section I offer an overview and draw some conclusions from each chapter in order.

8.1 Chapter 1, Responsible Innovation: An Overview

This chapter opens with an overview of the current definitions in common use within RI literature and practice. The von

Schomberg definition (Von Schomberg, 2011) is set within the context of his many years working within the European Commission and his working history and interest in Technology Assessment. The need described in von Schomberg's article for RI to address normative anchor points very much reflects this position, as the author gears his definition towards working towards the right impacts for innovation in terms of societal gain based upon a profound understanding of the aims of various EU treaties and publications.

The Stilgoe, Owen and MacNaghten definition is then described (Stilgoe, Owen and MacNaghten, 2013). Once more the definition is set within the context of the authors' background, in this case their work with the EPSRC in the UK, alongside its effect upon policy-making in the broader field of research funding (see EU links in chapter 3 for examples).

The third definition described comes from myself (Hankins, 2019). This definition demonstrates my interests in the local production of both artefacts and knowledge, and is very much borne from the research process carried out for my PhD. The influence of poiesis as described in the second section of this book is clearly visible within this definition. The aim is to offer a holistic conception of RI within which responsibility is a shared practice that is both local and global.

The definition offered by van Hoven is then described and put into context (van den Hoven, 2013). This definition is based upon the concept of moral overload, and is a rather stripped-down version of the others in use. This very much reflects the needs for which it was designed and van Hoven's own development of the concept of Value Sensitive Design (van den Hoven, 2013).

Pavie and Carthy's definition is then described and set within the context for its development (Pavie and Carthy, 2013). This definition is very much aimed at business operators with limited academic knowledge of the development of the concept.

The chapter continues with an in-depth description of background events that led to the development of the concept of RI and the definitions cited above, describing how this development can be seen as an intertwining of institutional aims and initiatives that have each affected the way the concept has shifted its interest and influence (Grunwald, 2014).

The chapter concludes with an investigation into definitions of RI that can be found in the public domain but are not in academic use. The Sutcliffe definition cited for example shows the influence of von Schomberg's thinking and its influence beyond the realm of EU policy-making (Sutcliffe, 2011).

The chapter concludes with an investigation into the academic and societal roots for the concept of RI. This section describes the influence of Technology Assessment (TA) (Grunwald, 2014), moving into Anticipatory Governance (Guston, 2008) and Constructive Technology Assessment and Real Time TA (Schot and Rip, 1996). This line of research has further developed into Socio Technical Integration Research and the concept of Midstream Modulation (Fisher, 2007).

The development and history of Governmental and Parliamentary Technology Assessment organizations are then described in detail, before brief conclusions are drawn. These include the underlying argument of this research, namely that RI definitions and practices have leaned towards representations of responsibility in pillar format rather than attempting to analyze the social construction of work narratives and their effects upon working practices. This has led to the academic community alongside the research funding community taking an interest in the governance of innovation in terms of responsibility, to the point of the dramatic underrepresentation of addressing the issue from the innovator's perspective, a perspective that this narrative approach takes as its point of departure.

8.2 Chapter 2, The Scholarly Narrative

The second chapter is a literature review of the current state of the art in academic RI.

The chapter begins with the first publications within the academic literature, *Responsible Innovation, Managing the Responsible Emergence of Science and Innovation in Society* edited by Owen, Bessant and Heintz (Owen, Bessant and Heintz, 2013). As the review demonstrates, this book was the first collection of scholarship directly related to the development of the concept of RI, and contains articles from almost all of the leaders in the field at that time.

As the title suggests, much of the focus is on governance, very much setting the agenda for the development of literature surrounding the concept that was to follow. It is however worthy of note that not all of the contributions come from academics, I myself wrote the endnotes, introducing the argument of building capacity within RI practices (Hankins, 2013).

The review continues with an analysis of the work of Bernd Stahl from the same year, outlining Stahl's arguments of RI as a meta or higher-level responsibility, a line that has been fundamental for the development of the concept of RI more broadly(Stahl, 2013).

The review then moves on to analyze the SNET series of publications. SNET is the Society for the Study of Nanoscience and Emerging Technologies and as such takes particular interest in scientific fields, a line that has very much developed in parallel to those described above. This standpoint has led to the development of RI studies into scientific practices, a field that my second case study fits into and I believe enriches, as it takes the actor's perceptions of right and correctness as its viewpoint.

This argument is further described in the review as organizational RI is introduced. Collective food purchasing groups are taken as the subject matter for a study conducted by myself and Cristina Grasseni (Hankins and Grasseni, 2014). This article differs from those previously cited as it calls for an analysis of working practices within a self-organized distribution and procurement scheme, taking a bottom up approach to RI in practice that has (with a few exceptions noted later in this review) remained largely undeveloped. This article precedes and very much lays the groundwork for this research in that it looks at know-how and the transmission of knowledge from an RI perspective.

The review then goes on to analyze several of the articles that have followed this approach. The articles all involve the use of case studies, setting the foundations for the approach adopted for my PhD research and this subsequent book (see also de Hoop, 2016).

Also included in the review is a description of my experience enrolled on a Delft University course; *Responsible Innovation: Ethics, Safety and Technology*. The completion of this course enabled me to view the problem from another and somewhat competing perspective that that of my own, strengthening my understanding of the concept of responsible design. However related to my own research this concept appears, it is very different in that it seems to look at design as a somewhat measurable process rather than a series of negotiated and shared actions and choices, a fact that I feel somewhat restricts its validity as a critical approach.

8.3 Chapter 3, The European Narrative

Chapter 3 is an investigation into the different ways that the European Commission has developed the concept of Responsible Innovation. It involves both literature-based research and interview transcription and analysis. The interview in question is between myself and René von Schomberg, the architect of the adoption of the use of this terminology in this field. The interview offers an insider perspective to support the literature research. The chapter also offers an overview on the various EU sponsored projects underway or completed that have taken RI as their focus.

The chapter opens with a description of how RI and RRI terminology came into use at EU level. It describes how the EU commitment to RI as promoted through von Schomberg led to the creation and use in EU literature of the derivate RRI (Responsible Research and Innovation), and the effect of this use within the EU funding structure.

This reconstruction is based upon documentation available in the public domain and through the systematic review of publications that have addressed this issue before me (see de Saille, 2015 for a comprehensive account of developments).

The chapter gathers together various examples of the use of the terminology, narrating the development of its positioning within both the economic policies of the EU and within its funding regime. An analysis of the Lund Declarations demonstrates how focus has remained on the issue while wording has changed over time as the concept has become better explained, as it gained in influence through the various FP5 to 8 funding programs, culminating in its cross cutting nature in the Horizon 2020 call (Lund, 2011).

The chapter also presents an overview of EU funded projects in order to expand upon an understanding of how the concept has been put into practice. Short descriptions of the RRI Tools, GREAT, ResAGora, Progress, Responsibility and Responsible Industry projects offer further understanding about how the calls have been interpreted, which projects have succeeded in obtaining funding, their approaches and results.

The chapter concludes with transcriptions of conversations and interviews that I conducted with René von Schomberg as part of my research for my PhD. The interview is introduced through an explanation of his RI matrix publications (Von Schomberg, 2011, 2012), setting the framework for the discussion, questions raised and responses offered.

My aim was to allow von Schomberg the freedom to narrate in his own words, and feel that the transcribed sections deepen the readers understanding of the literature cited above, narrate the development in sequence, point to turning points in the debate and offer a real insider's version of events.

8.4 Chapter 4, The Italian Narrative: The Bassetti Foundation in Milan

I have been extremely fortunate over recent years in being able to collaborate with the Bassetti Foundation in Milan. Chapter 4 represents research carried out both within the Foundation archives and during my working life, from conversations with colleagues and those with whom the foundation has come into contact and through long recorded interviews with President

Piero Bassetti.

I am indebted to Sally Randles of Manchester University who allowed me to use the transcription of an interview she conducted with President Bassetti as inspiration for my own work, and to my colleagues who have provided me with documentation and leads to follow that have allowed me to construct a history of approaches followed within the Foundation over the last twenty years.

The chapter presents the development of the concept of RI from its inception, charting its movement from Milan, through various meetings with like-minded persons across the globe, through the Foundation's participation in large global consortium such as the VIRI, its holding of a place on the Editorial Board of the Journal of Responsible Innovation and its central position within the global RI debate.

The historical overview of the family business sets the scene for the development of the Foundation and its thinking (Garruccio and Maifreda, 2004). The ethical issues that are topic for discussion every day within the Foundation today are in fact the same interests that those leading and managing the family business almost 100 years ago were interested in. The positioning in Milan, the Milanese work ethic and long history of 'la bottega' working practices set the scene for an analysis of the roots of this particular perspective on RI, a perspective that provides the basis for this book.

The chapter contains annotated transcriptions of several interviews and conversations that have taken place between President Bassetti and myself, and other public lectures and interviews that I have transcribed and translated from Italian. The notes refer to documentation that is available through the

Foundation archives, allowing a reconstruction of the historical development of the concept and the Foundation's operations over the last twenty years.

These transcriptions offer an incredible insight into the Foundation from its earliest inception to the present day, and as such an insight into the development of the concept of RI from the viewpoint of an organization that played a large part in its development. Merely from looking at some of the names of people that have collaborated over the years, the reader can understand this central position and the opportunities that it affords for a piece of research such as this. I also take the concept of Poiesis-Intensive Innovation, expanding upon it from my own perspective to form part of the methodological and analytical framework for this research.

One of the issues that is touched upon is the importance of the setting for the development of this particular conception of RI. Milan and the Region of Lombardy in general, offer stimulus for innovation research that cannot be so easily found in other situations. Coupled with president Bassetti's political and civic involvement over the last 50 years, this factor has helped in creating the conception of an active RI, one that has resulted in changes not only in working practices but also in political circles, with changes in local and regional legislation, the adoption of RI within the broader political sphere and the involvement of the Regional Government in the Foundation itself.

The analysis of the documents including the minutes of the original meeting that spawned the foundation demonstrates how forward thinking those present actually were, and how much of what was said on that day and pointed to as topics of study or development have actually come to fruition.

I demonstrate that the points discussed on that day, twenty years ago, are still the points that are under debate within RI today, one reason that the Foundation holds its central position. The analysis offered demonstrates the avant-garde nature of the vision at the time that underpinned the creation of the Foundation, and the influence of such qualities over the development of the concept in the following years.

8.5 Chapter 5, Poiesis Intensive Innovation

This chapter further describes the concept of Poiesis Intensive Innovation as developed by the Bassetti Foundation, offering my own interpretation of its possible meaning and proposing the extension concept of Poiesis Intensive Responsible Innovation (PIRI) (Hankins, 2019).

Having touched upon the concept of Poiesis-Intensive Innovation in chapter 4, this chapter deepens the analysis of the concept, placing its development within the interests and experiences of the Foundation as a whole and specifically President Bassetti, using case studies to demonstrate the model form. My aim is to demonstrate how the social setting and the narratives that prevail within that setting afford the development of particular perspectives, a fundamental idea for this research that repeats across the case studies.

Similarities are drawn between different forms of what has been variously described as rri and RRI (Randles and Loredo, 2013), de-facto RI (Rip, 2010) and grassroots or bottom up RI (Hankins and Grasseni, 2014), with these various models described in comparison to other more top down models of RI that are more prevalent in the academic literature.

The chapter argues that these forms of RI are generated through a process of enskillment through situated learning (Lave and Wenger, 1991, Ingold, 2010, Herzfeld, 2004, Grasseni and Ronzon, 2004). The concept of craftsmanship is described in terms of a learning process within which an individual learns not only the technicalities of the work, but also participates in the construction of a narrative that guides the choices made during the process.

The concept of skilled visions is then explained (Grasseni, 2007), a skilling of the eye gained through the apprenticeship experience that enables the shared understanding and appreciation of beauty within the process and artifacts produced.

The argument of skilled visions is further clarified as I argue that the skilled viewer sees the poiesis intensive process within the beauty of the artifact through their training, and that not only can the viewer learn to see the traits, the process and the decisions taken during that process, but that she can also see the reasoning that underlie those choices represented within a shared and socially constructed narrative that exists within each particular workplace.

In effect I am arguing that the apprentice learns to see the correctness of the production process as it is represented by the beauty of the artifact produced. It is tacit knowledge that is appreciated and shared, forms relationships and status, allows for the creation of networks and the procurement of specialist knowledge and materials on the basis of a shared understanding of a guiding narrative and experienced through beauty.

I then offer an example of how Poiesis-Intensive Innovation can be developed into a concept of Poiesis Intensive Responsible Innovation (PIRI) through two short case studies.

In both cases the case studies display many Poiesis-Intensive characteristics, alongside many RI characteristics. The first case study is that of Roadrunner Engineering, a specialized prosthetics developer in Milan. Their use of high technology accompanied by experimentation in mechanics was born from the fact that the founder himself began experimenting in order to find a solution for his own prosthetic needs. This displays many poiesis factors. The company's choice to work for the improvement of the prosthetic experience as a goal, to publish their finding through open access portals, and work towards creating international protocols for the mass application of their discoveries display several traits of an RI model. This allows me to argue that these examples could offer a basis for the development of a PIRI model, an argument further developed in chapter 7.

The second mini case study reported is that of Officina Corpuscoli, a laboratory experimenting in synthetic biology with fungus in Utrecht and Amsterdam (NL), in order to produce novel materials. Maurizio Montalti, the Director, has a non-conventional background in that he has come through the bio-hacking community. He has learned his trade in an informal setting, through sharing experience with amateur fungal producers, thus providing and learning a poiesis intensive research strategy. He produces materials with the aim of finding a replacement for plastics, shares the results of his work, and works towards educating the general public about the possibilities and perils of synthetic biology, displaying several RI traits. Once more I argue that this could form a model for PIRI.

8.6 Chapter 6, Apprenticeship, Learning to See, Learning to Do: The Upholsterer's Narrative

Chapter 6 is the first of two extended case studies, and is designed as a test of concept for Poiesis-Intensive Innovation and poiesis intensive forms of working, and the analysis and extension of the concept of skilled visions as a sharing of narrative understanding (Grasseni, 2007). The case study involves my return to the field where I conducted my Masters project in Manchester, my former workplace. As in the second case study that follows, this is predominantly based on a critical analysis of recorded conversation between myself and the co-producer of my data, in this case Adam, the senior apprentice from my own apprenticeship period who went on to employ me for several years in the late 1990's within his own business.

This chapter contains a brief description of my own apprenticeship period in terms of work and learning experience, political and economic background, and social experience. The basis of the argument that runs throughout this research can be found across all of these experiences; there is a correct way to do any job, and a skilled worker trained within the social setting in question (in this case a furniture restoration workshop) can learn to see if a particular job has been done correctly. The internal workplace narrative that is developed and maintained through everyday work conversation and embodied practices guides the decision-making process within working practices.

The choices made during the process are interesting in that they are morally laden, as many can only be seen by a trained eye, meaning that the quality of the job can be appreciated through an expert viewing from someone who knows the process. The shared appreciation of this decision-making process and its results creates an understanding of ability and status, which leads to supply opportunities that allow the business to grow and maintain access to high quality materials, in this case fabrics.

The case study also alludes to the fact that apprentices learn the trade through living in a social space, leading to the acquisition of tacit knowledge within a community of practice (Lave, 1993, Lave and Wenger, 1991). An example can be found in the text as the owner of the company where both myself and Adam trained feels that he did not teach us how to restore furniture, i.e. that we taught ourselves. The apprentice is given the possibility of learning through her placing within a social setting, learning through participating, rather than explanation.

Issues of responsibility run through the case study, not only in terms of the taking of responsibility and risk management but also in terms of the business's responsibility to its customers and surrounding community, which are also framed in terms of behavior and choices.

As with previous chapters this section also includes an annotated interview, in this case with the upholsterer Adam black. Before the transcription I explain my methodology, the technical and ethical aspects, describing the process as a co-construction (Oakley, 1981, Heyl, 2000, Dillard, 1982, Porter, 2000). The conversations were recorded at the workplace, giving them a contextual background in which they were not forced but the natural conversation forms of our working lives (Edwards and Holland, 2013).

The conversation addresses approaches to business, the apprenticeship experience, morality and shared understanding from the perspective of two people who share the same skilled vision and who trained together. Ideas surrounding poiesis, style and beauty are also discussed. An interesting aspect of the findings from these discussions is that style also relates to ethics, in that somebody who does not adopt a style that is flexible and can move with the times is seen as not maintaining a just 'moral' standpoint. Her work may be of high quality but not beautiful, and therefore can be criticized, leading to criticism of the worker herself. This supports my argument about skilled visions, but also raises the question of how the boundaries are drawn for this construction of right and wrong. Quality is not the only parameter, it must also be good choice of correct fabric and techniques and it must be beautiful, the beauty appreciated as representing these choices.

Workshop organization is also analyzed in terms of a tidiness and structure. A tidy well-structured workshop represents a structured approach to work and is reflected in the styles and quality of pieces produced. Tools are organized in functional terms as well as in displays of ability, with modern techniques hidden and traditional tools on display as a representation of the skill levels necessary to use them correctly.

Further issues addressed include the role of skill and its appreciation in family life, and more broadly the influence of having learned a trade (or methodology for problem solving) and its effect on our broader lives and outlook.

This chapter uses my own experience of the apprenticeship experience and skilled vision as a test of concept for the central arguments that run through this book. Its topic of investigation is the borderline between what can be explained and what can be shown (Sennett, 2008), and what can be understood and shared as a result. Within this case study beauty and morality are intertwined. An artefact or process cannot be beautiful if it is not moral, and experienced as correctly done, if corners were cut the skilled viewer will know, and its beauty will be impaired. Several aspects of the apprenticeship relationship come to the fore in terms of learning, risk and responsibility. The importance of doing the job right is fundamental, with the position of apprenticeship fundamental for doing the job right. An apprentice is paid a low salary precisely so that she has the opportunity to do the job right, almost regardless of the time needed. Her job is to get the job right at all costs, these costs being limited by the apprenticeship system, allowing the learning experience to sit within the workplace and its quality and beauty driven narrative.

In the case of the apprentice, the contradictions brought about by pricing a job are removed, she is paid the same amount per day regardless of the timeframe a job is completed in, the measurement is not financial but made in terms of result, of beauty. And this beauty is value laden, as it represents the choices made during the restoration process as well as the technical ability on display. I argue that this finding may be applicable to other fields and the other case studies.

A further finding relates to the apprenticeship and learning what tools can be used for, and the making of specific tools for specific jobs. Both of these aspects are also found across the other case studies, as is the element of risk management. In the case of the furniture restorer risk management is based upon economic damage in terms of making mistakes either with fabric or with the furniture itself, with the apprenticeship period bringing more and more responsibility as the years pass. This model can also be applied to the other case studies.

The importance of network, in this case for supplies is also raised. The shared understanding of a person's capacities in technical and relational terms enables different forms of network creation, a factor that is also related to that of risk cited above.

The case study also demonstrates the negotiated nature of the narrative of correctness. Small social working groups of this type rely on relationships of interdependency which leads to constant flux in negotiating status. At Christmas for example the owner is extremely reliant on the apprentice agreeing to work longer hours, giving her the upper hand in any negotiation. In a small working situation that relies on one or two pairs of hands, any refusal or inability to work dramatically affects production capability, leading to a relationship and decision-making process that is negotiated afresh on a daily basis from positions that are constantly in flux.

8.7 Chapter 7, the Scientist's Narrative

This chapter presents my second extended case study, that of Professor Jos Malda, based in the Hubrecht Institute at Utrecht University in the Netherlands. In this chapter I investigate the fit between the findings form the first case study and this setting, noting various similarities between the scientific setting and the workshop setting. The methodology used is similar to that in the first study, meetings and recorded conversations that were then transcribed and annotated.

Although the settings may seem very different, I argue that this case study fits into a model of poiesis intensive working practices and by extension Poiesis-Intensive Innovation, and given the aims and working practices also offers a model that can be analyzed in terms of a Poiesis Intensive Responsible Innovation model and approach (PIRI).

Similarities noted between this working model and that of the previous case study include the organization of tools into historic positioning, the display of products and processes for wider consumption and viewing as part of a shared skilled vision, and the distribution of responsibility and risk amongst several internal and external actors.

The most striking similarities are easy to see in some cases. Prof Malda works in the fabrication of bio materials, the design of which relates to producing an artefact that must then grow. The production of the implant is merely a part of a process, not a final aim. The implant must then be able to grow once transplanted, and its design must bear this in mind leading to design that has to bear possible future use in mind. This is similar to a furniture restorer or designer in that she must design an object bearing in mind the effect of use upon that object. The choice of materials and techniques is not only geared towards beauty, but also to wear. The furniture is not seen or designed as a finished product but is designed with its degeneration in mind, in a similar way to the implant (although that is with growth as well as consumption). The artifact is produced within a perceived future use, with this perceived future forming part of the design process from its inception.

The hierarchical setting also shows similarities, as does the management of risk and responsibility taking. In the case of the furniture maker these relate to physical damage, whereas in the bio fabrication setting it refers to the delegation of responsibility to people with completely different specializations, the following of protocols and the ongoing maintenance and development of tools (3D printers and bio inks).

The physical layouts are also comparable as noted above. The laying out of machinery in chronological order in terms of development, and the way that the users speak about these tools in terms of what they are capable of is also very similar.

The positioning of a 3D printed bone in one case, and a series of photos documenting traditional furniture restoration on show to those who visit the work space in another setting, also represent the sharing of a skilled vision within the workplace. In the case of what may appear to the untrained eye a plastic toy bone in a laboratory setting, a skilled vision reveals an exact replica of a human bone, produced using a 3D printer after a scan, a tool for testing the resistance of an implant. It is not just a plastic bone, it is a work tool. The photos and half-done antique pieces in the workshop setting represent a display of ability, the capability to do but also the will that leads someone to invest days of time into work that can only be appreciated by another professional restorer. No corners were cut. It was done right. They are described as tools to display capabilities to the trained eye, important in promoting conversation between skilled practitioners in possession of a shared skilled vision. This is an argument that can be applied to both situations.

This shared understanding has also allowed Professor Malda to build up a network that allows him to operate at such a high level. Agreements with 3D machine manufacturers as well as sharing developments and learning from others is possible due to the shared understanding of the quality of work and the capabilities that his team possesses. This also applies to both the scientific and artisanal situations.

Many of the problem-solving techniques can also be compared. The use of a strengthening technique for the 3D printed structure that comes from furniture production, and the use of a piled surface taken from textile production both demonstrate how solutions pass between seemingly distant operations. These solutions are not distant however, they have their bases in antique technology, in knowing how to strengthen things, in experience. The application of this know-how in a science laboratory is no different to the application of the same know-how in a furniture workshop.

The second part of this chapter describes Professor Malda's professional development, before introducing an annotated conversation taken from recordings made in his laboratory. Malda touches upon many of the topics that have been discussed and debated within RI and RRI literature. From debate over the possibilities and possible problems that technological developments might bring, to the importance of networks and sharing of information, Malda is well aware of the broad debates within RI literature.

The rationale that Malda offers for the underlying goals and aims of his research seem to match ideas of RI on several levels. His goal to improve surgical techniques in order to avoid secondary repair surgery and improve quality of life certainly seems to resonate with the EU defined global challenges (EC, 2012). The related effect of lowering cost also resonates with this policy (Treaty of Lisbon, 2007). His incorporation of specialists from across a spectrum of disciplines within his project team and his willingness to participate in my research and the broader project of the Bassetti Foundation demonstrate his commitment to such ideas and models.

He also talks about standardization and the need to be able to measure quality in order to use the results of his work on a large scale, as well as discussing the governance of such regimes. He shows a great deal of insight into ethical issues, teaching ethics to all of his students and investing heavily in minimizing and improving upon animal use in experimentation. All of these things could be described as showing similarities to an RI approach, allowing me to make the argument that his work could be seen as offering a possible model for a PIRI analysis.

In sum I have offered an argument and case studies that may be able to form the basis of a model for PIRI. The argument made, building upon Grasseni's 'skilled visions' approach (Grasseni, 2007), is that a workplace narrative that is generated through everyday work conversation use concepts such as functional beauty or precision (and their shared appreciation) as a partial representation of the aim of the process. Those working within the processes experience their learning through a form of apprenticeship, formalized as such in the case of artisan workers and in the scientific community seen through project collaborations and network, both of which are based upon peer review and participation. Each workplace develops its own narrative that guides the shared understanding of correct procedure, developed and shared through in-situ conversation. These narratives all have goals and a specific language of categorization.

In the case of the craft workshop the narrative aim is the production of beauty, an aesthetic value, its appreciation allowing the sharing of status and the appreciation of ability and quality throughout the network that enables the production of such beauty. I believe that a deeper analysis of the science laboratory setting in the second case study would lead to the discovery of similar categories of functional judgement that are shared within these different workplaces and guide working practices. In the case of Officina Corpuscoli, one of the smaller science case studies presented in this book, the aim of the production of beauty is clear to see, alongside that of provoking public debate, two facets of the narrative developed in that particular laboratory.

When Professor Malda explains that actions taken in the laboratory become norms, procedures are guided not only by the existing (old) norms and best practices, but by the team's understanding of what a responsible approach to their shared workshop narrative looks like.

BIBLIOGRAPHY

A

Asante, K., Owen, R. and Williamson, G. 2014. Governance of new product development and perceptions of responsible innovation in the financial sector: insights from an ethnographic case study, *Journal of Responsible Innovation*, 1:1, 9-30.

Anderson, C. 2012. *Makers: The New Industrial Revolution,* McClelland & Stewart, Toronto.

Anzaldo Montoya, M., and Chauvet, M. 2016. Technical Standards in Nanotechnology as an

Instrument of Subordinated Governance: Mexico Case Study. *Journal of Responsible Innovation* 3:3, 132–150.

Atkinson, P. and Silverman, D. 1997. Kundera's Immortality: The Interview. Society and the Invention of the Self, *Qualitative Inquiry* 3:3, 304–25.

B

Bächler, G. 2001. Conflict Transformation Through State Reform. In: *Berghof Handbook for Conflict Transformation.* Available at: http://www.berghof-handbook.net/documents/publications/ baechler_handbook.pdf (accessed 31-01-2017).

Balmer, A., Calvert, J., Marris, C., Molyneux-Hodgson, S., Frow, E., Kearnes, M., Bulpin, K., Schyfter, P., Mackenzie, A, and Martin, P. 2016. Five Rules of Thumb for post-ELSI Interdisciplinary Collaborations, *Journal of Responsible Innovation*, 3:1, 73-80.

Barben, D., Fisher, E., Selin, D. and Guston, D. 2008. Anticipatory Governance of Nanotechnology: Foresight, Engagement, and Integration in E. Hackett, M. Lynch, J. Wajcman (Eds.), *The Handbook of Science and Technology Studies* (third ed.), MIT Press, Cambridge, MA , pp. 979–1000

Bennett, G. 2015. The Moral Economy of Biotechnical Facility, *Journal of Responsible Innovation*, 2:1, 128-132.

Bergen, J. P. 2014. On Engineers Engaging Ethics Through Dislocation and Reconnection, *Journal of Responsible Innovation*, 1:2, 242-244.

Bertagna, G. 2006. *Pensiero manuale. La scommessa di un Sistema Educativo di Istruzione e di Formazione di Pari Dignità.* Milan. Rubbettino

Bessant, J. 2013. Innovation in the Twenty-First Century in Owen, Richard, Bessant, John and Heintz, Maggie (eds). 2013. *Responsible Innovation: Managing the Responsible Emergence of Science and Innovation in Society*, Chichester, Wiley

Biddle, J. 2014. New Frontiers in the Philosophy of Intellectual Property, *Journal of Responsible Innovation*, 1:3, 331-335.

Bijker, W. E. 2010. How is Technology Made?-That is the Question! *Cambridge Journal of Economics* 2010, 34, 63–76.

Bimber, B.A. 1996. *The Politics of Expertise in Congress: The rise and fall of the office of technology assessment.* Albany: State university of New York Press.

Blackstone, A. 2017. *Principles of Sociological Inquiry: Qualitative and Quantitative Methods, v. 1.0*, FlatWorld inc. Maine.

Blok, V. 2019. From Participation to Interuption: Towards an Ethics of Stakeholder Engagement, Participation and

Partnership in Corporate Social Responsibility and Responsible Innovation in von Schomberg, R. and Hankins, J. (eds) *International Handbook on Responsible Innovation. A Global Resource.* Edward Elgar Publishing, Cheltenham (UK) and Northampton (USA).

Blok, V. 2014. Look Who's Talking: responsible innovation, the paradox of dialogue and the voice of the other in communication and negotiation processes, *Journal of Responsible Innovation*, 1:2, 171-190.

Bohannan, P. 1995. *How Culture Works,* New York, Simon and Schuster Free Press.

Bos, C., Walhout, B,. Peine, A. and van Lente, H. 2014. Steering with Big Words: articulating ideographs in research programs, *Journal of Responsible Innovation*, 1:2, 151-170.

Bos, C., Peine, A., and Van Lente, H. 2012. Articulation of Sustainability in Nanotechnology: Funnels of Articulation in Konrad, K., Coenen, C., Dijkstra, A., Milburn, C. and van Lente, H. (eds) 2012. *Shaping Emerging technologies: Governance, Innovation, Discourse.* Akademische Verlagsgesellschaft AKA GmbH, Berlin.

Bosso, C. 2014. Nano risk Governance, Soft Law and the US Regulalatory Regime in Coenen, Christopher, Anne Dijkstra, Camilo Fautz, Julia Guivant, Kornelia Konrad, Colin Milburn and Harro van Lente. 2014. *Innovation and Responsibility: Engaging with New and Emerging Technologies*, pages 7-19, Akademische Verlagsgesellschaft AKA GmbH, Berlin.

Brian, J. D. 2015. Special Perspectives Section: responsible research and innovation for synthetic biology, *Journal of Responsible Innovation*, 2:1, 78-80.

Britt Holbrook, J. and Briggle, A. 2014. Knowledge Kills Action – why principles should play a limited role in policy-making, *Journal of Responsible Innovation*, 1:1, 51-66.

Bronk D.W. 1975. The National Science Foundation: Origins, hopes, and aspirations. *Science*

188(4187), 409–414.

Bronson, K. 2015. Responsible to Whom? Seed Innovations and the Corporatization of Agriculture, *Journal of Responsible Innovation*, 2:1, 62-77.

C

C. (2011). 5023. 2011. Science in Society Work Programme 2012 Part 5 – Capacities. Downloadable at http://ec.europa.eu/research/participants/portal/doc/call/fp7/common/31557–5._science_in_society_wp2012_en.pdf.

Callon, M., Méadel, C. and Rabeharisoa, V. 2002. The economy of qualities, *Economy and Society*, 31:2, 194-217.

Campa, M. F., Wolfe, A.K., Bjornstad, D.J. and Shumpert, B.L. 2014. From Lab Bench to Fuel Pump: Researchers' Choices in the Development of Lignocellulosic Biofuels in Coenen, Christopher, Anne Dijkstra, Camilo Fautz, Julia Guivant, Kornelia Konrad, Colin Milburn and Harro van Lente. 2014. *Innovation and Responsibility: Engaging with New and Emerging Technologies*, pages 39-53, Akademische Verlagsgesellschaft AKA GmbH, Berlin.

Carson, R. 1962 *Silent Spring*. Boston MA: Houghton Mifflin

Cassia, L., Tommaso Minola and Stefano Paleari. 2011. *EntrepRenéurship and Technological Change*, Cheltenham, Edward Elgar

Čeičytė, J. 2015. Responsible innovation, *Journal of Responsible Innovation*, 2:2, 237-241.

Chalmers, D., McWhirter, R.E., Nicol, D., Whitton, T., Otlowski, M., Burgess, M.M., Foote, S.J., Critchley, C. and Dickinson, J.L. 2014. New Avenues Within Community Engagement: addressing the ingenuity gap in our approach to health research and future provision of health care, *Journal of Responsible Innovation*, 1:3, 321-328.

Chilvers, J. 2010 Sustainable Participation? Mapping Out and Reflecting on the Field of Public Dialogue in Science and Technology, *Sciencewise-ERC*, Harwell

Coenen, C., Dijkstra, A. Fautz, C. Guivant, J. Konrad, K. Milburn, C. and van Lente, H. 2014. *Innovation and Responsibility: Engaging with New and Emerging Technologies,* Akademische Verlagsgesellschaft AKA GmbH, Berlin.

Collingridge, D. 1980. *The Social Control of technology*, Open University Press, Milton Keynes.

Collins, H. 2010. *Tacit and Explicit Knowledge*, University of Chicago Press, Chicago

COM. 2011. Proposal for a Regulation of the European Parliament and of the Council: Establishing Horizon 2020 – the Framework Programme for Research and Innovation (2014–2020). Brussels: Official Journal of the European Union

Cussins, C. M. 1998. 'Ontological Choreography: agency for women patients in an infertility clinic', in M. Berg and S. Mol (eds) *Diff erences in Medicine: Unraveling Practices, Techniques, and Bodies*, Durham NC: Duke University Press.

D

Deblonde, M. 2015. Responsible research and innovation:

building knowledge arenas for glocal sustainability research, *Journal of Responsible Innovation*, 2:1, 20-38.

de Hoop, E., Pols, A. and Romijn, H. 2016. Limits to responsible innovation, *Journal of Responsible Innovation*, 3:2, 110-134.

Demers-Payette, O., Lehoux, P. and Daudelin, G. 2016. Responsible Research and Innovation: A productive model for the future of medical innovation. Journal of Responsible Innovation 3:3, 1-21.

De Boer, B., Hoek, J. and Kudina, O. 2018. Can the technological mediation approach improve technology assessment? A critical view from 'within', *Journal ofResponsible Innovation*, 5:3, 299-315.

de Jong, I., Kupper, F. and Broerse, J. 2016. Inclusive deliberation and action in emerging RRI practices: the case of neuroimaging in security management, *Journal of Responsible Innovation,* 3:1, 26-49.

de Saille, S. 2015. Innovating innovation policy: the emergence of 'Responsible Research and Innovation', *Journal of Responsible Innovation, 2:2*, 152-168,

Di Giulio, D., Groves, C., Monteiro, M and Taddei, R. 2016. Communicating Through Vulnerability: knowledge politics, inclusion and responsiveness in responsible research and innovation, *Journal of Responsible Innovation*, 3:2, 92-109.

Dillard, A. 1982. *Living By Fiction*. New York, Harper & Row.

E

EC. 1997. Research and Technological Development Activities of the European Union: Annual Report 1996 (CG-NA-17–242-EN-C).

EC. 2009. Preparing Europe for a New Renaissance: A Strategic View of the European Research Area: First Report of the European Research Area Board 2009 (KI-NA-23905-EN-C).

EC. 2011. Newsletter, DG Research Workshop on Responsible Research & Innovation in Europe. May 16– 17, 2001.

EC. 2012. Responsible Research and Innovation: Europe's Ability to Respond to Societal Challenges (KI- 31-12-921-EN-C)

EC. 2013. Options for Strengthening Responsible Research and Innovation (KI-NA-25-766-EN-C).

Edwards, R. and Holland, J. 2013. *What is Qualitative Interviewing?* London, Bloomsbury.

Eggleson, K. and Berry, S. A. 2015. Macroethics Exploration with Impact: technological innovators reconsider profound personal and societal questions after viewing the film FIXED: The Science/Fiction of Human Enhancement , *Journal of Responsible Innovation, 2:2,* 220-233.

EEA, 2001. *Late Lessons from early Warning: the precautionary principle 1896–2000.* Copenhagen

F

Fisher, E. 2006. Midstream Modulation of Technology: Governance From Within, *Bulletin of Science Technology Society,* 26:6. 485-496.

Fisher, E. 2007. Ethnographic Invention: probing the capacity of laboratory decisions. *Nanoethics* 1:2: 155-165.

Fisher, E. and Rip, A. 2013. Responsible Innovation: Multi-Level Dynamics and Soft Innovation Practices in Owen, R. Bessant, J. and Heintz, M. (eds). 2013. *Responsible Innovation:*

Managing the Responsible Emergence of Science and Innovation in Society, Chichester, Wiley

E. Fisher, E., Mahajan, R and Mitcham, C. 2006. Midstream modulation of technology: governance from within, *Bulletin of Science, Technology & Society*, 26, 485–496.

Fisher, E., O'Rourke, M., Evans, R., Kennedy, E.B., Gorman, M.E. and Seager, T.P. 2015. Mapping the Integrative Field: taking stock of socio-technical collaborations, *Journal of Responsible Innovation*, 2:1, 39-61.

Fisher, E. 2016. Mission Impossible? Developing responsible innovation in a global context, *Journal of Responsible Innovation*, 3:2, 89-91.

Fleming Miller, L, 2014. Better humans? Understanding the enhancement project, *Journal of Responsible Innovation*, 1:2, 220-224.

Fleming Miller, L. 2015. Anticipating the ultimate innovation, volitional evolution: can it not be promoted or attempted responsibly? *Journal of Responsible Innovation*, 2:3, 280-300.

Foley, R. W., Bernstein, M.J. and Wiek, A. 2016. Towards an Alignment of Activities, Aspirations and Stakeholders for Responsible Innovation. *Journal of Responsible Innovation* 3:3, 209-232.

Forsberg, E.M. 2019. Responsible Research and Innovation in the Broader Innovation System: Reflections on Responsibility in Standardization, Assessment and Patenting Practices in von Schomberg, R. and Hankins, J. (eds) *International Handbook on Responsible Innovation. A Global Resource.* Edward Elgar Publishing, Cheltenham (UK) and Northampton (USA).

Frankel, M.S. 2015 .An empirical exploration of scientists' social responsibilities, *Journal of Responsible Innovation*, 2:3.

Friedman, B. 1996 Value-sensitive design in *ACM Interactions*, 3:6, 17–23.

Fuller, S. 2009. *Review of the handbook of science and technology studies*. Isis 100:1, 207–209.

G

Gabriela C., Longstaff, H., Hanney, P., and Secko, D.M. 2015 Responsible innovation: an approach for extracting public values concerning advanced biofuels, *Journal of Responsible Innovation*, 2:3, 246-265.

Ganzevles, J., van Est, R., and Nentwich, M.. 2014. Embracing Variety: introducing the inclusive modelling of (Parliamentary) technology assessment, *Journal of Responsible Innovation*, 1:3, 292-313.

Garfinkel, H. 1996. Ethnomethodology's Program, *Social PsychologyQuarterly* 59:1, 5–21.

Garruccio, R. and Maifreda, G. 2004. *Giannino Bassetti. L' imprenditore raccontato*. Milan, Rubbettino.

Gibson, J. 1979. *Ecological Approach to Visual Perception,* London, Lawrence Erlbaum

Glerup, C. and Horst, M. 2014. Mapping 'Social Responsibility' in science, *Journal of Responsible Innovation*, 1:1, 31-50.

Grimpe, B., Hartswood, M., and Jirotka, M. 2014. "Towards a Closer Dialogue Between Policy and Practice: Responsible Design in HCI. *Proceedings of the SIGCHI Conference on Human Factors in Computing Systems,* 2965-2974.

Grimpe, B., Hartswood, M., Asante, K., Owen, R. and Jirotka, M. 2014b. "Responsible Innovation in Financial Markets: A Research Programme". *SIGCHI Extended Abstracts*.

Grasseni, C. and Ronzon, F. 2004. *Pratiche e cognizione. Note di ecologia della cultura*. Roma, Meltemi

Grasseni, C. (ed). 2007. *Skilled Visions: Between Apprenticeship and Standards*. Oxford, Berghahn Publishers.

Grasseni, C. 2009. *Developing Skill, Developing Vision. Practices of Locality at the Foot of the Alps*. Oxford, Berghahn.

Grinbaum, A. and Groves, C. 2013. What is "Responsible" about Responsible Innovation? Understanding the Ethical Issues in Owen, R. Bessant, J. and Heintz, M. (eds). 2013. *Responsible Innovation: Managing the Responsible Emergence of Science and Innovation in Society*, Chichester, Wiley

Groves, C. 2009. "Future Ethics: Risk, Care and Non-Reciprocal Responsibility." Journal of Global Ethics 5:1, 17–31.

Groves, C. 2014. *Care, Uncertainty and Intergenerational Ethics*. London: Palgrave

Macmillan.

Groves, C., Henwood, K., Shirani, F., Butler, C., Parkhill, K. and Pidgeon, N. 2016. The Grit in the Oyster: using energy biographies to question socio-technical imaginaries of 'smartness', *Journal of Responsible Innovation*, 3:1, 4-25,

Grunwald, A. 2014. The hermeneutic side of responsible research and innovation, *Journal of Responsible Innovation*, 1:3, 274-291.

Grunwald, A. 2014b. Technology Assessment for Responsible Innovation, in Van den Hoeven et.al (eds.), *Responsible innovation 1: Innovative Solutions for Global Issues*: London, Springer.

Gupta, A. 2001. Searching for shared norms: Global anticipatory governance of biotechnology. PhD Thesis, Yale University, New Haven, CT.

Guston, D. 2013. "Daddy, Can I Have A Puddle Gator?": Creativity, Anticipation and Responsible Innovation in Owen, R. Bessant, J. and Heintz, M. (eds). 2013. *Responsible Innovation: Managing the Responsible Emergence of Science and Innovation in Society*, Chichester, Wiley

Guston D. 2014. Responsible innovation: a going concern, *Journal of Responsible Innovation*, 1:2, 147-150.

Guston D. 2014a. Giving content to responsible innovation, *Journal of Responsible Innovation*, 1:3, 251-253.

Guston, D. 2014b. Understanding 'Anticipatory Governance', *Social Studies of Science*, Vol. 44:2 218–242

Guston, D. 2015. Responsible innovation: who could be against that?, *Journal of Responsible Innovation*, 2:1, 1-4.

Guston, D., Fisher, E., Grunwald, A., Owen, R., Swierstra, T., and van der Burg, S. 2014. Responsible Innovation: motivations for a new journal, *Journal of Responsible Innovation*, 1:1, 1-8.

Guston, D. 2015. Want, Settle, Get, *Journal of Responsible Innovation*, 2:2, 149-151.

Guston, D. 2015. People, persons and publics, Journal of Responsible Innovation, 2:3, 243-245.

Guston, D. and Sarewitz, D. 2002. Real Time Technology Assessment. *Technology in Culture* 24, 93-109

H

Hartswood, M., Grimpe, B., Jirotka, M. and Anderson, S. 2014. Towards the Ethical Governance of Smart Society In Daniele Miorandi, Vincenzo Maltese, Micheal Rovatsos, Anton Nijhold and James Stewart (eds): *Social Collective Intellegence: Combining the Powers of Humans and Machines to Build a Smarter Society*. Springer.

Hartswood, M., Grimpe, B. and Jirotka, M. 2013. Towards Ethical Governance of Social Machines, International Conference on Cloud and Green Computing (CGC), 426-427.

Hankins, J. 2012. *A Handbook for Responsible Innovation.* I Libri Della fondazione Giannino Bassetti, Milan.

Hankins, J. 2013. Endnotes: Building Capacity for Responsible Innovation in Owen, R. Bessant, J. and Heintz, M. (eds). 2013. *Responsible Innovation: Managing the Responsible Emergence of Science and Innovation in Society*, Chichester, Wiley

Hankins, J. 2014. Notes from the S.NET conference, *Journal of Responsible Innovation*, 1:1, 125-128

Hankins, J. 2015. The GM Food Debate within Responsible Innovation, *Formazione, Lavoro, Persona*, 4:14, 201-206.

Hankins, J. 2019. Grass-roots case studies in 'Poiesis Intensive' responsible innovation (PIRI) von Schomberg, R. and Hankins, J. (eds) *International Handbook on Responsible Innovation. A Global Resource.* Edward Elgar Publishing, Cheltenham (UK) and Northampton (USA).

Hankins, J. 2015. Innovation and Responsibility: engaging with new and emerging technologies, *Journal of Responsible Innovation*, 2:2, 234-237.

Hankins, J and Grasseni, C. 2014. Collective Food Purchasing Networks in Italy as a Case Study of Responsible Innovation in

Glocalism, 2014:1, Online.

Hemphill, T. A. 2014. Responsible Innovation and Patent Assertion entities, *Journal of Responsible Innovation*, 1:3, 314-320.

Hemphill, T. A. 2016. Responsible innovation in industry: a cautionary note on corporate social responsibility, *Journal of Responsible Innovation*, 3:1, 81-87.

Herzfeld, M. 2004. *The Body Impolitic: Artisans and Artifice in the Global Hierarchy of Value*, Chicago, Chicago University Press.

Heyl, B.S. 2000. Ethnographic Interviewing, in Atkinson, P, Coffey, A., Delamont, S., Lofland, J. and Lofland, L. (eds). *Handbook of Ethnography*. London: Sage.

Hodges, K. and Angelos, P. 2014 Responsible Innovation in Surgery: a proposal for an anonymous registry of surgical innovation, *Journal of Responsible Innovation*, 1:2, 208-213.

Holbrook, J. 2014. Early Engagement and New Technologies: opening up the laboratory, *Journal of Responsible Innovation*, 1:2, 224-227.

Hoop, E., Pols, A. and Romijn, H (2016) Limits to responsible innovation, Journal of Responsible Innovation, 3:2, 110-134

Hoople, G. 2014. Engineering Ethics in every Decision, *Journal of Responsible Innovation*, 1:2, 241-242.

Hurlbut, J.B. 2015. Reimagining Responsibility in Synthetic Biology, *Journal of Responsible Innovation*, 2:1, 113-116.

Hutchins, E. 1995. *Cognition in the Wild*, MIT Press, Cambridge MA.

I

Ingold, T. 2000. *The Perception of the Environment: Essays on Livelihood, Dwelling, and Skill*. London, Routledge.

Ingold, T. 2010. The Textility of Making. In *Cambridge Journal of Economics* 2010, 34, 63–76

J

Jasanoff, S. 2003. Technologies of humility: citizen participation in governing science

Minerva, 41, 223–244.

K

Kahl, Linda J. 2015 Realizing Positive Network Effects in Synthetic Biology, *Journal of Responsible Innovation*, 2:1, 137-139.

Kay, Luciano. 2016. We Need to Innovate Fast. *Journal of Responsible Innovation* 3:3, 269-265

Karinen, R and Guston, D. 2010. Toward anticipatory governance: the experience with nanotechnology. Governing future technologies in *Sociology of the Sciences Yearbook,* 27, 217–232.

Kiran, A. H., Oudshoorn, N. and Verbeek, P. 2015. Beyond Checklists: toward an ethical-constructive technology assessment, *Journal of Responsible Innovation*, 2:1, 5-19

Konrad, K., Coenen, C., Dijkstra, A., Milburn, C. and van Lente, H. (eds) 2012. *Shaping Emerging technologies: Governance, Innovation, Discourse,* Berlin, Akademische Verlagsgesellschaft AKA GmbH.

Kuzma, J. 2015 Translational governance research for synthetic biology, *Journal of Responsible Innovation*, 2:1, 109-112.

L

Lave, J. 1988. *Cognition in practice. Mind, mathematics and culture in everyday life*, Cambridge, Cambridge University Press.

Lave, J. 1993. The Practice of Learning, in Chaiklin S. e Lave J. (ed), *Understanding Practice. Perspectives on Activity and Context*, Cambridge, Cambridge University Press, 3-32.

Lave, J. and Wenger, E. 1991. *Situated Learning. Legitimate Peripheral Participation*, Cambridge, Cambridge University Press

Lawler, S. 2002. Narrative in social research, in T. May (ed.) *Qualitative Research in Action*, London: Sage.

Lee, R.G. and Petts, J. 2013 Adaptive Governance for responsible Innovation in Owen, R. Bessant, J. and Heintz, M. (eds). 2013. *Responsible Innovation: Managing the Responsible Emergence of Science and Innovation in Society*, Chichester, Wiley

Li, F., Owen, R. and Simakova, E. 2015. Framing responsible innovation in synthetic biology: the need for a critical discourse analysis approach, *Journal of Responsible Innovation,* 2:1, 104-108.

Li, N., Brossard, D., Yi-Fan Su, L., Liang, X., Xenos, M. And Scheufele, D.A. 2015. Policy Decision-making, Public Involvement and Nuclear Energy: what do expert stakeholders think and why? *Journal of Responsible Innovation,* 2:3, 266-279.

Lindner, R., Kuhlmann, S., Randles, S., Bedsted,B., Gorgoni, G., Griessler, E., Loconto, A. And Mejlgaard, N. 2016. *Navigating Towards Shared Responsibility: Navigating Towards Shared Responsibility in Research and Innovation -*

Approach, Process and Results of the Res-AGorA Project, Karlsruhe, Fraunhofer Institute foe Systems and Innovation Research

Liu, J.A. 2015. Synthetic biology in Global Health: lessons from history and anthropology, *Journal of Responsible Innovation,* 2:1, 96-99.

M

Macnaghten, P., Owen, R., Stilgoe, J., Wynne, B., Azevedo, A. de Campos, A., Chilvers, J., Dagnino, R., di Giulio, G., Frow, E., Garvey, B., Groves, C., Hartley, S., Knobel, M., Kobayashi, E., Lehtonen, M., Lezaun, J., Mello, L., Monteiro, M., Pamplona da Costa, M, Rigolin, C., Rondani, B., Staykova, M., Taddei, R., Till, C., Tyfield, D., Wilford, S. and Velho, L.. 2014. Responsible Innovation Across Borders: tensions, paradoxes and possibilities, *Journal of Responsible Innovation,* 1:2, 191-199.

Macnaghten, P. and Chilvers, J. 2013. The future of science governance: publics, policies, practices in *Environment and Planning* C: 32: 530–548

Macnaghten, P. 2016. Responsible Innovation and the Reshaping of Existing Technological Trajectories: The Hard Case of Genetically Modified Crops. *Journal of Responsible Innovation* 3:3, 282-289

Malda, J., Visser, J., Melchels, F.P., Jüngst, T., Hennink, W.E., Dhert, W.J.A., Groll, J.and Hutmacher D.W. 2013. 25th Anniversary Article: Engineering Hydrogels for Biofabrication in *Advanced Materials,* 25:36, 5011–5028

Mampuys, R. and Brom, F.W.A. 2015. Governance Strategies for Responding to Alarming Studies on the Safety of GM Crops, *Journal of Responsible Innovation*, 2:2, 201-219.

Mason, J. 2002. *Qualitative Researching , Six Strategies for Mixing Methods and Linking Data in Social Science Research* , Real Life Methods NCRM Node Working Paper. Online publication accessed 31.3.17 www.socialsciences.manchester.ac.uk/morgancentre/realities/wps/4–2006–07-rlm-

Montoya, M.A. and Chauvet, M. 2016. Technical Standards in Nanotechnology as an Instrument of Subordinated Governance: Mexico case study, *Journal of Responsible Innovation*, 3:2, 135-153.

Meyer, M. 2015. Devices and Trajectories of Responsible Innovation: problematising synthetic biology, *Journal of Responsible Innovation*, 2:1, 100-103.

Miller, C. A. 2015. Modeling Risk in Complex Bioeconomies, *Journal of Responsible Innovation*, 2:1, 124-127.

Muniesa, F. and Lenglet, M. 2013 Responsible Innovation in Finance: Directions and implications in Owen, R. Bessant, J. and Heintz, M. (eds). 2013. *Responsible Innovation: Managing the Responsible Emergence of Science and Innovation in Society*, Chichester, Wiley

N

Nordmann, A. 2019. The ties that bind: collective experimentation and participatory design as paradigms for responsible innovation von Schomberg, R. and Hankins, J. (eds) *International Handbook on Responsible Innovation. A Global Resource.* Edward Elgar Publishing, Cheltenham (UK) and

Northampton (USA).

Nordmann, A. 2014. Responsible Innovation, the Art and Craft of Anticipation, *Journal of Responsible Innovation*, 1:1, 87-98.

Nordmann, A. 2007. If and then: A critique of speculative nanoethics. *NanoEthics* 1:1, 31–46

O

Oakley, A. 1981. Interviewing women: a contradiction in terms, in H. Roberts (ed.) *Doing Feminist Research* , London, Routledge.

Oudheusden, M. van. 2014. Where are the politics in responsible innovation? European governance, technology assessments, and beyond, *Journal of Responsible Innovation*, 1:1, 67-86.

Owen, R., Macnaghten, P. and Stilgoe, J. 2012 Responsible Research and Innovation: from science in society to science for society, with society. *Science and Public policy* 6. 751-760

Owen, R. Stilgoe, J. Macnaghten, P. Gorman, M. Fisher, E. and Guston, D. 2013. A Framework for Responsible Innovation in Owen, R. Bessant, J. and Heintz, M. (eds). 2013. *Responsible Innovation: Managing the Responsible Emergence of Science and Innovation in Society*, Chichester, Wiley

Owen, R, Bessant, John and Heintz, Maggie (eds). 2013. *Responsible Innovation: Managing the Responsible Emergence of Science and Innovation in Society*, Chichester, Wiley

Owen, R. 2014. The UK Engineering and Physical Sciences Research Council's commitment to a framework for responsible innovation, *Journal of Responsible Innovation*, 1:1, 113-117.

P

Parkhill, K., Pidgeon, N., Corner, A. and Vaughan, N. 2013. Deliberation and Responsibility: a Geoengineering Case Study in Owen, R. Bessant, J. and Heintz, M. (eds). 2013. *Responsible Innovation: Managing the Responsible Emergence of Science and Innovation in Society*, Chichester, Wiley

Pavie, X. and Carthy, D. 2013 Responsible-Innovation in Practice: How to implement Responsibility Across an Organization, Cahier Innovation & Society

Pellé, S. 2016. Responsibility as Care for Research and Innovation. *Proceedings of the*

PACITA conference, The next horizon of Technology assessment. 25–27 February 2015.

Pellé, S. 2016a. Process, Outcomes, Virtues: The Normative Strategies of Responsible Research and Innovation and the Challenge of Moral Pluralism. *Journal of Responsible Innovation* 3:3, 233-254.

Pellé, S. 2017a. *Business, Innovation and Responsibility*. London, Wiley-ISTE.

Pellé, S. 2017b. Responsibility in Research and Innovation: The Potential of Care Ethics. In Robert, G., Reber, B. and Pearson, J. (eds) *RRI. Concept and Practices*, London, Routledge.

Pinch, T. 2010. On making infrastructure visible: putting to non-humans to rights. In *Cambridge Journal of Economics* 34, 63–76.

Polanyi, M. 1966. *The Tacit Dimension*, Chicago, University of Chicago Press.

Porter, E.J. 2000. Setting Aside the Identity-Furor: Staying her Story-Course of Same-ness, *Qualitative Inquiry* 6:2, 238–50.

Poznic, M. 2014. Technological Models: epistemic and responsible perspectives, *Journal of Responsible Innovation*, 1:2, 244-246.

R

Rainey, S., Stahl, B., Shaw, M. and Reinsborough, M. 2019. Ethics Management and Responsible Research and Innovation in the Human Brain Project in Responsible Innovation in ICT: Challenges for Industry in von Schomberg, R. and Hankins, J. (eds) *International Handbook on Responsible Innovation. A Global Resource.* Edward Elgar Publishing, Cheltenham (UK) and Northampton (USA).

Raman, S. 2014. Responsible Innovation: from Concept to Practice, *Journal of Responsible Innovation*, 1:3, 329-331.

Raman, S. 2015 Responsive Novelty: taking innovation seriously in societal research agendas for synthetic biology, *Journal of Responsible Innovation*, 2:1, 117-120.

Randles, S. 2019. Interview with Piero Bassetti, President of Fondazione Giannino Bassetti in von Schomberg, R. and Hankins, J. (eds) *International Handbook on Responsible Innovation. A Global Resource.* Edward Elgar Publishing, Cheltenham (UK) and Northampton (USA).

Randles, S., Youtie, J., Guston, D., Harthorn, B., Newfield, C., Shapira, P., Wickson, F., Rip, A. von Schomberg, R. and Pidgeon, N. 2012. A Trans-Atlantic Conversation on Responsible Innovation and Responsible Governance. in: Van Lente, H., Coenen, C., Fleischer, T., Konrad, K., Krabbenborg, L., Milburn, C., Thoreau, F. and Zülsdorf, T. (Eds.) *Little by Little: Expansions of Nanoscience and Emerging Technologies.* Heidelberg: Akademische Verlagsgesellschaft, 2012. 169-180.

Randles, S. and Laredo, P. 2013. 'Doing Good/Being Good: Five Building Blocks of an Institutionalist Sociology of Responsible Innovation', Presentation to the S.NET Conference, Boston 27-29 October 2013.

Randles, S., Dorbeck-Jung, B.R., Lindner, R. and Rip, A. 2014 *Where to Next for Responsible Innovation?* In: C. Coenen & A. Dijkstra & C. Fautz & J. Guivant & C. Milburn & H. van Lente (Eds.), *Innovation and Responsibility: Engaging with New and Emerging Technologies. Studies of New and Emerging Technologies* (vol. 5). IOS Press, 19 - 37. ISBN 9781614994305

Randles, S and Laasch, O. 2015. *Theorising the Normative Business Model in Organization & Environment, London: sage.*

Randles, S., Laredo, P., Laconto, A., Walhout, B., Lindner, R. 2016. Framings and frameworks: six grand narratives of de facto rri in Lindner, R., Kuhlmann, S., Randles, S., Bedsted, B., Gorgoni, G., Griessler, E., Loconto, A. and Mejlgaard, N. (eds), *Navigating Towards Shared Responsibility in Research and Innovation: Approach, Process and Results of the Res-AGorA Project,* Fraunhofer ISI

Reale, G. 2003. *Per una nuova interpretazione di Platone*: Milan: V&P Universita'.

Reichow, A. and Dorbeck-jung, B. 2014. How Can We Characterize Nano Specific Soft regulation? Lessons From Occupational Health and Safety Governance, In Coenen, C., Dijkstra, A., Fautz, C., Guivant, J., Milburn, C., and van Lente, H. (Eds.), *Innovation and Responsibility: Engaging with New and Emerging Technologies. Studies of New and Emerging Technologies* (vol5). IOS Press, (pp. 83-102)

Riessman, C. K. 1993. Narrative Analysis, *Qualitative Research*

Methods Volume 30, London/New Delhi: Sage.

Rip, A., Misa, T. and Schot, G. (eds). 1995. *Managing technology in Society*. London, Pinter Publishers.

Rip, A. 2016. The Clothes of the Emperor. An Essay on RRI in and Around Brussels. *Journal of Responsible Innovation* 3:3, 290-304.

Robaey, Z. 2014. A Commentary on Engineering Ethics Education, or how to bring about change without needing scandals, *Journal of Responsible Innovation*, 1:2, 248-249.

Robinson, D. K. R. 2009. Co-Evolutionary Scenarios: An Application to Prospecting Futures of the Responsible Development of Nanotechnology in *Technological Forecasting and Social Change* 76:9, 1222–1239.

Rolfe, D. 2014. No Field is an Island: why we should have been having an interdisciplinary discussion about nano-ethics all along, *Journal of Responsible Innovation*, 1:2, 240-241.

Ruggiu, D. 2013. A Rights based Model of governance: The Case of Human Enhancement and the Role of Ethics in Europe in Konrad, K., Coenen, C., Dijkstra, A., Milburn, C. and van Lente, H. (eds) 2012. *Shaping Emerging technologies: Governance, Innovation, Discourse,* Berlin, Akademische Verlagsgesellschaft AKA GmbH. 103-117

S

Sadowski, J. 2014. Exoskeletons in a disabilities context: the need for social and ethical research, *Journal of Responsible Innovation*, 1:2, 214-219.

Sayer, A. 2011. *Why things matter to people: Social science, values and ethical life*. Cambridge, England: Cambridge University Press.

Schot, J. and Rip, A. 1996. The Past and Future of Constructive Technology Assessment in *Technological Forecasting and Social Change* 54, 251-268.

Schroeder, D and Ladikas, M. 2015. Towards principled Responsible Research and Innovation: employing the Difference Principle in funding decisions, *Journal of Responsible Innovation*, 2:2, 169-183.

Schuurbiers, D. 2011. What Happens in the Lab: applying midstream modulation to enhance critical reflection in the laboratory in *Science and Engineering Ethics*, 17, 769–788.

Selin, C. 2014. On not forgetting futures, *Journal of Responsible Innovation*, 1:1, 103-108.

Sennett, R. 2008. *The Craftsman*, London, Penguin

Shapira, P., Youtie, J. and Li, Y. 2015. Social Science Contributions Compared in Synthetic Biology and Nanotechnology, *Journal of Responsible Innovation*, 2:1, 143-148.

Simakove, E. and Coenen, C. 2013. Visions, Hype, and Expectations: a Place for Responsibility in Owen, R. Bessant, J. and Heintz, M. (eds). 2013. *Responsible Innovation: Managing the Responsible Emergence of Science and Innovation in Society*, Chichester, Wiley

Simirenko, L., Harmon-Smith, M., Visel, A., Rubin, E.M. and Hillson, N.J. 2015. The Joint Genome Institute's synthetic biology internal review process, *Journal of Responsible Innovation*, 2:1, 133-136.

Smits, R. and den Hertog, P. 2007. TA and the Management of Innovation in economy and society In *International Journal on Foresight and innovation Policy 3*, 28–52.

Spruit, S. 2014. Responsible Innovation through Ethics Education: educating to change research practice, *Journal of Responsible Innovation*, 1:2, 246-247.

Stahl, B., Borsella, E., Porcari, A. And Mantovani, E. 2019. Responsible Innovation in ICT: Challenges for Industry in von Schomberg, R. and Hankins, J. (eds). *International Handbook on Responsible Innovation. A Global Resource.* Edward Elgar Publishing, Cheltenham (UK) and Northampton (USA).

Stahl, B. 2013. The role of privacy in an emerging framework, *Science and Public Policy journal*, 40:6, 708-716

Stahl, B. Eden, G. and Jirokta, J. 2013. Responsible Research and Innovation in Information and communication Technology: Identifying and Engaging with the Ethical Implications of ICT's in Owen, R. Bessant, J. and Heintz, M. (eds). 2013. *Responsible Innovation: Managing the Responsible Emergence of Science and Innovation in Society*, Chichester, Wiley

Stahl, B, McBride, N., Wakunuma, K. and Flick, C. 2014. The Empathic Care Robot: A prototype of responsible research and innovation, *Technological Forecasting and Social Change*, 84, 74–85.

Stanley, L, and Wise, S, 1993. *Breaking out again.* London, Routledge.

Stemerding. D. 2019. From Technology Assessment to Responsible Research and Innovation in Synthetic Biology in von Schomberg, R. and Hankins, J. (eds) *International Handbook on Responsible Innovation. A Global Resource* Edward Elgar Publishing, Cheltenham (UK) and Northampton (USA).

Stemerding, D. 2015. iGEM as Laboratory in Responsible

Research and Innovation, *Journal of Responsible Innovation*, 2:1, 140-142.

Stilgoe, J. 2011. A Question of Intent. *Nature Climate Change 1*, 325 – 326.

Stilgoe, J. Owen, R. MacNaghten, P. 2013. Developing a framework for responsible innovation. *Res. Policy,* Volume 42, Issue 9, November 2013, Pages 1568–1580.

Stirling, A. 2016. Addressing Scarcities in Responsible Innovation. *Journal of Responsible Innovation* 3:3, 132-150.

Strauss, L. 1962. *The Savage Mind.* Chicago, Chicago University Press

Suchman, L. 2007. *Human-Machine Reconfigurations, Plans and Situated Actions*. Cambridge, Cambridge University Press.

Sunderland, M. E, Taebi, B., Carson, C. and Kastenberg, W. 2014. Teaching Global Perspectives: engineering ethics across international and academic borders, *Journal of Responsible Innovation,* 1:2, 228-239.

Sutcliffe, Hilary. 2011. A Report on Responsible Research and Innovation. Matter. https://ec.europa.eu/research/science-society/document_library/pdf_06/rri-report-hilary-sutcliffe_en.pdf
Last accessed 14/11/2019

Sutton, V. 2014. Hydrogen: A model for Regulating Emerging Technologies in Coenen, C., Dijkstra, A., Fautz, C., Guivant, J., Konrad, K., Milburn, C. and van Lente, H. 2014. *Innovation and Responsibility: Engaging with New and Emerging Technologies*, Akademische Verlagsgesellschaft AKA GmbH, Berlin. 53-61.

Sykes, K. and Macnaghten, P. 2013. Responsible Innovation –

Opening Up Dialogue and Debate, in Owen, R. Bessant, J. and Heintz, M. (eds). 2013. *Responsible Innovation: Managing the Responsible Emergence of Science and Innovation in Society*, Chichester, Wiley

T

Tait, J. 2009. Upstream Engagement and the Governance of Science. The shadow of the genetically modified crops experience in *Europe EMBO Rep. 2009 Aug; 10(Suppl 1):* S18-S22.doi:10.1038/embor.2009.138

Taebi, B, A., Cuppen, C., Dignum, M. and Pesch, U. 2014 Responsible innovation as an endorsement of public values: the need for interdisciplinary research, *Journal of Responsible Innovation*, 1:1, 118-124.

Thomas, J. 2015. Constructing a 'futurology from below': a civil society contribution toward a research agenda, *Journal of Responsible Innovation*, 2:1, 92-95.

Thompson, P. 2008. Life stories, history and social change', in R. Edwards (ed.) *Researching Lives Through Time: Time, Generation and Life Stories* , Timescapes Working Paper No. 1 www.timescapes.leeds.ac.uk/assets/fi   les/timescapes/WP1-Researching-Lives-Th rough-Time-June-2008.pdf .

Thompson, P., Lummis, T. and Wailey, T. 1983. *Living the Fishing*, London: Routledge and Kegan Paul.

Thorstensen, E. and Forsberg, E. 2016. Social Life Cycle Assessment as a resource for Responsible Research and Innovation, *Journal of Responsible Innovation*, 3:1, 50-72.

Toffler, A. 1970. *Future Shock* Random House, New York

Treaty of Lisbon. 2007. Amending the Treaty on European Union and the Treaty Establishing the European Community.

2007/C 306/01, 17.12.2007. Brussels: Official Journal of the European Union

Turnbull, D. 2009. Maps and Plans in 'Learning to See: the London Underground and Chatres Cathederal as Examples of Performing Design in Grasseni, C. (ed). *Skilled visions, Between Apprenticeship and Standards*. Oxford, Berghahn Books

V

Van den Hoven, J., Lokhorst, G., van de Poel, I. 2012. Engineering and the problem of moral overload in *Science and Engineering Ethics*, 18, 1–13.

Van den Hoven, J. 2013. Value Sensitive Design and Responsible Innovation in Owen, R. Bessant, J. and Heintz, M. (eds). 2013. *Responsible Innovation: Managing the Responsible Emergence of Science and Innovation in Society*, Chichester, Wiley

Van den Hoeven, J. 2014. Responsible Innovation: A New Look at Technology and Ethics in Van den Hoeven, J., Doorn, N., Swierstra, T., Koops, B. and Romijn, H. (eds.), *Responsible innovation 1: Innovative Solutions for Global Issues*: London, Springer.

Van der Burg, S and Swierstra, T. 2013. *Ethics on the laboratory floor*, Hampshire, England, Palgrave-Macmillan.

Van der Burg, S. 2014. On the Hermeneutic Need for Future Anticipation, *Journal of Responsible Innovation,* 1:1, 99-102.

Vogel, K. M. 2015. More Socio-technical Assessments of Synthetic Biology to Inform Security Deliberations, *Journal of Responsible Innovation*, 2:1, 85-87.

Vogt, T. 2016. How Fast Should We Innovate? *Journal of Responsible Innovation* 3:3, 255-259.

Von Schomberg, R. 2019. Why Responsible Innovation? In von Schomberg, R. and Hankins, J. (eds). 2019. *International Handbook on Responsible Innovation. A Global Resource.* Edward Elgar Publishing, Cheltenham (UK) and Northampton (USA)

von Schomberg, R. and Hankins, J. (eds). 2019. *International Handbook on Responsible Innovation. A Global Resource.* Edward Elgar Publishing, Cheltenham (UK) and Northampton (USA)

Von Schomberg, R. 2007. *From the Ethics of Technology Towards an Ethics of Knowledge Policy & Knowledge Assessment.* Report prepared for European Commission, Directorate-General for Research and Innovation.

Von Schomberg, R. 2011, Prospects for Technology Assessment in a framework of responsible research and innovation, in Dusseldorp, M. and Beecroft, R. (ed.), *Technikfolgen abschätzen lehren: Bildungspotenziale transdisziplinärer Methoden*, Wiesbaden: Vs Verlag, 2011.

Von Schomberg, R. 2013. A Vision of Responsible Research and Innovation in Owen, R. Bessant, J. and Heintz, M. (eds). 2013. *Responsible Innovation: Managing the Responsible Emergence of Science and Innovation in Society*, Chichester, Wiley

Von Schomberg, R. 2014. The Quest for the "Right" Impacts of Science and Technology: A Framework for Responsible Research and Innovation. In van den Hoven, J. Doorn, N. Swierstra, T. Koops, B-W. and Romiyn, H. (eds*) Responsible innovation 1, Innovative Solutions for Global Issues*, Springer, New York.

W

Weiss Evans, S. 2015. What's the Matter with Biosecurity? *Journal of Responsible Innovation,* 2:1, 88-91.

Wender, B. A., Foley, R.A., Hottle, T.A., Sadowski, J., Prado-Lopez, V., Eisenberg, D.A., Laurin, L. and Seager, T.P. 2014.Anticipatory Life-cycle Assessment for Responsible Research and Innovation, *Journal of Responsible Innovation,* 1:2, 200-207.

Wickson, F. and Carew, A.L. 2014. Quality Criteria and Indicators for Responsible Research and Innovation: learning from transdisciplinarity, *Journal of Responsible Innovation,* 1:3, 254-273.

Wilsdon J. and Willis R. 2004. *See-Through Science: Why Public Engagement Needs to Move Upstream.* London, UK: Demos

Wilsdon, J. 2014. From Foresight to Hindsight: the promise of history in responsible innovation, *Journal of Responsible Innovation,* 1:1, 109-112.

Winickoff, D. E., Jamal, L and Anderson, N.R. 2016. New Modes of Engagement for Big Data Research, *Journal of Responsible Innovation,* 3:2, 169-177.

Withycombe K, L. and Foley, R.W. 2015. The Monster and the polar bears: constructing the future knowledge landscape of synthetic biology to inform responsible innovation, *Journal of Responsible Innovation,* 2:1, 81-84.

Wolfe, A. K. 2015. Societal Aspects of Synthetic Biology: organisms and applications matter!, *Journal of Responsible Innovation, 2:1,* 121-123.

Wong, P.H. 2016. Responsible Innovation for Decent Nonliberal Peoples: a dilemma? *Journal of Responsible*

Innovation, 3:2, 154-168.

Woodhouse, E. J. 2016. Slowing the Pace of Technological Change? *Journal of Responsible Innovation* 3:3, 266-273.

Wynne, B. 1992. Misunderstood Misunderstandings: social identities and the public uptake of science in *Public Understanding of Science*, 1, 281–304

Wynne, B. 1993. Public Uptake of Science: a case for institutional reflexivity in *Public Understanding of Science*, 2, 321–337

Wynne, B. 2002. Risk and Environment as Legitimatory Discourses of Science and Technology: reflexivity inside-out? In *Current Sociology*, 50, 459–477

Wynne, B. 2006. Public Engagement as a Means of Restoring Public Trust in Science: hitting the notes but missing the music. *Community Genet* 9, 211–220

Y

Yanow, D. and Schwartz-Shea, P. 2006. *Interpretation and Method: Empirical Research Methods and the Interpretive Turn*, New York, M.E. Sharp.

Z

Ziegler, R. 2015. Justice and Innovation – towards principles for creating a fair space for innovation, *Journal of Responsible Innovation*, 2:2, 184-200.

List of Figures

Figure 1. An overview of the workshop with Gordon at work175

Figure 2. Diverse generations of springing techniques 206

Figure 3. A series of planes on display.....................................206

Figure 4. Modern finishing techniques.....................................207

Figure 5. Traditional finishing techniques................................207

Figure 6. 3D cell printing technique...234

Figure 7. A series of 3D printers in a row in Prof. Malda's
laboratory..237

Figure 8. 3D printed objects sitting on display.........................238

Figure 9. An early printer with wires and tools........................239

Figure 10. A further developed version, still with associated
tools 241

Figure 11. Prof. Malda with his latest printing technology 242

Figure 12. Photo of antique restoration process 246